SPINNING
on the
axis
of evil

America's war against Iraq

By Scott Taylor

D1057766

ABOUT THE AUTHOR

Scott Taylor, a former soldier, is the editor and publisher of *Esprit de Corps*, an Ottawa-based magazine celebrated for its unflinching scrutiny of the Canadian military. As a war correspondent, Taylor reported from the Persian Gulf during the 1991 *Operation Desert Storm*. He has since made 14 trips into Iraq – before and after Saddam's regime was toppled.

Taylor appears regularly in the Canadian media as a military analyst and is the recipient of the 1996 Quill Award, for outstanding work in the field of Canadian communications. That same year he won the Alexander Mackenzie Award for journalistic excellence.

A columnist for the *Halifax Herald*, the *Windsor Star*, and Osprey newspapers, Taylor has been a contributor to the *Globe and Mail*, *Reader's Digest* and *Media Magazine*. Some of the on-site reporting that appears in this book was produced while on freelance assignments for *the Ottawa Citizen, Toronto Sun, Maclean's, Aljazeera* (English-language news web service), *Dnevnik* (*Macedonian Daily*) and *Magyar Nemzet* (*The Hungarian Nation*).

OTHER WORKS BY SCOTT TAYLOR:

Tarnished Brass: Crime and Corruption in the Canadian Military (co-author with Brian Nolan), 1996 (reprinted paperback 1997)

Tested Mettle: Canada's Peacekeepers at War (co-author with Brian Nolan), 1998

Inat: Images of Serbia and the Kosovo Conflict (author), 2000

Canada at War and Peace, II: A Millennium of Military Heritage (editor-in-chief), 2001

Diary of an Uncivil War: The Violent Aftermath of the Kosovo Conflict (author), 2002

SPINNING
on the
aXIS
of evil

America's war against Iraq

By Scott Taylor

"Oil is much too important
a commodity to be left in the
hands of the Arabs."

Henry Kissinger, U.S. Secretary of State, 1973

Printed in Canada

NATIONAL LIBRARY OF CANADA CATALOGUING IN PUBLICATION DATA
Taylor, Scott, 1960-
Spinning on the axis of evil: America's war against Iraq/ScottTaylor
Includes index.
ISBN 1-895896-22-3
1. Iraq--History--1991 2. Iraq War, 2003--Causes.
3. Reconstruction--Iraq. I. Title

DS79.76.T39 2003   956.7044'3   C2003-905446-2

Printed and bound in Canada
Esprit de Corps Books
1066 Somerset Street West, Suite 204, Ottawa, Ontario, Canada K1Y 4T3
1-800-361-2791
www.espritdecorps.ca / e-mail: espritdecorp@idirect.com
From outside Canada
Tel: (613) 725-5060 / Fax: (613) 725-1019

ACKNOWLEDGEMENTS

The author wishes to acknowledge the contributions of those individuals whose generous assistance made this project possible. At the top of the list would have to be Najeeb (Nick) Shallal, who first encouraged me to report on the post-Gulf War conditions inside Iraq – and helped to facilitate my initial visits.

As for administrative support during my numerous trips into Iraq, I wish to thank Anmar, Lela, Jabar, Sami, Mustafa and Dr. Al-Hashimi (wherever you are hiding). Margarita Papandreou was an inspiration and I wish to thank her for her hospitality and support.

For believing in my ventures, credit is due to my editors: Bruce Garvey (*Ottawa Citizen*), Terry O'Neill (*Halifax Herald*), Mike Burke-Gaffney (*Toronto Sun*), Tom Fennel (*Maclean's*), Yvonne Ridley (*Aljazeera*) and Global TV producer George Browne.

The last-minute edit by Penelope Body really helped to smooth out the rougher edges, and it was great to have her involved in the project. The *Esprit de Corps* production team, Julie Simoneau, Cathy Hingley, Bill Twatio and Donna Tillotson, did a superb job in bringing this book to fruition.

Special thanks is also due to Anne Trinneer, Arthur Millholland, Mazen Chouaib, Donn Lovett, Lenore and Herb Forestal, Miriam, Kirk, Mary, Raymond and the Kirkness family for their support.

Last, but not least, I wish to acknowledge the efforts made by Katherine Taylor to promote and market this book. (On a personal level I must admit that, without her continued support, none of this would be possible).

*Dedicated to all the innocents
that have suffered and died in Iraq:
First as the victims of their own
brutal dictator and then as the
collateral damage of international
power-brokering, lies and greed.*

ABOUT THIS BOOK

In order to justify its war against Iraq, George Bush's administration needed to first frighten the American public into believing that Saddam Hussein posed a "clear and present danger." In addition to "sexing up" intelligence dossiers regarding Saddam's alleged weapons of mass destruction (WMDs), it was also necessary to somewhat distort and simplify Iraq's complex ethnic, political, social and religious structures.

Unfortunately, it seemed as though the U.S. military officials actually started to believe their own propaganda, and were genuinely shocked when the Iraqi people did not welcome them as liberators. In contrast to the American naïveté, the post-Saddam anarchy, violence and inter-ethnic combat that has occurred were all accurately predicted by the Iraqi people. Although fearful of Saddam's regime, most Iraqis had even greater concerns over what would ensue should his Baath Party ever be toppled.

This book, consisting primarily of Scott Taylor's first-hand observations and interviews with the people who have become an integral part of this conflict, is a very personal account of America's war against Iraq.

Put into historical context and with a rare inside view of Saddam's regime, *Spinning on the Axis of Evil* provides a unique perspective on President Bush's ill-conceived intervention in Iraq.

SOURCES

While most of this book is presented as a first-person narrative, with attributed quotes denoting the source, historical references were drawn largely from:

Paris: 1919, Margaret MacMillan (Random House, 2001)

Challenge to Genocide, Ramsey Clark (IAC Press, 1998)

Iraq at the Crossroads, Toby Dodge and Steven Simon (Oxford University Press, 2003)

Iraq: 30 Years of Progress, Saddam Hussein (1998)

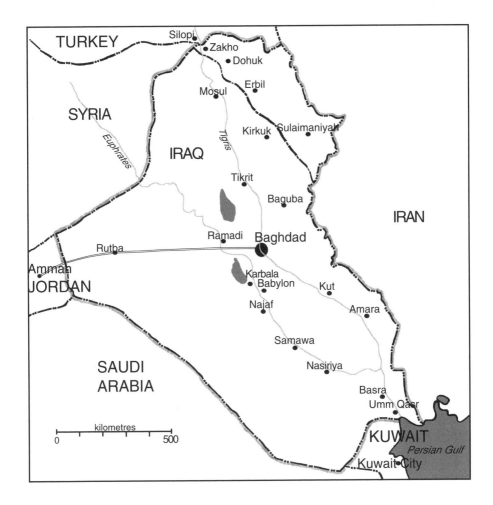

ABOVE: Map of Iraq depicting the cities and places visited by the author on his 14 trips into the region.

NOTE TO READERS: *The place names on this map – and throughout the book – may differ from other official sources. The English spellings in* Spinning on the Axis of Evil *are based on phonetic translations of the original Arabic or Kurdish names. The same applies to names of individuals.*

PHOTOGRAPHY

FRONT COVER: *Oil fires burning in Kuwait.*

BACK COVER (CLOCKWISE FROM TOP LEFT): *An Iraqi prisoner is consoled by a comrade (PETER DEJONG/AP); Americans drag a wounded Iraqi to safety (CHERYL DIAZ MEYER/ CORBIS); Iraqi women flee an allied airstrike (BRITISH MINISTRY OF DEFENCE); an Iraqi man comforts his son and observes the destruction of his house. (DAVID GUTTENFELDER/AP)*

ABOVE: *Funeral of four-year-old Dijana Pavlovic who was killed by an errant NATO bomb during 1999 airstrikes against Belgrade.* (*S.TAYLOR*)

OPPOSITE PAGE: *On the night of June 3, 1999, NATO airstrikes knocked out the power grid, plunging Belgrade into yet another blackout* (*S.TAYLOR*)

CHAPTER ONE

From Belgrade to Baghdad

BELGRADE, YUGOSLAVIA, JUNE 3, 1999   The air raid sirens had sounded just after dusk and the Yugoslav anti-aircraft gunners were sending up streams of tracer fire into the sky above Belgrade. This was the 72nd day of the NATO air campaign, and for Serbs, these airstrikes had long since become part of their daily routine. I had already filed my story for the *Ottawa Citizen* and was sitting in my tiny, sweltering room at the Moskva Hotel when the telephone rang.

As one of only a handful of North American journalists reporting from inside war-torn Yugoslavia, I had provided updates for a number of television and radio outlets whenever the phone lines were operable. This call was from a young research assistant at the CBC. "Can you comment on the mood tonight among the [Albanian] refugees now that they have finally signed a peace agreement?" she asked.

Startled by her ignorance of both geography and the ongoing crisis in Kosovo, I took a few minutes to enlighten her. I explained that the Serbian capital is over 400 kilometres from Macedonia, where the refugees were and, despite peace talks, the Yugoslav Army was still engaged in a bloody confrontation with the Albanian Kosovo Liberation Army (KLA). When the NATO airstrikes (in support of the KLA) started on March 24, they had precipitated a flood of refugees that poured into neighbouring Macedonia. As the Kosovo crisis escalated, thousands of reporters rushed to the Balkans only to find themselves unable to officially enter either Kosovo or Yugoslavia. As a result, the majority of 'war' reports filed were about the plight of the Albanian refugees, the only story to which the press had easy access.

Once the CBC researcher realized I was nowhere near the Albanians, she switched questions. "What do the Serbs in Belgrade think about the refugees going home to Kosovo now that the peace deal is signed? Are they happy for them?"

I explained to her that, at that very moment, the two million inhabitants of Belgrade were without power and water and were on the receiving end of yet another air attack. My guess, I said, was that the Serbs probably had more pressing concerns than the mood of the Albanians.

"That is rather insensitive of them don't you think?" she asked without sarcasm. Rather than voice an opinion, I suggested that maybe her producer would be interested in the fact that the air raids on Belgrade were continuing, despite the announced peace deal. I waited on the line while she checked with her boss. "No thanks," was her response. "Tonight's lead story is about the peace celebrations, so the air attack would only be confusing to the viewers."

By this point, the Western media had long since started to believe its own jingoism and there was no longer even the pretense of providing a balanced report. Official spokespersons – such as James Rubin at the U.S. State Department and Jamie Shea at NATO – were so successful in demonizing the Serbs that it reached the point where Serbian civilian casualties were routinely referred to as mere collateral damage. Being inside Serbia, suffering hardship alongside the Serbs and seeing the blown-apart bodies of innocent civilians killed by NATO bombs, it was difficult for me not to resent the distortions and exaggerations put forward in the name of an alliance I had once proudly served as an active Canadian soldier. What I resented most, however, was that the majority of the media willingly provided the Sheas and Rubins with a largely unchallenged platform.

When the peace negotiations stalled, I headed south from Belgrade to Kosovo with several dozen Serbian-accredited foreign journalists. It was here that I had a ringside view of the NATO forces finally rolling in to Pristina. Following close on the armoured vanguard's heels was a media horde of some 2700 NATO-authorized journalists. Having spent the previous weeks churning out unconfirmed tales of genocide, torture and rape, these reporters were anxious to uncover evidence to support their tales.

The top three things these journalists wanted to find were the mass graves (the final U.S. State Department estimate had put the body count of murdered Albanians "in excess of 100,000"); the rape camps, where Jamie Shea claimed Serbian soldiers had conducted the systematic violation of tens of thousands of Albanian women; and the shattered remains of the Yugoslav Army, which, according to official NATO statistics, included 150 destroyed tanks, 400 artillery pieces and an equal number of logistic vehicles.

On all three counts, the media 'treasure hunt' would come up empty-handed. Despite allied satellite photographs of purported mass graves and eyewitness accounts by Albanian refugees of alleged slaughter, no evidence was ever discovered of any genocide.

One site where such atrocities were said to have occurred was the Trepca mine. Countless Albanians had told harrowing tales of Serbs bussing Albanians to the mine, slaughtering them and then throwing their bodies down the shafts. It was believed that as many as 700 corpses lay at the bottom of these pits. UN forensic experts, trailed by eager journalists, descended into the mine. After an extensive search, the investigators failed to uncover a single body.

Of all the sites reported to be mass graves, only one, at Ljubenic, was found to contain multiple bodies. A comprehensive examination of the site uncovered only seven bodies, a far cry from the 350 corpses alleged to have been buried there.

By 2002, after an exhaustive search of all possible sites, the Kosovo death toll stood at around 2000. This number included 700 Serbs and gypsies (no distinction was made between combatants and civilians), those who had been killed during the guerrilla war in 1998 as well as those hit by NATO airstrikes. The final tally showed NATO had killed nearly as many innocent civilians as had the warring Serbs and Albanians, all in the name of preventing a genocide that had never happened.

Likewise, the mythical rape camps failed to materialize. One female British journalist had found a number of Serbian pornographic magazines in a looted kiosk in downtown Pristina. She and her producer were in the foyer of the Grand Hotel discussing the find. She believed this constituted further proof of Serbian sexual deviancy.

Overhearing their conversation, I felt obliged to remind them that, during the 78-day campaign, Pristina had been a virtual ghost town populated almost exclusively by male soldiers. In my opinion, I said, the shopkeeper was probably just catering to a rather frustrated clientele. Annoyed by my interruption, the reporter asked, "Do you really think that Serbian soldiers were using these magazines to masturbate?" I replied that, as a former soldier, I was convinced of it, and furthermore, such pornography could be found in the armoured vehicles of all NATO armies.

"You are so naive!" she replied.

Slowly, many journalists began to realize they had been duped during the war. A CBC news crew had produced a moving documentary on a female guerrilla fighter. Through tears, the young Albanian had explained how Serbs had raped and killed her sister. After being forced to witness the atrocity, she said, she had enlisted in the Kosovo Liberation Army.

After the Serbs withdrew from Kosovo, the producer decided to do a follow-up piece on the young guerrilla fighter. When the television crew arrived at her home, they were shocked to discover her sister was very much alive. Furthermore, she denied ever having been raped. Asked about the fabrication, the Albanian family was unrepentant. "We did what we had to do. We could not beat the Serbs ourselves," they explained.

When United Nations investigators sought out the testimony of rape victims only a few Albanian girls, not the thousands predicted, came forward. To explain the discrepancy, NATO officials claimed that, as Muslims, the victims were too ashamed to admit they had been violated. Of course, no one could explain – or was even asked – why these women who had been so willing to give explicit details to reporters during the war, were now too cowed to give evidence that would bring the rapists to justice.

Physical evidence to support NATO's wartime claims of material success were also hard to find. Given that NATO had expended nearly $12 billion worth of explosive ordnance, most reporters expected to come across the smoking, cratered graveyard of the Serbian military. While there was plenty of evidence of shattered buildings and infrastructure, there were very few abandoned or destroyed armoured vehicles. In fact, only 13 tank hulks were eventually found: five had been destroyed by KLA landmines, while four were actual World War II vintage museum pieces. Some NATO officials had hinted that Yugoslav President Slobodan Milosevic had withdrawn the remainder of his disabled tanks back into Serbia during the retreat. However, those of us who had accompanied the Serb withdrawal had also witnessed the security forces pulling back virtually intact and unscathed after 78 days of aerial bombardment.

The biggest lie of the Kosovo crisis, however, would not be exposed until April 2000. That was when the final edition of the Finnish forensic report was released on the alleged massacre at Racak. It was in this small village north of Pristina that 45 bodies had been discovered on January 16, 1999.

Based on initial evidence supplied by U.S. Special Envoy William Walker, President Bill Clinton had denounced the Racak incident as a Serbian atrocity. In gory detail, Clinton told American viewers that innocent Albanians had been forced from their homes and "made to kneel in the dirt" where they were shot or "had their throats slit." Clinton said such atrocities could no longer be tolerated, and that the countdown to war in Yugoslavia had begun.

The forensic report did not substantiate President Clinton's version of events. The Albanians were all males of military age, and none had either been shot at close range or had their throats slit. According to the report, the evidence revealed that most had been shot at long range and, most important, 94 per cent (i.e., all but one victim) had gunpowder residue on their fingers, indicating they had fired their weapons near the time of death. This showed that Racak had been not a massacre, but rather a KLA ploy. The dumping of the soldiers killed in action into a single ditch was a deliberate attempt by the KLA to fake an atrocity and lay blame on the Serbian security forces.

As disturbing as it was to realize that the U.S. government was capable of stage-managing a fabricated incident into justification for war, it was equally disheartening to see the media no longer cared. When the Finnish forensic report was released in the spring of 2000, it caused barely a ripple in the North American press.

After returning to Canada, I catalogued my observations on the Balkan war in *Inat: Images of Serbia and the Kosovo Conflict*, a book that was published in March 2000. To thank me for presenting the largely untold Serbian side of the war, the first consul at the Yugoslav embassy had invited me out for a special lunch.

I had met with Ljiljana Milojevic Borovcanin on many previous occasions and she had been instrumental in approving my travel visas. Since Borovcanin was not a member of the Communist Party and was active in Serbia's underground opposition movement, she had introduced me to many top Serbian democratic leaders. As reported in *Inat*, they had candidly, and accurately, predicted the demise of Slobodan Milosevic's rule in the fall of 2000.

The lunch Borovcanin arranged took place at La Favorita. The restaurant's proprietor, Najeeb Shallal, an Iraqi-Canadian who had set up shop in Ottawa back in 1985, had studied cooking at the University of Belgrade after emigrating from Iraq. Najeeb speaks fluent Serbian and many of his staff are recent Yugoslav immigrants, so he had no trouble preparing a special off-menu Serbian feast for us.

Instantly likeable, Najeeb is a generous host who wears his heart on his sleeve. Having spent so much time living in Belgrade, he had followed the war in Kosovo closely and was genuinely interested in my book. When he asked why I wasn't exposing the same sort of lies about Iraq, I explained that, as a reporter, I wrote about events as they happened, not issues that had long since been resolved. Although aware that an abortive showdown had taken place between Iraq and the U.S. in 1998, the whole issue of Iraq's readmission of UN weapons inspectors had subsequently disappeared from the news.

"Old news?" Najeeb sputtered incredulously. "They are bombing Iraq every-day!"

Sensing that I found the idea that a war could be underway without anyone in the Western media reporting it incredulous, Najeeb disappeared into his office. He returned, brandishing a number of wire reports and e-mail messages detailing the ongoing U.S. and British airstrikes. I was immediately intrigued and pledged to visit Iraq if Najeeb could assist with arranging a travel visa. This would prove to be a major stumbling block as one of the first requests from the Iraqi embassy was that I submit all of the articles I had written about the Gulf War and Iraq.

In 1991, I had made a total of four trips to the Persian Gulf theatre. *Operation Desert Storm* was the first war I had ever covered. As a reporter for *Esprit de Corps*, a magazine aimed at the military community, my coverage of the buildup for war and the actual combat had admittedly been naive and heavy on the rah-rah. In fact, immediately following the cease-fire *Esprit de Corps* published the book *Desert Cats*, which profiled the Canadian fighter squadron and its Persian Gulf exploits. I had never bothered to do any research on the conflict from an historical perspective. And from the mainstream media reports I had read, the reasons for the crisis had seemed pretty clear-cut: Iraqi President Saddam Hussein was a madman who had invaded his innocent neighbour and U.S. President George Bush Senior – armed with a UN mandate and an international coalition force – was out to set the world straight again

As the U.S.-led forces built up in the region, American defence analysts took to the airwaves to convince everyone this would prove to be an epic struggle. On paper, the balance of forces appeared to support them. Iraq, with its conscripted army, was able to put 950,000 soldiers in the field – nearly double the number deployed by the coalition forces. In terms of armoured vehicles, the Iraqis possessed 5,500 tanks and 9,000 armoured personnel carriers (APCs). By comparison, it was estimated the U.S.-led coalition only had about 4,000 tanks and a similar number of APCs in the Persian Gulf theatre.

Although the allies possessed a massive array of air power – 1,700 attack helicopters and 1,800 fighter jets – the Iraqi air force had a respectable collection of 160 helicopters and 700 combat aircraft. In addition to their graph-chart comparisons, analysts pointed out that the Iraqi army was comprised of "battle-tested" veterans after their decade-long war with Iran. Plus, as a wild card, Saddam had nearly 1000 Scud missiles in his arsenal.

As history revealed, once the war began, all the analysts' predictions were proven wrong. The slaughter of Iraq's forces during Operation *Desert Storm* ranks as one of the most one-sided conflicts of all time. Nearly 200,000 Iraqi soldiers were killed, wounded or captured during the three-day ground war. During that short period, allied forces destroyed over 4,000 Iraqi tanks, 2,140 artillery pieces, 1,856 armoured personnel carriers, 7 helicopters and 240 combat aircraft.

Losses on the allied side were shockingly light in comparison. Only four tanks were reportedly destroyed by enemy fire (another four U.S. tanks were lost when an ammunition dump exploded in Kuwait after the war). Only one artillery piece and nine APCs were destroyed, all of them as a result of friendly fire. Of the 148 allied casualties, 31 per cent were the result of friendly fire, while the rest occurred during the clean-up operations and resulted primarily from unexploded landmines and ordnance – not from combat.

In fact, the Mother of All Battles proved so one-sided that Major General Patrick Cordingley, commander of the British "Desert Rats" brigade, cautioned his peers in the aftermath: "We must be careful about the lessons we take from a war where we defeated a technologically inferior enemy on featureless terrain and met very few reverses."

In his autobiography *In the Eye of the Storm*, General Cordingley reflected that many of his soldiers "were disturbed by what they had seen or done" during the battle. "The collapse of the Iraqi army was on a scale no one had anticipated... The Iraqis, without night vision, were at a terrible disadvantage; the only thing they could fire back at was the flash of [our] muzzles, but they were out of range... as fast as they could pour vehicles in [we] destroyed them... The lucky few withdrew."

When I entered Kuwait shortly after its liberation the grim evidence of this wholesale slaughter was everywhere. The blackened hulks of obsolete Iraqi tanks and the rubble of primitive defensive structures indicated just how one-sided the battles had been. As a former soldier I could not help but pity all those Iraqis because they had never stood a chance of survival – let alone victory.

It was on this same trip that I had met up with the soldiers of 1 Canadian Engineer Regiment (1CER). They had been deployed to Kuwait to clear safe routes through the unexploded ordnance in the bomb-strewn desert. As part of the UN observer mission UNIKOM, these troops were not part of the U.S.-led coalition forces that had remained poised along the Iraqi border.

Toiling in the terrible heat beneath billowing black clouds caused by the still-burning oil fires, the soldiers of 1CER had dubbed themselves "The Lost Boys." In the flurry of post-war celebrations, all of the media's focus was on the Yellow Ribbon homecoming parades, not on those still performing dangerous duty in Kuwait. While I was there, reporting on their mission, 1CER discovered an abandoned Iraqi Silkworm anti-ship missile battery. In the compound, a total of 17 Silkworm missiles were found. Similar to the famed Exocet, the Silkworm is made in China, has a sophisticated guidance system, and a range of some 60 kilometres.

As UN troops, 1CER was not permitted to remove the weapons, but the Canadian commander dutifully reported the missiles' location to the local U.S. military authority. Over the course of the next four days, 1CER patrols witnessed small groups of Iraqis cross the frontier at night to reclaim their rockets. Obviously still short of transport, the Iraqis could only remove a few Silkworms at a time. The Canadians continued to report this activity to the Americans, who, unbelievably, took no measures to either secure the Silkworms or apprehend the Iraqis. These nocturnal incursions were undeniably in violation of the cease-fire agreement, but the American troops in Kuwait turned a wilful blind eye to the Iraqis' rearmament.

While I was perplexed as to why the U.S. would have openly allowed Saddam Hussein to re-equip his battered army, I was thoroughly incensed 18 months later. On January 13, 1993, following George Bush Senior's November 1992 election defeat – but prior to President-elect Bill Clinton's taking office – the U.S. launched a punitive round of airstrikes against Iraq. Four days later, on the second anniversary of the start of the Gulf War and with just 72 hours remaining in his stint as U.S. Commander in Chief, Bush ordered another military strike against Iraq. About 50 Cruise missiles smashed into Baghdad, including one that hit a conference room where Saddam was supposed to be making a speech. The explanation given by Pentagon officials was that they had caught Saddam's operatives inside Kuwait attempting to recover military hardware.

Furious at their duplicity, I had fired off an immediate press release accusing the U.S. of staging a "propaganda ploy." I included the information about the Silkworm missiles and stated that either the U.S. wanted to get rid of Saddam Hussein or this attack was a last hurrah by outgoing President Bush. The rearming of Iraq's army was old news, and certainly not the real reason for these attacks.

Several Canadian media outlets picked up the story and called the Pentagon for a response. "We respect [Scott Taylor's] opinion but we do not share it," replied spokesman Colonel Dave Garner. "U.S. President George Bush has given his reasons for the action, and those words stand on their own."

This was the first time that I had challenged the Pentagon, but it certainly wouldn't be the last. Neglecting to include my early Gulf War articles, I forwarded only the press clips that were associated with the 1992 "propaganda ploy" with my visa request to the Iraqi embassy.

On the strength of Najeeb's recommendation and my deliberately thin résumé of reports on Iraq, my credentials were approved. There certainly wasn't a lot of North American media interest in Iraq, but by using the ten-year anniversary of the Kuwait invasion as a hook – and given that it was the dog days of summer – I was able to persuade news editor Bruce Garvey at the *Ottawa Citizen* to publish a four-part series. With little money for expenses, my best hope was to break even on the trip. But the more I began to research Iraq and her people, the more I felt this was a story that needed to be told.

TOP: *Iraqi soldiers surrender en masse to coalition forces during the allied ground offensive of Operation Desert Storm in 1991. (RICHARD KEMP)*

ABOVE: *Canadian soldiers inspect the carnage on the Highway of Death following Operation Desert Storm in June 1991. Many coalition soldiers were "sickened" by the slaughter of Iraqi troops. (S. TAYLOR)*

THIS PAGE: *Throughout history, the Arabs of Iraq have excelled at mobile hit-and-run guerrilla tactics, a lesson hard-learned by many an invader. (FROM THE BOOK IRAQ: 30 YEARS OF PROGRESS)*

OPPOSITE PAGE: *The British occupation of Iraq (from 1919-58) would prove a costly affair. (RAF MUSEUM)*

CHAPTER TWO:
All About Oil

Of all the ridiculous pre-war rhetoric uttered by U.S. officials, Secretary of Defense Donald Rumsfeld would certainly take the gold medal in the history-revision category for grandly proclaiming, "We are going to bring democracy back to Iraq!"

Straddling the Tigris and Euphrates rivers, modern-day Iraq can certainly lay claim to being the "cradle of civilization," but never in its storied 6000-year history has this land ever been a democracy. From the glory days of the Babylonian and Assyrian empires to the numerous occupations by invading armies, Iraq has always been ruled by an iron fist. Another hallmark of Iraqi history has been violent resistance to outside authority.

It was in the northern foothills around present-day Mosul that the original "assassins" first plied their deadly trade. Derived from the word for users of hashish, these warriors would carry out their mission to the death. Unable to match their opponents' large field armies, the assassins used the threat of terror in the form of murdering political opponents to retain their own independence.

Not to be outshone by his boss, on the eve of war U.S. Deputy Secretary of Defense Paul Wolfowitz captured gold in the geopolitical naïveté category by declaring "Iraq is not like the Balkans... they are one people, unified in a single cause [the ousting of President Saddam Hussein]." In response to reporters' questions about the potential duration of an American occupation of Iraq. Wolfowitz confidently predicted U.S. soldiers would be welcomed as "liberators" and would begin pulling out of Iraq "within six months."

Wolfowitz's statement could be interpreted as wishful thinking; in reality, however, it was a shocking admission of dangerous ignorance. Iraq's present borders had been arbitrarily defined in the post-World War I Treaty of Sèvres. The boundaries were determined more by the British desire to dismantle the Turkish Ottoman empire than by existing ethnic divisions.

As a result, modern Iraq is a complex mixture of races, tribes and religions. The long history of mutual hatred and distrust between many of these factions make the Balkans seem copacetic by comparison. For instance, in Iraq, the majority of the Arab population is divided by region into three main groups: the fundamentalist Shiite Muslims, the Sunni Muslims and the Christians (Chaldean and Assyrian denominations).

The three northernmost provinces remain under the control of the Kurds. About 3.5 million in number, the Kurds represent the largest minority group in Iraq. Although they are autonomous and have not been under the control of Saddam Hussein's regime since the 1991 uprising, these "free" Kurds are hardly one big, happy family. In the past eleven years, two rival factions have clashed eleven times in territorial disputes.

Added to this mix is the large Turkmen population. Nearly two million in number, the Turkmen represent the second-largest minority in Iraq. Distinct from both the Kurds and the Arabs, these descendants of ancient Turkey found their community divided by the same administrative boundary that separated the Kurds from Saddam's regime. Also affected by this division are the Yazidi, an ancient religious order. Denigrated by some of their Arab neighbours as "devil worshippers," the reclusive Iraqi-Yazidi number about 300,000.

Although there are no accurate statistics on the number of Marsh-Arabs still residing along the Shatt-Al-Arab waterway, these tribesmen live as they did in biblical times – fishing from dugout canoes and residing in tiny stone houses. Similarly, Bedouin nomads still traverse the vast expanses of the Syrian desert, herding goats, sheep and camels.

Although they probably represent the smallest group in terms of numbers, the Sabia, or "Water Worshippers," are perhaps the most unique faction in Iraq. Thought to number barely 100,000, this religious sect believes that all life springs from water. As water is part of all their religious rites, the Sabia live along the banks of the Tigris and Euphrates rivers.

To keep a lid on this diverse and fractious population, Saddam Hussein and his ruling Baath party had relied on an elaborate system of patronage. At the top of the pyramid was the extended clan group of Sunni Arabs known as the Al-bu Nasir. This "extended family" consisted of about 30,000 people based in Saddam's hometown of Tikrit. During the 34 years of Baath Party rule, the Al-bu Nasir were elevated to hold the top Iraqi civil and military positions. Secondary positions were granted to other tribes from Tikrit – the Al-Tikritis and Sunni Arabs. In addition, Saddam carefully chose a select few minorities to be part of his inner circle. For example, Tariq Aziz, Iraq's longstanding Deputy Prime Minister, was an Assyrian Christian. By keeping the Shia majority resentful of the minorities' status, the Baath Party deliberately cultivated what Middle East experts dubbed "a coalition of guilt" that underpinned its continued rule with corruption and the great fear of what would happen if it were even toppled.

In a pre-war published report, the London-based International Institute for Strategic Studies had a far different assessment of Iraq than Paul Wolfowitz. "Iraq cannot easily be mapped onto a neat diagram of sect, tribe or party. The rentier structure of the state economy, the regime's manipulation of group identity to control the population, the emergence of a shadow state that distributes public goods to advance regime interests and pervasive violence have transformed Iraq's sociopolitical landscape into dangerous and unfamiliar ground for intervention."

WHILE THE STATEMENTS ISSUED by Rumsfeld and Wolfowitz were both unfounded, the most oft-repeated falsehood could fairly be claimed by every member of George W. Bush's inner circle. Virtually without exception, they all took every possible opportunity to proclaim the war in Iraq was not about oil. Of course, ever since oil was first discovered in 1919 in the vicinity of Basra, everything about Iraq had been inextricably linked to oil.

At the turn of the 20th century, coal was the fuel of the industrial revolution, but over the next two decades oil increasingly gained prominence. World War One had played a part, certainly, and Lord George Curzon, a British politician, went so far as to claim the Allies had floated to victory upon a wave of oil. Ironically, it was only to protect their supply of British Petroleum resources in Iran that the British had first launched military attacks against the Turks in neighbouring Mesopotamia.

This region, consisting of three Ottoman provinces – Basra, Baghdad and Mosul – was not known to possess its own oil resources. By the time the British had forced the Turks out of the area, however, the burning natural-gas fires around Baba Gurgur in the north and the pools of black oil bubbling out of the sand in the south led British navy officials to proclaim Mesopotamia's petroleum assets "the greatest in the world."

Organized and led by the legendary T.E. Lawrence (of Arabia), the Arabs had proved to be valuable allies to the British and French expeditionary forces in the Middle East. The most prominent among the Arab leaders was Faisal, son of Sherif Hussein. He believed his contribution to the war effort would be rewarded by the creation of an Arab kingdom, under his control, stretching from Syria into Lebanon and Mesopotamia.

But wartime promises gave way to the Allies' own post-war ambitions. The French wanted to retain Syria as a colony and the British had no wish to part with the new-found oil deposits in Mesopotamia. In September 1919, Faisal visited London and Paris only to discover that he was being cut out of the spoils. Returning to Damascus, Faisal devoted his energies to the Arab independence movement. Despite the continued occupation by Allied troops, the Syrian congress pronounced Faisal the King of Syria on March 7, 1920.

Shortly thereafter, a second congress in Damascus proclaimed Faisal's brother, Abdullah, ruler of Mesopotamia. King Adbullah's first official act was to denounce the occupation and order British troops out of his country. When the British ignored his request and the French military crushed King Faisal's small army in Syria, rebellions erupted throughout Mesopotamia. In scenes of violence remarkably similar to those encountered by the coalition forces in 2003, Arab guerrillas ransacked railway lines, destroyed telegraph poles, murdered British officers and besieged small garrisons.

In response, the British launched a series of punitive strikes, bombing and machine-gunning villages thought to harbour resistance fighters. Winston Churchill was the British Colonial Secretary. Frustrated at the military's inability to bring the fractious tribes into line, Churchill reportedly advocated poison gas be dropped from aircraft onto rebellious Kurdish villages.

Unable to suppress the unrest, and with the British public growing weary of the mounting casualty lists it was decided that a pliable Arab should be appointed as a ruling figurehead. Having gone into exile following the defeat of his troops in Syria, King Faisal was deemed the most likely candidate and was summoned to Mesopotamia.

The British convinced Faisal of his domestic popularity by staging a referendum in which he acquired an implausible 96 per cent of the votes. On August 23, 1921, Faisal became king of the territory that would henceforth be called Iraq.

Faisal would prove to be less pliable than the British had imagined, however, and his quest for self-government would continue until Iraq was declared an independent state in 1932. Nevertheless, the fledgling kingdom would remain a protectorate, with a small garrison of British troops and aircraft on hand to protect their mutual interests – namely, Faisal's regime and the British Petroleum resources.

When Faisal died in 1933, his son ascended the throne. Although considered a playboy, in 1938 King Ghazi became the first Iraqi leader to lay claim over Kuwait's sovereignty. Not by coincidence, this was the same year that oil was discovered in the neighbouring sheikdom. With both states still under British protection, Ghazi's attempted annexation of Kuwait was easily thwarted. In 1939, Ghazi was killed in a suspicious automobile accident (the Iraqis believed the British were responsible) and his three-year-old son, Faisal II, became king. With his uncle, Abdul Illah, serving as regent, the infant Faisal's monarchy would soon face its first serious challenge.

In March 1941, at the height of the Second World War, with British military resources stretched thin around the globe, Iraqi military officers staged a brief rebellion. With their oil supply at stake, Britain quickly mobilized troops and bloodily suppressed the insurrection. The major conspirators were rounded up and executed, and Faisal's kingdom was restored by British military force. Although the Iraqi royal family denounced the executed officers as traitors, most Iraqis viewed them as martyrs, and sporadic killing of British soldiers ensued.

By 1958, Iraqi nationalism had grown into a full-blown revolution. Led by Abdul Karim Kassem, popular forces rose up and killed 23-year-old King Faisal II in a coup, and proclaimed Iraq a republic. Weary of it all, the British finally recognized Iraq's independence and withdrew their troops. The U.S., however, was not as complacent about this development.

In 1953, after Britain had withdrawn from neighbouring Iran, newly-installed Iranian Prime Minister Mohammed Mossadegh had similarly declared his country to be a republic. In an effort to fill the power vacuum left by Britain's withdrawal and to secure future oil supplies, the U.S. quickly moved in. With the backing of the Central Intelligence Agency (CIA), the Shah of Iran, Muhammed Reza Pahlavi, overthrew Mossadegh's government and placed himself atop the Iranian throne where he would remain, thanks to billions of dollars in U.S. weaponry and training for his security forces, until 1979.

Although its control over the Shah was secure, the U.S. wanted to hedge its bets. When Kassem took power in Iraq in 1958, the CIA established a covert cell known as the "Health Alteration Committee." Pentagon officials conspired with their Turkish counterparts on a number of military contingency plans. Dubbed *Operation Cannonbone*, in the event of a disruption in Iraqi oil exports, a joint U.S.-Turkey task force was to invade northern Iraq and seize the oilfields.

While the invasion proved unnecessary, Kassem's rule came to a bloody end in 1963. Sponsored by the CIA, the Iraqi Baath party staged its own coup and murdered thousands of Kassem's followers. The CIA never denied its involvement in bringing the Baathists to power, nor did they appear repentant over the bloodshed. Testifying before a U.S. Senate committee, one CIA agent actually quipped, "the target [Abdul Kassem] suffered a terminal illness before a firing squad in Baghdad." The Baathists themselves were only briefly in power before their fledgling administration was in turn overthrown by army officer Abdul Salim Arif. Five years later, however, following a bloodless coup, the Baath party was once again back in power, and this time, able to solidify its hold on Iraq. While President Ahmed Hasa Al-Bakr was the nominal head of the socialist regime, it was his young deputy, Saddam Hussein, who emerged as the power behind the Baath Party.

Although he was perceived by most Iraqis as pro-American, by the time Saddam replaced Al-Bakr as president in 1979, he had already run afoul of Washington. When Iraq took the lead role in the Arab world by privatizing Iraq's oil in 1972, Saddam earned himself the personal enmity of the White House. In response, the CIA had placed Iraq on its list of countries it claimed supported terrorism. In an effort to destabilize the Baath regime and to force political concessions, the Shah of Iran and the CIA had begun arming and equipping Kurdish rebels in northern Iraq. Forced to the bargaining table in 1975, Saddam negotiated a deal in Algiers whereby Iraq would share control of the vital Shatt-al-Arab waterway with Iran.

In exchange, the U.S. and Iran agreed to terminate their support of the Kurdish rebels, and allowed the Iraqis a free hand in suppressing the insurrection. Although their former Kurdish allies were summarily destroyed by Iraqi forces, the senseless sacrifice was callously viewed by the U.S. State Department as a means to an end. Secretary of State Henry Kissinger summed up the U.S. betrayal of the Kurds with the phrase "covert operations should not be confused with missionary work."

Despite growing violent unrest in Iran, the U.S. continued to prop up the Shah until the very end. It was estimated that in his final year of power, the Shah's security forces killed nearly 45,000 insurgents. By February 1979, he could no longer stave off the inevitable and fled into exile.

Under the leadership of the Ayatollah Ruhollah Khomeini, the Shiite fundamentalists seized control in Tehran, and America's longstanding ally suddenly became an enemy. In November 1979, when U.S. diplomats were seized and held hostage by Iranian students, the whole world watched anxiously to see how President Jimmy Carter would handle this challenge to America's authority.

Suddenly, Saddam Hussein was no longer seen as a bogeyman, but as a potential ally. U.S. National Security Advisor Zbigniew Brzezinski openly urged the Baghdad regime to attack Iran. If Saddam complied, then the U.S. would once again recognize Iraq's sovereignty over the Shatt-al-Arab waterway.

The once-powerful Iranian military had been purged of many of its top officers who had been summarily executed, under orders from the Ayatollah Khomeini. As a result, Saddam believed his own formidable army could achieve a quick victory. After some initial gains, however, the Iraqi offensive bogged down in the face of Iranian numerical superiority. The Iraqis dug in and the war became a bloody battle of attrition.

Washington was no friend of Iraq's, but as long as Saddam was weakening Iran then he would be supported. The CIA eventually removed Iraq from its list of countries that supported terror, clearing the way for official arms shipments. However, it soon became clear that the U.S. State Department and the Pentagon did not want either Iran or Iraq to achieve victory. Simply put, their objective was to keep a balance between combatants and let them bleed each other white. "It's too bad they both can't lose," said Henry Kissinger at the start of the Iran-Iraq War. By covertly playing both sides of the conflict, America ensured the ultimate result would be precisely that.

By 1984, with his troops pushed back to the banks of the Shatt al-Arab, Saddam Hussein began having serious doubts about the war's outcome. Believing that Iraq might be on the verge of ceasing hostilities, President Ronald Reagan dispatched Special Envoy Donald Rumsfeld to Baghdad. In top-level meetings with Saddam, Rumsfeld assured the Iraqi dictator that the U.S. would do "anything and everything" to help Iraq in the war effort.

The U.S. agreed to substantially increase purchases of Iraqi oil to pay for billions of dollars worth of military hardware. Then-Vice President George Bush Senior – the former head of the CIA – was instrumental in lobbying for intelligence sharing with Iraq, and in 1986 the CIA dispatched a team of advisors to Baghdad. While openly providing Saddam with military support, the Reagan administration was secretly arming and equipping the Iranians. Colonel Oliver North had been the Pentagon's point man in negotiating indirect support to Tehran in what became known as the Iran-Contra affair.

Also kept under wraps was the American complicity in equipping Saddam Hussein with chemical weapons. In the latter stages of the war, both Iran and Iraq used nerve agents and mustard gas on each other's troops. In March 1988, in the north of Iraq, during a major battle with Iranian-sponsored Kurdish troops, Saddam's artillery unleashed a devastating mustard gas bombardment on the town of Halabja.

Although as many as 5,000 Kurds perished in this atrocity there was no protest from the U.S. State Department, nor was there any cessation in America's arms shipments to Iraq. Following the signing of the cease-fire on August 20, 1988, the Americans began quietly drawing up battle plans for a military intervention in Iraq.

Although the Soviet Union was still intact, the CIA knew it was faltering and the Cold War was drawing to a close. When he served as Director of the CIA, George Bush Senior had been suspicious of his agency's assessment of the Soviets. Believing that reports had underestimated the level of threat, Bush set up an independent committee. Dubbed Special Project 'B' and headed by an ambitious young man named Paul Wolfowitz, the numbers had been radically adjusted. Detailed intelligence reports compiled by Wolfowitz painted a frightening picture of the Soviets' secret military buildup. Special Project B's assessment led President Reagan to dramatically increase U.S. defence spending to the point where the Soviet Union had to collapse out of the arms race. In the end, it was discovered that the bankrupt Soviets had nothing near the arsenal Wolfowitz had claimed. Knowing better than to believe their own fabrications, in the late 1980s the CIA considered the threat posed by Saddam to America's oil supply greater than that of any Communist invasion.

As a first step, the U.S. began to systematically demonize Saddam Hussein. In September 1988, just one month after the cease-fire, Iraq's Foreign Minister Sa'dun Hammadi was invited to Washington. Although billed as a friendly meeting with U.S. Secretary of State George Shultz, the whole thing was a stage-managed ambush. Two hours before the scheduled meeting, the State Department released photographs of the Halabja massacre. The U.S. press were brought in to question the unsuspecting Iraqi Foreign Minister on this "abhorrent" atrocity. Taken completely by surprise, the Iraqi was unable to respond to reporters' questions. Without questioning why the State Department had waited six months to pass judgement on the incident, the U.S. Senate imposed trade sanctions prohibiting sales of food and weapons to Iraq. Meanwhile, General Norman Schwarzkopf was already conducting large-scale computer war games based on the premise of Iraq invading Kuwait. As events unfolded, this scenario evolved from the hypothetically plausible to imminently probable.

Economically vulnerable as a result of his massive war debt and the unilateral U.S. trade sanctions, Saddam was suddenly pressured by Kuwait which demanded immediate repayment of a $30 billion loan that had been forwarded to Iraq to bootstrap massive U.S. arms purchases. While pushing for repayment, the Kuwaitis themselves had come under U.S. diplomatic pressure to overproduce oil. The U.S. was battling a terrible recession and threatened oil price hikes by the Organization of Petroleum Exporting Countries (OPEC) would seriously undermine the U.S. economy. By slant drilling into shared Iraq-Kuwait oil fields, the Kuwaitis were able to flood the world market, thereby keeping the price per barrel within U.S. expectations.

With these lower oil prices, Saddam's oil industry, even at maximum production, could barely generate enough money to pay the interest on the national debt. Despite repeated warnings to desist, the Kuwaitis continued to provoke Saddam. Meanwhile, the U.S. was sending Iraq mixed signals. In January 1990, Assistant Secretary of State John Kelly met with Saddam and assured him that the U.S. "wanted to improve relations."

By July 25, with the Kuwaiti crisis coming to a head, Iraqi troops massed along the border. Before acting however, Saddam deliberately sought clarification of the United States' position. Ambassador April Glaspie met with the Iraqi President in Baghdad and said, "We [the USA] have no opinion on Arab-Arab conflicts, like your border disagreement with Kuwait... [Secretary of State] James Baker has directed our official spokesman to emphasize this instruction." Taking this to be a green light, Saddam Hussein invaded Kuwait on August 2, 1990.

It did not take long for the U.S. to develop a position on Arab-Arab affairs. By August 6, the U.S. took the lead at the UN Security Council, imposing full economic sanctions against Iraq. On the military front, General Schwarzkopf immediately began beefing up forces in the Persian Gulf.

Selling the American people on the idea of going to war to liberate Kuwait, however, would not prove easy. Since the 1973 oil crisis, the Gulf Arabs had been collectively vilified in the American media as "rich fat cats" who had crippled the U.S. economy. It was, therefore, easier to demonize the Iraqis. This was accomplished in part through the gripping televised testimony of a young Kuwaiti girl.

Claiming to have escaped following the Iraqi invasion, she described in excruciating detail how Saddam's soldiers had entered the neo-natal ward at the Kuwaiti City hospital, thrown sick babies out of their incubators, and left them to die.

Only after the war would it be discovered that this was a complete fabrication scripted and produced by the American public relations firm Ruder Finn. The young girl turned out to be the Kuwaiti ambassador's daughter who had been in Washington the whole time. No babies had ever been left to die. But the deception had worked and public support for military action in the Gulf soared.

In September 1990, U.S. President Bush Senior was still maintaining that the U.S. buildup in the Gulf was "purely defensive" and aimed at curbing Saddam's potential aggression against Saudi Arabia. Air Force Chief of Staff General Michael Dugan, however, prematurely let the cat out of the bag. In an interview with the

Washington Post, Dugan had revealed that the list of U.S. targets was topped by "downtown Baghdad." In addition, Dugan had noted that the U.S. Air Force would destroy "Iraqi power grids, roads, railroads, and domestic petroleum refineries." What was interesting was that Dugan stressed his pilots "would not target the oil fields."

Following this interview, Secretary of Defense Dick Cheney hastily fired the loose-lipped Dugan, claiming his comments were "inappropriate." But when the first airstrikes of *Desert Storm* began on January 17, 1991, it didn't take long for analysts to realize that Dugan had been telling the truth. The liberation of Kuwait was secondary to the United States' primary objective. To paraphrase Wold War II General Curtis Lemay, the U.S. was going to bomb Iraq back into the stone age.

ABOVE: *Winston Churchill was Britain's post-World War I colonial secretary. With conventional forces unable to contain the Iraqi revolt of 1920, Churchill resorted to punitive airstrikes. (BBC HULTON PICTURE)*

LEFT: *King Faisal I with Lawrence of Arabia at the 1919 Paris Peace Conference. Contrary to their wartime promises, both Britain and France reneged on the creation of an Arab kingdom. (IMPERIAL WAR MUSEUM)*

TOP: *In 1988, during the Iran-Iraq War, Saddam Hussein's forces used chemical weapons against the Kurdish village of Halabja. It is estimated that 5,000 civilians perished in the massacre. (IRAN PHOTO FOUNDATION).*

ABOVE, LEFT: *The devastation of the first Gulf War — oil fires burned for months, depleted uranium seeped into the soil and water table — would be repeated 12 years later. (S. TAYLOR)*

ABOVE, RIGHT: *Although Iran had been on the path to becoming a Republic in 1953, U.S. intervention placed Reza Pahlavi, pictured with U.S. President Richard Nixon, into power as the Shah. (CORBIS)*

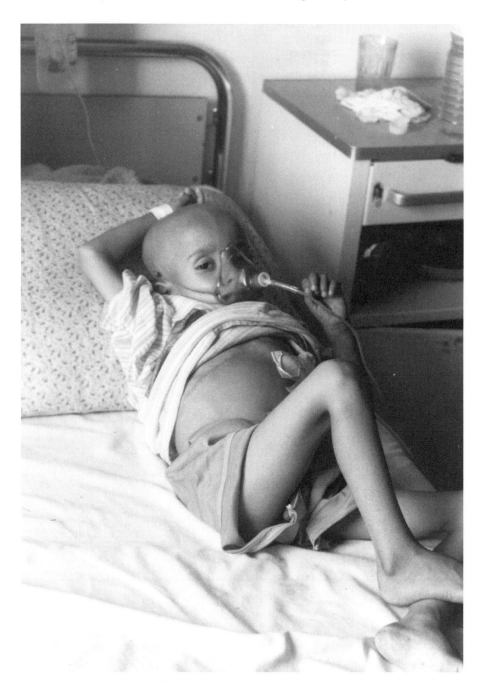

THIS PAGE: *A young boy lies dying of leukemia at the Saddam Central Teaching Hospital for Children in August 2000. (S. TAYLOR)*

OPPOSITE PAGE: *At one time the fourth largest army in the world, after Operation Desert Storm Iraq's military was but a shattered hulk of its former self. A shepherd walks past a tank graveyard in Southern Iraq. (LAURENT REBOURS, ASSOCIATED PRESS)*

CHAPTER THREE:
Sanctions and Suffering

BAGHDAD, AUGUST 11-18, 2000   Massive explosions suddenly lit up the desert sky as British and U.S. aircraft pounded an Iraqi warehouse complex in Samawa, just south of Baghdad. The following morning, additional attacks were mounted against a nearby railway junction. When the dust had settled, it was reported that two Iraqi civilians had been killed and another 19 seriously injured. A journalist working for Reuters visited the bombed site and concluded the target had been, in fact, a food depot.

Back in Washington, Pentagon spokesman Lieutenant Commander Ernest Duplessis did not deny the report of civilian casualties nor the fact that several adjacent homes had been destroyed. In his statement, Duplessis said U.S. pilots had not intentionally conducted strikes against civilians or non-military buildings. He stressed such attacks were carried out only in response to ground fire directed at planes enforcing the U.S.-imposed no-fly zones over northern and southern Iraq.

Three days later, American and British aircraft launched 14 combat sorties against Iraqi military targets on the outskirts of the northeastern city of Mosul. According to press releases issued by the Iraqi Defence Ministry, those attacks brought the number of airstrikes launched against Iraq since August 1998 to a total of 2,799 – or an average of four per day.

While there was no way for me to independently verify the ministry's figure, the scale and scope of the air campaign came as a shock to most North Americans. Unlike the extensive media coverage of *Operation Desert Storm* in 1991 or the 1999 NATO campaign against Yugoslavia, by the summer of 2000, Iraq had long since become a forgotten war zone. No foreign journalists were permanently based in Baghdad and the tightly controlled visa process, coupled with its geographical isolation made Iraq all but inaccessible to the Western media.

Ironically, during the same week as the Samawa airstrikes, Iraq announced the opening of Saddam International airport in the capital even though there were no aircraft, passengers or cargo to handle. A week earlier, Venezuelan President Hugo Chavez had broken the ten-year ban on flying into Iraq when he was ferried in from the Iranian border aboard Saddam Hussein's personal helicopter.

The scant international media coverage of the incident focussed solely on the implications of Chavez's violation of the U.S.-imposed blockade. However, as interim head of OPEC, the staunchly anti-American Chavez was making more than just a political statement with this official visit. Discussions between the two leaders centred on the possibility of converting their future oil exports from U.S. dollars to Euros the following spring after that currency had been brought into official circulation. At the airport's opening ceremony, Transport Minister Ahmed Murtadha Ahmed Khalil said Iraq was expecting the imminent arrival of flights from friendly countries. With Iraq surrounded by hostile neighbours and terrain and still subject to the U.S. air embargo, however, the only viable route into Baghdad was over land from Jordan.

From the Jordanian capital of Amman, one had to charter a taxi – or take a chance on a bus – to make the gruelling 1000-kilometre trek across the Syrian Desert. Daytime temperatures at this time of year average 55° Celsius. Depending on the make of vehicle and its condition, the trip could take up to 22 hours. Although drivers preferred to make the crossing at night, competition for a fare meant they worked virtually around the clock. (Those who drove the few modern Chevy Suburbans available were in great demand, making two 10-hour crossings every day with a mere four hours downtime between trips.)

For reasons known only to airline schedulers, the flights from Europe to Jordan always seem to arrive in the middle of the night. For the uninitiated like me, arriving at a strange airport, exhausted and without any means of arranging transportation in advance, the situation was a little intimidating. Although Iraqi shuttle drivers were not permitted direct access to the airport, there was no shortage of Jordanian taxis willing to take me to one of the Baghdad transport depots.

Because of the economic embargo against Iraq, no financial transactions could be conducted after crossing the border. There would be no way of using a credit card or travellers' cheques, or even of picking up a wire transfer. With no access to any banking services whatsoever in Iraq, there was no alternative but to travel with large quantities of cash. (Ironically, the only foreign currency accepted in Iraq at that time was U.S. dollars.) For most travellers, the thought of carrying a large amount of cash is not reassuring. And in this case anyone aware of my destination would also know I must be carrying all my travel funds on me – in American dollars. Making my way by Jordanian taxi to the transport depot with a driver who spoke no English, my apprehension heightened as we drove for more than 30 minutes across nothing but empty desert. When we finally pulled into the shuttle depot, a variety of vehicles were parked in the lot. From battered old Chevy coupes to brand new Suburbans, all were painted in the distinctive orange and white pattern that I would soon learn denoted Iraqi taxis.

Inside a small cement building, about a dozen drivers were sleeping on floor mats. My 3:00 a.m. arrival caused a commotion. From the back of the room, Mooky, the 24-year-old foreman, clapped his hands and yelled at the drivers to rouse themselves and clear a passage to his desk.

As the drivers gathered around Mooky's desk, a tray of tea (chi) was brought in from a small anteroom. I had been told by Iraqi-Canadian acquaintances that a one-way passage to Baghdad should cost no more than $100 US, Mooky's price, however, was 5 times that. With my Jordanian cabbie having already left, I found myself alone in the middle of nowhere, surrounded by a sullen-looking crowd – hardly a strong bargaining position. Since I was on an extremely tight budget and had no way of knowing what costs to expect over the course of my two-week trip, I bartered as best I could.

Throughout protracted negotiations, the tousle-haired Mooky revealed he had been educated in Belgrade and had fled Yugoslavia at the start of the 1999 air strikes. When I told him I had reported from inside Serbia and Kosovo during the NATO campaign, Mooky's attitude softened. We eventually agreed I would make the trip in an old Crown Victoria rather than a Suburban and that I would pay $250 U.S. up front for return passage.

As it turned out, my designated driver was the only one still sleeping on the office floor. Mooky had to prod him with his foot several times before he woke up. Unshaven and completely exhausted, the youngster was angered by the manner in which he had been awoken. He nevertheless accepted his assignment and a beaming Mooky assured me Mohammed was fit to make the 12-hour drive.

There were still roughly three hours until dawn when we finally set out toward the Iraqi border. Mohammed spoke no English, but through hand signals he repeatedly indicated I should climb into the backseat and go to sleep. Despite my own exhaustion, I had serious concerns about Mohammed's fatigue and, more important, I still feared that I might end up robbed and murdered somewhere on that barren stretch of roadway.

The desert highway into Baghdad was like a scene from an old Mad Max movie. Strewn about the barren landscape were numerous hulks of vehicles that had either broken down or been damaged beyond repair in collisions presumably caused by driver fatigue. Passing motorists had quickly stripped anything usable from these wrecks, often leaving nothing more than a skeletal chassis.

On a road running parallel to the eerily empty main four-lane highway, a continual stream of petrol trucks hurtled along in both directions. At intervals, robed drivers would park their tankers in a cluster to create a brief shady repair from the sun, scorching even in these mid-morning hours. Their colleagues, meanwhile, continued to rumble by in dust-raising columns that stretched across the horizon. For Iraq, this "rolling pipeline" constituted a precious link: In exchange for vast quantities of oil sold to Jordan at below market prices, Iraq was able to trade for essential goods prohibited under restrictive UN sanctions.

Ever since the invasion of Kuwait on August 2, 1990, the UN had imposed severe trade sanctions against Iraq. Following the military success of the Gulf War, the UN embargo had been tightened in an effort to destabilize Saddam Hussein's regime. Ten years later, these measures had taken a terrible toll on the Iraqi people, but Saddam remained firmly in control.

The crippling combined effects of sanctions and the massive destruction caused by allied bombers during *Desert Storm* were evident everywhere in Baghdad. Rotating power failures regularly blacked out entire districts of the Iraqi capital for two-hour periods twice a day. With a bomb-damaged power grid and a shortage of spare turbine parts, the Iraqis had no choice but to tightly curb their use of electricity. (In rural areas, many people have been without power since 1991.)

Rampant inflation had caused the devaluation of the Iraqi dinar (ID) by an astounding 7000 per cent. (In 1990, one ID was the equivalent of $3.60 U.S.; by August 2000, $1 U.S. was worth 2,000 ID). Although aware of the exchange rate, I was still shocked the first time I exchanged a $100 U.S. bill into dinars at my hotel. With the largest denomination being a 250 Iraqi dinar note, the teller handed me several four-inch thick wads of cash. The money more than filled my briefcase and the remaining bills made unsightly bulges in my pant pockets.

With a complete ban on automobile imports, the streets of Baghdad were clogged with ancient relics, the newest cars dated back to 1990. And, thanks to ten years of sanctions, modern technology had bypassed Iraq. Cellular phones were non-existent and the Internet was a closely controlled, almost inaccessible resource. Use of the only Internet cafe in Baghdad required prior photo registration and security clearance from the Mukhabarat, Iraq's secret police.

After my arrival in Baghdad, it did not take long for the Mukhabarat to find me. Although ostensibly working for the Foreign Ministry, Jabar Abu Marwan was actually a senior officer with Iraqi intelligence who had been assigned to be my 'guide' during my stay. Short and slight of build, the 40-year-old Jabar was hardly intimidating, yet his mere presence commanded fear and respect from the average Iraqi. Like the rest of the population, Jabar drove a broken-down old car that had no air conditioning. As a result of having spent several years as a diplomat at the Iraqi embassy in Ottawa, however, he had been able to procure several modern electronic goods for himself, not the least of which was a portable computer.

While computers themselves were banned by the embargo, spare parts were not. As a result, enterprising entrepreneurs had begun acquiring all the parts, then assembling them in Baghdad. It was a laborious process, but Iraqi merchants boasted their finished products cost less and worked better than the few pre-assembled models available in Iraq.

Shortages of printing ink and paper had drastically reduced the publication of all but essential material – and government propaganda. With no tourist trade to speak of and only a trickle of foreign visitors, even maps of Iraq were hard to find. The most recent edition I could find had been published in 1980. The Iraqi government, the vendor quipped, was waiting for the Chinese to build a new embassy before printing new maps, so the Americans wouldn't make the same mistake they had made in Belgrade.

In speaking with them, it became apparent that many Iraqis had closely followed the conflict in Kosovo and had felt a deep affinity with the Serbs.

"Even though we are a Muslim country, we supported the Serbian people. Not only in their fight against NATO, but in their right to suppress insurrection in their sovereign territory," said Nasra Al-Sadoon. "We also empathize with (the Serbs) for their suffering under trade sanctions."

Short and stocky, the fifty-something Al-Sadoon was one of the few female officials working at the Iraqi Ministry of Information and was editor of the state-published *Baghdad Observer.* The day following my meeting with Nasra I was surprised to learn my interview with her had been a two-way affair; a photo of me accompanied by a story about my "mission" graced the front page of her paper.

According to the article, I was in Iraq to record "American imperialist aggression" and to see for myself the "Zionist plot against Iraq." While such fabrication of quotes was very unsettling, the article did serve the purpose of letting the tiny English-speaking international community know that I was in Iraq. And, subsequently, when conducting interviews with UN or diplomatic officials, someone would invariably jokingly refer to my 'anti-U.S. mission.'

Nevertheless, as I would soon discover for myself, for Nasra to describe the Iraqis as "suffering" was to put it mildly. In one decade, what was once a progressive, emerging middle-class society had been transformed into an impoverished and often desperate population. Immediately after the Gulf War, hard-pressed Iraqis had been forced to find new means to simply feed their families. Children were pulled from schools to help sell on the streets. To raise money, many families had no choice but to sell heirlooms and prized furniture. Virtually overnight, Baghdad abounded with new auction houses, where desperate Iraqis would accept minimal bids on cherished belongings.

This situation was brought home to me one evening at a dinner party. My host, Sami Shallal, was the older brother of my old friend Najeeb who had instructed his sibling to "treat me right" while I was in Baghdad. The Shallals are Christian and Jabar, my guide, had been eager to accompany me to their home. (Although a Shiite Muslim, Jabar had developed a taste for whisky during his stay in Canada.) The extended Shallal family was in attendance that evening, all of them eager to gawk at the Westerner, try their limited English and hear news of relatives in Canada.

Following an enormous feast, Sami's eldest son arrived – with dinner. Jabar politely explained that the first course had been a mere appetizer. When I told him I couldn't possibly eat another bite, Jabar dropped his voice to a whisper. "You had better make an attempt because this family sold a coffee table to buy you this food," he explained.

A former nuclear scientist, Sami had lost his career when the Israeli air force attacked and destroyed Iraq's Tamuze reactors in a 1981 air strike. Although his family still lived in an upper middle-class neighbourhood, Sami now operated a small stationery store. To make ends meet, the Shallals also relied upon occasional donations from relatives living abroad. Seeing the extent to which this family would go to make me, a total stranger, feel welcome was enough to incite me to eat another helping.

~ ~ ~ ~ ~ ~ ~ ~ ~ ~

The extensive bomb damage to Iraq's infrastructure during the Gulf War had proved difficult to repair. And the resultant breakdown in power, water and sewage systems had created a lethal path across the country. The combination of broken sewers and water mains – irreparable without spare parts delayed by the economic sanctions – had led not only to a shortage of drinking water but to widespread dysentery. Unable to irrigate fields without operable pumping stations, Iraq's already insufficient domestic food production had plummeted.

The humanitarian crisis inside Iraq had become so widespread by 1995 that the UN recognized the need to 'relax' the sanctions. The UN Security Council drafted a policy that would allow Iraq to export certain quantities of oil in exchange for limited, UN-controlled purchases of basic foodstuffs and medicine. Although agreed to in principle in May 1996, the first humanitarian shipment did not reach Iraq until March 1997.

Under the terms of the oil-for-food program, all revenues from Iraq's oil production were paid into an escrow account managed by the UN in New York. Thirty per cent of the revenue was paid into the Kuwait Reparation Fund, a further three per cent was deducted by theUN as an administration fee and an additional one per cent was levied as a bank service charge by the UN's Banque Nationale de Paris in New York. Of the 66 per cent remaining, 53 per cent was allocated to the Iraqi government and 13 per cent was directed to the autonomous Kurdish region in northern Iraq, administered by the UN. When these terms were first explained to me by a UN official in Baghdad, his tone was apologetic and he made no attempt to justify the conditions.

"The 30 per cent paid to Kuwait is potentially in perpetuity because there is no fixed final sum," the official explained. "As long as the U.S. is enforcing the no-fly zones and 'protecting' Kuwait, then those costs will be added to the total bill. Essentially, the U.S. is using Iraq's oil exports to pay for bombing Iraq."

Given that more than $20 billion U.S. worth of oil had been sold, the UN administration fee of 3 per cent had already provided the perpetually cash-strapped international agency with a $600 million windfall. This certainly helped explain why no one on the UN Security Council was in any hurry to alter the status quo.

"In theory, we are taking away one dollar, handing 53 cents back to the Iraqis and calling it humanitarian aid," said the UN official. "But in reality, due to the excessive controls, it is even worse than that."

With their share of the revenue, the Iraqis were free to contract for goods (or purchase goods) that were not specifically banned (i.e., prohibited weapons).Once the contracts had been approved by the supplying nation, they had to be cleared by the 15 members of the UN Security Council. Each member could veto or postpone, pending further review, any of the submitted orders. Most of the rejections were instigated by the United Kingdom or the United States. According to the

UN's 2000 figures, more than 7,000 contracts worth $1.7 billion U.S. had been postponed. This explains the drastic shortages of vital goods in Iraq.

Moreover, much of the material being delayed was essential to the operation of the oil industry itself. If production had to be further reduced, as predicted by a senior Iraqi oil ministry official, it would compromise Iraq's ability to purchase even vital necessities. Benon Sevan, then head of the UN's oil-for-food program in Iraq, had long since recognized the danger posed by any further delay in obtaining oil production parts.

"Iraq is producing and exporting oil at a very high cost to its own industry," said Sevan. "It is damaging its wells, some of them irrevocably."

Sevan had taken the Security Council to task for delaying the process: "We are trying hard to persuade all concerned that the issue should be humanitarian, and we must maintain this stance despite all differences among members of the Security Council. The (oil-for-food) program was never meant to solve all the problems of the Iraqi people, and not all the needs of Iraq. It is becoming worse because, as the years go by, the needs are becoming more acute."

At that time, food distribution centres established as part of the oil-for-food program still failed to meet basic requirements. Ration cards entitled Iraqis to a small quantity of six basic items: rice, wheat (flour), sugar, tea, vegetable oil and chickpeas. There was a separate ration allotment for milk, with priority given to children and nursing mothers. There was no meat or vegetables, forcing many families to sell precious belongings at auction just to acquire sufficient food.

George Somerwill, formerly with the CBC in Toronto, was the spokesman for the UN office in Baghdad. He admitted the situation needed to be improved, but stressed progress that had been made. When he first arrived in 1998, the UN had just issued a special report urging drastic steps be taken to "stop the rapid decline in the Iraqi situation."

Somerwill believed this goal had been achieved, but admitted the situation, "while no longer worsening, remains critical." The UN humanitarian mission's role in Iraq was, admittedly, a difficult one. They were there to mete out rations and aid to a population that would not have required assistance had their organization not imposed sanctions in the first place.

Despite the UN's dual role, Somerwill said the mission in Baghdad was receiving full co-operation from Iraqi officials. "We are granted access any time we request it, in order to follow up on the delivery process of goods. There has never been any attempt by the Iraqis to divert any of the shipments for military purposes," said Somerwill. "By establishing even closer monitoring, we're hoping to convince the Security Council to speed things up."

Although Somerwill's information and assessment would be repeated by many senior UN officials over the course of the next three years, the U.S. State Department consistently claimed otherwise. Despite evidence to the contrary from those on the ground monitoring the situation, the U.S. steadfastly maintained Saddam Hussein was siphoning off funds to produce weapons of mass destruction and to build himself more palaces. The only reason Iraqis were suffering and dying, they said, was because of Saddam's personal greed and power mongering, not because the sanctions had created shortages.

For the average Iraqi, however, the delays and sanctions became a focus for simmering anger and frustration. If the United States' intention was to undermine the people's support for Saddam Hussein, then the plan backfired. The misery and despair felt by the people was not being blamed on "His Excellency" or "The Leader." There was no civil disobedience in the streets. The massive portraits and statues of Saddam Hussein seen throughout the capital remained unvandalized. Instead, the object of the Iraqis' animosity was the United States, the country they blamed for the ongoing embargo.

To capitalize on this sentiment, Saddam embarked on a campaign aimed at keeping the memories of the Gulf War's destruction vivid in Iraqi minds. Collectively, the Iraqi people take an immense pride in having rebuilt much of their country's physical infrastructure –bridges, roads, and schools – in a very short time. To commemorate this 'victory,' Saddam ordered the building of a museum dedicated solely to the reconstruction effort in central Baghdad.

A more gruesome reminder of the first Gulf War has been preserved at the Amirya Bunker. This is the site where two U.S. 900-kilogram smart bombs plunged through the layered concrete and detonated inside a shelter packed full of civilians. Preserved since 1991 as a memorial to the women and children who died within its confines, Amirya had become a 'must-see' guided tour for foreign journalists. Even allowing for the heavily slanted diatribe of the museum commentator, the graphic and grisly remains of the bunker – where at least 315 people were killed, 130 of them children – were a disturbing sight.

Of the hundreds who took shelter there on February 13, 1991, the night the bombs fell, only 14 escaped. Concussions from the explosions triggered the automatic locks on the heavy steel doors, so when fires ignited, the people were trapped inside. Children still alive after the initial explosion, frantically tried to claw their way through solid concrete. Tiny hand- and footprints of melted skin and pieces of hair mark the ceiling and walls in one corner of the blackened shelter, permanently baked into the concrete. (To counter this grisly evidence of collateral damage, the Americans maintain the Amirya facility had contained a legitimate military target. While they've never denied the civilian death toll, the Pentagon has asserted Saddam Hussein was to blame for using his people as human shields.)

At the turn of the 21st century, with sanctions a part of daily life and U.S. and British airstrikes still an all-too-real possibility, no one in Iraq could possibly forget the Gulf War. On my first night in Baghdad, I ventured out onto my hotel room balcony to watch the sunset. Only then did I notice the shadowy figures on the adjacent rooftop. After a few moments, I realized the men were air defence gunners removing muzzle covers from a battery of 35-mm cannons. As I scanned the capital's skyline, I could see this same drill being repeated atop many government buildings. Everywhere, Iraqi soldiers were uncrating ammunition and training their guns skyward; they remained on full alert until the all-clear sounded at dawn.

~ ~ ~ ~ ~ ~ ~ ~ ~ ~

Accompanying a small delegation of British peace activists, I had not yet entered the cancer ward at Baghdad's hospital for sick children when a series of mournful cries filled the corridor. Slumped on the floor, an Iraqi woman wept inconsolably as a young orderly brushed past, carrying the lifeless form of her 12-year-old son, Kamar Salih.

At that moment, I recognized a vulnerability in myself I had not previously known. Seeing that grief-stricken mother trying to hold on to the orderly's leg as though trying to will back the life of her child, I was overcome. Although I knew I should record this image, I simply couldn't. I froze. I could not bring myself to take a photograph and I was suddenly very aware that our little group was invading the privacy of this woman at a very painful moment.

As nurses and some of the British women in the group rushed to console the mother, I moved further away down the hall. In Kamar's room, a team of orderlies had already begun to strip the sheets from his bed, making room for the next patient.

Ravaged by leukemia for the past 14 months, the young boy's tiny body appeared grotesquely disfigured and frail. Surrounding the now-vacant bed were five other young patients and their mothers, all of whom seemed more apprehensive than upset by Kamar's death.

"They are waiting to see if they will be moved to the bed beside the door," said Dr. Basim Al-Abili, chief of residents at the Saddam Central Teaching Hospital for Children. "They know the worst cases are moved there and that they are usually the next to die."

Thin and gaunt, the 27-year-old Dr. Al-Abili looked at least a dozen years older. The stress of providing care on this death row for children had obviously taken a toll on him. Prior to the Gulf War in 1991, leukemia was virtually non-existent in Iraq. By the summer of 2000, it was reaching alarming proportions with more than 1,500 cases diagnosed in children.

"We have no modern technology to conduct bone marrow transplants or transfusions," Dr. Al-Abili explained.

With access to such treatments, the remission rate for leukemia in developed countries is 60 to 80 per cent. For Iraqi doctors, the situation is difficult to accept. During the mid-1980s, Iraq's health care system was one of the best in the Middle East. There are ample funds to purchase equipment and there are well-qualified medical specialists anxious to administer the treatments

Unfortunately, the machines they need were banned under the decade-long United Nations trade sanctions. Since the UN Security Council considers anything that produces radiation potentially "dual purpose" (i.e., it could be used to make a weapon of mass destruction), radiation units were forbidden. Tragically, there is mounting evidence that the coalition bombardment, including large quantities of depleted uranium (DU) warheads used during *Desert Storm*, may have caused widespread cancer. In a report issued in July 2000, the World Health Organization (WHO) confirmed that the United States and Britain had, in fact, employed DU shells against Iraq and noted a potential link to the increased incidence of leukemia in particular.

The UN's ban on dual-purpose items also applied to a large number of vaccines considered to be potential biological agents. One direct result of the embargo on vaccines was the 1999 outbreak of polio, a disease that had all but been eliminated in the late 1980s. In a report issued by the UN Humanitarian Mission in Baghdad, the blame for the outbreak was placed squarely on UN Security Council sanctions.

"Iraq is the only country in the world that has no control over its revenues, although well committed to the polio eradication initiative. Unfortunately, this could not be translated into programmatic areas because the needed resources are controlled somewhere else," the report states. Since 1996, the UN Security Council has controlled all funds and purchase approval for Iraq.

While the increased rate of cancer and diseases among Iraqi children was alarming, an even more pressing concern was the widespread malnutrition that claimed up to 140 lives a day. Dysentery had become rampant, particularly among children. With little meat, fruit or vegetables available, many children succumbed to malnutrition, becoming more susceptible to infection. Under normal circumstances, antibiotics could be administered successfully. Under the embargo, however, the antibiotics that were shipped to Iraq were of insufficient quantity and, more important, of insufficient quality to reverse infections. "Since we cannot control what they ship to us, we often receive first-generation antibiotics to which many common germs have long since developed immunity," said Dr. Al-Abili. "In the West, you are using fifth-generation drugs."

Prior to the Gulf War, Iraq's pharmaceutical plants had produced and exported antibiotics throughout the Middle East. Now Iraqi doctors were often unable to prevent routine ailments from becoming fatal.

Pregnant women were also hard hit by the food shortages. The overcrowded wards of the neo-natal intensive care unit at the Baghdad children's hospital were filled with premature babies and malnourished newborns. With no air-conditioning, due to the UN's ban on essential spare parts, the heat was almost unbearable. Still, with a chronic shortage of nurses, the mothers were all in attendance to watch over and fan their tiny babies.

In a room next to the neo-natal unit, a husband tried to comfort his sobbing wife as she clutched the motionless body of their doll-sized infant. An orderly holding a blanket stood by patiently, waiting to wrap up the tiny corpse and take it away.

Dr. Al-Abili explained his staff used to cry with the families, "but now we lose an average of three children a day. After a while, you are just numb."

The 1999 UNICEF child and maternal mortality survey revealed the scope of this humanitarian crisis. The incidence of malnutrition had doubled since 1991, while the mortality rate for children under the age of five had tripled to 13 per 1000.

"That amounts to nearly 500,000 children lost over the past 10 years," Nasra Al-Sadoon, editor of the *Baghdad Observer*, had explained to me when we met earlier. "In a population of 22 million, that means every family has suffered a loss."

Although Al-Sadoon's comments to me were filled with anti-American rhetoric, the numbers she quoted were backed by independent UN reports. Incredibly, the U.S. State Department never questioned the death toll, nor did any representative ever publicly challenge the UN assertion that this was directly attributable to ongoing sanctions. In late 1995, when asked on the U.S. news program *60 Minutes* whether the U.S. policy toward Iraq could possibly justify the death of 500,000 children, then-Secretary of State Madeleine Albright didn't hesitate: "Yes, the price is worth it."

Children were not the only ones suffering under the sanctions and in the war's aftermath. An estimated 1.5 million Iraqis have died in the last decade as a direct result of the Gulf conflict and the ensuing embargo.

In addition, many of the Iraqi soldiers who fought in the Kuwait campaign have been diagnosed with a variety of illnesses similar to those afflicting Canadian and U.S. soldiers suffering from what has been termed Gulf War Syndrome. (The World Health Organization's initial report on depleted uranium called for a probe to further study the adverse health effects caused by these munitions. At the time, however, the U.S. government continued to block the agency's efforts to launch an investigation.)

"The high rate of birth defects among the children of our soldiers and from the region around Basra [where heavy fighting took place], would strongly suggest a link to depleted uranium," said Dr. Al-Abili. "However, we don't have the means necessary to investigate it."

As Dr. Al-Abili concluded his tour, a woman's piercing cry from the floor above signalled another child's death. It was not even noon and the Saddam Central Teaching Hospital for Children had already reached its daily average.

~ ~ ~ ~ ~ ~ ~ ~ ~ ~

SAMAWA, AUGUST 18-20, 2000   It was mid-morning when the air raid sirens sounded throughout the Samawa market square. At the governor's headquarters, several Iraqi soldiers in the courtyard stared skyward trying to spot any trace of approaching U.S. aircraft, while an anti-aircraft gunner atop the roof anxiously traversed his automatic weapon at the unseen foe. Several seconds later, the sound of jets high overhead indicated this was no false alarm.

Everyone braced for an imminent attack. When the sound of the aircraft engines faded and there were no explosions, the people in the market and the Iraqi soldiers who had been frozen in anticipation, quickly resumed their activities as though nothing had ever happened.

Just one week earlier, U.S. and British bombers had pounded this same town in two separate attacks. The Pentagon's explanation for those attacks was that, while patrolling the southern no-fly zone, their jets had been fired upon by Iraqi forces. (Ever since the 1991 Gulf War, the U.S. had imposed and enforced strict no-fly zones in the north of Iraq – above the 36th parallel – and in the south below the 35th parallel.)

In spite of the constant presence of Jabar, my Mukhabarat 'guide,' I had to present myself daily to the Ministry of Information's protocol section. These visits had quickly grown tiresome. As all requests to interview senior officials had to be accompanied by a list of questions, I spent hours completing forms only to see them sit untranslated for days on end. There was no other foreign reporter in Iraq at that time and, although a local journalist working for Reuters had been granted access to Samawa after the attack, I had to make repeated requests to be granted the same access. In the end, permission was granted and I combined my trip to Samawa with one to the southern city of Basra.

On this particular trip, Jabar did not accompany me since his presence was considered redundant as Mohammed Hassan, my state-appointed translator, and his cousin who was hired on as driver, accompanied me. With much of the Iraqi telephone system in a state of disrepair since the Gulf War, communication between cities was virtually non-existent. Adding to my difficulties was a rigid bureaucracy that displayed little inter-departmental co-operation. As a result, the unexpected arrival of our little party set off a flurry of activity. Unable to decide whether I should be under the control of civil or military headquarters, the Samawa authorities simply gave us the benefit of the doubt and allowed us to proceed to the bombsite unescorted.

Immediately following the August 11 airstrikes, Lieutenant Commander Ernest Duplessis, spokesman for the United States Central Command, claimed the attack on Samawa had destroyed a building "used to store air defence equipment and weapons." My inspection of the site, however, did not substantiate this claim. Two large blackened craters marked the point of impact in an empty lot, some 300 meters in front of the train station. The shrapnel from the bombs damaged nearby houses, but caused only superficial damage to the warehouse. If this lightly damaged warehouse was the U.S. jets' intended target (and it was the only building even close to the impact area), then the Pentagon's initial intelligence reports were clearly faulty.

A portion of the Samawa warehouse was now being used as an administrative office for food distribution, while the remainder – formerly an auto parts centre – had long stood empty, as evidenced by the mounds of pigeon droppings on the floor.

As I crawled around the craters picking up scraps of the shattered U.S. missile, a crowd of villagers gathered to watch. Given that the village had just been bombed and that there had been civilian casualties, I was not sure what sort of reception I would receive. With the heat topping 60° Celsius, I must have been showing the effects of the sun for, within minutes, one of the elders came forward. With Mohammed translating, the man invited me to his home for a drink.

A dozen men gathered inside the man's crowded living room. They all waited patiently as I struggled to remove my combat boots before entering, the effort of which left me sweating even more. Once I was seated on a floor mat, a young boy approached with a metal goblet, frosted from the ice-cold water it contained. With no electricity in the village, I could not fathom how they had chilled the water.

Although I had serious reservations about drinking local well water, under the expectant gaze of so many I simply couldn't refuse. Realizing I would probably fall victim to dysentery, I downed the tumbler in a single gulp. My hosts were pleased and quickly offered any assistance they could. Although burials had already been conducted for the two warehouse employees killed in the attack, my new acquaintances made arrangements for me to visit with a number of those injured in the blast.

In total, 19 civilians had been wounded in the attack. I interviewed several of them, and they all said they had heard no sirens or anti-aircraft fire preceding the attack. The blasts came as a shock. "I was just taking a smoke break beside my car when there was a giant flash in front of me," explained Talib Lamir Sahib, a 56-year-old railway worker. "The shock threw me to the ground about 20 feet away."

Sahib received a 20-centimetre gash to his forehead from a piece of shrapnel when a second rocket exploded, even closer to him, just seconds later.

Rad Hazal-Kareem, a 24-year-old security guard at the station, received injuries to his arms and wrists when he was blown out of his cot and onto the roadway. "I was sound asleep at the time," he admitted sheepishly.

Several days after my report on Samawa was published in the *Ottawa Citizen*, the Pentagon released a series of satellite photographs purportedly showing the remains of Iraqi air defence guns destroyed during the attack. I have no idea where those photos were taken, but they were not taken at Samawa. The American media, however, was apparently convinced by the photographs that the U.S. pilots had attacked only in self-defence. From that point on, I would no longer trust any photographic 'evidence' offered by Pentagon officials.

Even if Iraqi forces had fired at the U.S. planes, such a gesture would have been merely an act of futile defiance. With its aircraft either destroyed or still being held by the Iranian government (135 Iraqi fighter pilots flew their planes to what they believed to be a safe Iranian haven during the Gulf War; they remain there to this day), Iraq's only challenge to the no-fly patrols must come from ground forces.

The Iraqi air defences, which had proved woefully inadequate during *Operation Desert Storm* 10 years earlier, had been neither replaced nor modernized. In the no-fly zones, the majority of Iraq's anti-aircraft weapons consisted of 23-millimetre automatic cannons and 14.5-millimetre heavy machine guns. Around major military installations, these weapons were grouped together in four-gun batteries directed by primitive radar units. However, most of the air defences consisted simply of single cannons mounted atop the facility they were intended to protect.

While neither the 23-mm or 14.5-mm guns are effective above 6000 feet, the majority of the U.S. patrol flights were flown between 15,000 and 23,000 feet. The state-run Iraqi press reported daily on the number of sorties flown against Iraq by the "U.S. and British aggressors." These attacking jets were derogatorily referred to as "ravens" and the pilots as "cowards," but through the jingoistic bravado, the importance of the Iraqi air defence effort in maintaining the country's morale was readily apparent.

"Our brave soldiers chased away the hostile intruders" was the common closing line for most of these articles, while any claim of downed U.S. aircraft was accompanied by an explanation that the wreckage could not be seen because it had gone down outside Iraq's borders.

In the central region between the 35th and 36th parallels, which was not part of the no-fly zones, Saddam Hussein had retained the best of what little air defence he had left. Larger 35-mm cannons, which are effective to 10,000 feet, and guided missile batteries were in evidence throughout Baghdad and the surrounding region. Privately, however, Iraqi officials admitted even these heavier weapons were virtually useless against U.S. warplanes. Despite an estimated 7,000 rockets fired at allied aircraft over the past 10 years, the U.S. and British militaries deny any of their planes has ever been successfully downed by the Iraqis.

It is also in the relatively secure central region that the remains of Saddam Hussein's armoured personnel carriers were housed in covered vehicle parks. In 1991 they failed to put up any resistance against the U.S. coalition forces. Ten years later, the vehicles were starved for spare parts due to the decade-long trade sanctions. As a result, the Iraqi military had to seriously curtail use of their armoured vehicles. Instead, roving army patrols used civilian Toyota pickup trucks with a light machine gun mounted above the cab, while armoured personnel carriers (APCs) could often be seen dug into sand berm perimeters established as permanent bunkers around military encampments.

As I travelled further south to Basra, the destruction levelled against Iraqi forces during the 1991 bombing campaign and in subsequent airstrikes became all too apparent. Every current Iraqi military facility sat adjacent to its obliterated predecessor. Huge lots of twisted metal and destroyed vehicles remained as grim testimony to the havoc unleashed by allied warplanes. Inside the rebuilt compounds, herds of sheep slept under canopies meant to house Iraq's once vaunted armoured regiments.

With the best of Saddam Hussein's military hardware hidden away from U.S. air force patrol zones, the calibre of soldiers deployed into these regions was somewhat more impressive. The Republican Guard and airborne units stationed in Basra and Samawa, for example, were far more martial in their demeanour than the rag-tag units that provided security around Baghdad's official buildings (with the exclusion of the elite military police units that patrolled certain key intersections).

Of the nearly 500,000 troops in the Iraqi army the vast majority were conscripts doing a mandatory two-year term of national service. But those who desired more money ($15 US a month instead of $10) and better food could volunteer for the more strenuous job of serving in the Republican Guard. However, even among the elite units there was a shortage of basic equipment: Footwear was by no means standardized, with civilian leather shoes being the norm; body armour or flak jackets were non-existent; ammunition pouches were shared between on- and off-duty sentries; and the wooden stocks of personal weapons were badly scarred and worn.

The officer corps remained the only professional element of the Iraqi army with all of its senior commanders having had some combat experience over the past twenty years of constant warfare.

As an ex-soldier and publisher of a military magazine, I had submitted daily requests with the Ministry of Information's protocol office in the hope of obtaining an interview with a senior military official. I doubt any of my applications was even passed along to the Iraqi military, however, as the Ministry seemingly acted outside of any civilian administrative control. My official guide, Jabar Abu Marwan, had a different kind of clout, though, and, after a few rounds of Scotch, I managed to persuade him to bring me to a military facility.

The facility wasn't much of a site; it was just a storage area for Iranian weaponry and vehicles captured during the Iran-Iraq war of the 1980s. The garrison, however, consisted of several hundred conscripts. The commanding officer held the rank of brigadier general and knew Jabar well since they had served together in the Gulf War. He offered me what little hospitality he could.

The heat was almost unbearable in the small wooden office that served as headquarters, and the brigadier apologized for the lack of air conditioning. As a matter of courtesy, the Iraqi commander had put on a uniform shirt, although he had not bothered to button it. He wore only khaki boxer briefs and, pointing to his swollen stump, the general explained he had lost his right foot during an attack by an American helicopter gunship during the retreat from Kuwait in 1991. Explaining that the heat played havoc with his prosthetic foot, he also apologized for the informality of his appearance.

For the next hour, as we sat in his office drinking tea and exchanging war stories, a steady procession of wide-eyed young conscripts would stop and stare at me from the doorway and window. "They have never seen an American in real life before," explained the general. "You are a curiosity to my men – an enemy right here in our camp."

Although I explained I was not an American but a former Canadian soldier, the old officer said it did not matter. "When we fought the Americans, these boys," pointing to the young soldiers staring from the window, "were just seven years old. All they know about the Americans is air raid sirens, explosions and the horror stories passed on to them by disabled veterans like myself," he explained. "When we fought the Iranians, courage meant something on the battlefield. But against the technological might of the Americans, it was meaningless."

When the 1980-90 war with Iran ended, Saddam Hussein declared a tremendous victory for Iraq. As part of the victory celebrations, Saddam staged a massive parade of military power at a purpose-built reviewing stand in the centre of Baghdad. Unfortunately, these pre-Gulf War images of massed tanks being overflown by hundreds of fighter aircraft, which 10 years later were still being aired nightly on television, served only to illustrate how thoroughly Iraq's armed forces had been ravaged.

What was once the fourth largest army in the world was now just a shattered hulk, unable to defend its own territory and people from ongoing airstrikes.

~ ~ ~ ~ ~ ~ ~ ~ ~ ~

BAGHDAD, AUGUST 21-22, 2000   On August 22, 2000, Taha Yassin Ramadan, Iraq's Vice-President and a key adviser to Saddam Hussein, gave a rare briefing to the Iraqi parliament. The reason for Ramadan's appearance was to officially outline the problems Iraq was experiencing as a result of the decade-long United Nations sanctions. In particular, the Vice-President wanted to claim UN Security Council "corruption" was responsible for the current "postponement" of numerous contracts of vital necessities under the oil-for-food program.

The UN's latest figures showed that over $1.7 billion worth of essential spare parts and medicine contracts were being indefinitely "postponed" at the Security Council level, primarily by British and U.S. vetoes. Vice-President Ramadan alleged to his parliament that many of these potential contractors were being forced to pay UN officials "bribes" in order to avoid these "postponements" and to conduct business with Iraq.

My attendance at Ramadan's presentation had been offered as a last-minute stopgap solution by the office of the Ministry of Information. After two weeks of filling out questionnaires and interview requests, my first trip to Iraq was fast coming to an end without my ever having met any senior officials. Upon learning of Ramadan's planned speech, the protocol officials reluctantly agreed to my presence in the parliament, so long as I remained in the press gallery.

The first 30 minutes of the presentation had been a vicious anti-West, anti-media diatribe and was greeted by hearty applause and cheers from the Iraqi parliamentarians. When Mohammed Hassan translated the vice-president's allegations of bribery at the UN, I was genuinely intrigued and eager to find out if Ramadan could substantiate the accusation. Canada was one of the 15-member Security Council and, presumably, included in this claim of bribery.

Not knowing whether there would be a question period following the briefing, I waited for a pause in Ramadan's speech and asked in a loud voice from the back of the hall for proof. Sitting next to me, Mohammed turned white as, in a single motion, the 200 politicians wheeled around in their seats to see who had had the audacity to interrupt the presentation and call out in English. There was a long pause as the vice-president stared at me from the podium. When he demanded a translation of my question, I thought Mohammed was going to faint. Stammering through a "with all due respect" phrase in Arabic, my request for proof was reiterated.

You could have heard a pin drop during the moments that followed. After a lengthy pause, Ramadan issued a statement in Arabic that my petrified translator scribbled nervously onto his pad. I would be unable to ask a summary question for, as the vice-president resumed his speech, Mohammed pulled me towards the exit. He told me Ramadan had not given any direct evidence of bribery but, as for Canada's role in the Security Council, the vice president had said that "we cannot conclude, from their actions to date, that Canada is an enemy of Iraq. However, Canada is very much under the influence of our enemy – the U.S.A. – and we can only hope that in the future [Canada's] government will improve their behaviour."

As a member of the Mukhabarat, Jabar had spent a number of years at the Iraqi embassy in Ottawa. He still followed events in Canada closely and he explained that many senior Baghdad officials had felt betrayed by Foreign Affairs Minister Lloyd Axworthy.

"In 1990, Axworthy was one of the three Canadian members of parliament who ventured [to Iraq] to seek a peaceful solution to the Gulf crisis," explained Jabar. "Now that he's the Minister, why is he not using his voice to challenge the U.S. on their policy of sanctions?"

In the previous months there had been a growing movement in Canada to publicize the suffering of the Iraqi people and to push for a lifting of the UN sanctions. Spearheaded by Arthur Millholland, an executive with a Calgary-based oil company, and organized by long-time Liberal party fixer Donn Lovett, the Iraqi initiative had found a parliamentary champion in Colleen Beaumier, the Liberal Member of Parliament for Brampton-West Mississauga.

The group had been able to arrange a series of presentations to a parliamentary Foreign Affairs committee, outlining the dire circumstances caused by the embargo against Iraq. Most who testified were former UN officials who had worked in Baghdad and who had resigned in protest. The evidence was convincing enough to generate a unanimous resolution from the committee urging a lifting of the sanctions against Iraq and Beaumier's initiative was lauded in an August 15, 2000 *Calgary Herald* editorial. Axworthy knew that such a motion, if passed, would enrage the Americans, so no further effort was made to table such a bill in the House of Commons.

In the spring of 2000, Iraq's relations with Canada were further strained when the Iraqis claimed bacteria was discovered in Canadian wheat obtained under the oil-for-food program. Canadian inspectors insisted the bacteria was merely a harmless mould that frequently grows on wheat husks and that would be eliminated in the milling process. However, following the incident, the Canadian government announced a one-million dollar humanitarian shipment of pharmaceutical supplies to Iraq.

Instead of being eagerly received as a welcome antidote to Iraq's health care crisis, however, Canada's unsolicited offer was rejected by the Iraqi government.

"This was done in keeping with our policy regarding such donations," explained Dr. Abdul Razzaq Al-Hashimi, a former Iraqi cabinet minister and currently director of the Organization of Friendship, Peace and Solidarity. "We are not about to let Lloyd Axworthy or others like him assuage their conscience by giving us the medicine that their own sanctions prevent us from buying for ourselves. If Axworthy sincerely wants to help the Iraqi people, he will break with the U.S.-imposed policy."

Prior to my trip I had been given Al-Hashimi's name and home address by Margarita Papandreou. Although I had not yet met the former First Lady of Greece, mutual acquaintances who were trying to gain wider publicity for the plight of the Iraqis had put us in touch. Margarita had launched a number of initiatives to help the Iraqi people and her introduction had served me well with Dr. Al-Hashimi.

During the course of my stay in Baghdad, Al-Hashimi a former ambassador to Paris, had proven to be as approachable as he was opinionated. Although officially the head of a non-governmental organization (NGO), Al-Hashimi was very well connected to the senior Baath party leadership in Iraq. On a more personal note, Al-Hashimi wanted to make it very clear that Iraq did not require 'charity' since it was exporting billions of dollars in oil. "The world will not listen to America forever," he said. (Admittedly, there had been an increasing number of developments in recent weeks suggesting that other countries were already breaking ranks with the U.S. and re-establishing normal relations with Iraq.)

The August 2000 visit to Baghdad by Venezuelan President Hugo Chavez and a visit in September of that year by Indonesian President Abdurrahman Wahid had both sparked stern rebukes from the U.S. State Department. The U.S. government remained steadfast in its insistence that Saddam Hussein's regime remain in isolation.

While the Venezuelans and Indonesians had publicly disregarded U.S. pressure, behind the scenes many key American allies had been quietly cozying up to Saddam Hussein. The Germans, who never formally broke diplomatic relations with Baghdad during the Gulf War, had recently, and without fanfare, reinstated their ambassador in Iraq's capital. Of the few businessmen in evidence in Iraq, Germans constituted the majority. The Japanese had also reopened their embassy and heralded the return of their chargé d'affaires with a formal reception on August 20 for the entire Baghdad diplomatic community.

In addition to making some inroads with the international community, one of the key regional strategic gains Saddam Hussein had made was the normalizing of relations with Syria. A long-standing enemy of Iraq – Syria supported Iran during the 1980-90 war with Iraq – the new-found tentative economic co-operation between these two neighbouring countries had come as a shock to many Middle East analysts.

"Five years ago, no one would have imagined Iraq reopening their railway lines and oil pipelines to Syria," stated Enko Karabegovic, the Yugoslav ambassador in Baghdad. Although not formally allied, the Yugoslavs had suffered through their own decade of sanctions and had conducted considerable trade with Iraq prior to the Gulf War. Under President Slobodan Milosevic, Yugoslavia had maintained close diplomatic ties with Baghdad.

"If Saddam can shore up his ties with Syria, he will have won a major victory over the U.S., whose policy is to keep him bottled up," said Karabegovic, a career diplomat who had spent many years in the Middle East. His insight proved to be invaluable to me in those first fact-finding days. I had been provided a contact with the Yugoslav diplomat through my friend Ljilijana Borovcanin at the embassy in Ottawa. Equally eager to hear news of the post-war situation in his home country, Karabegovic hosted me on several occasions at his residence during my stay.

OVER THE PAST DECADE, it had been Iraq's alleged possession of or ability to produce weapons of mass destruction that had been the nub of the rationale for justifying continued sanctions against Iraq.

Although the UN had continually deployed teams of inspectors inside Iraq following the Gulf War (until they were pulled out during the crisis in 1998), there had been little tangible proof of such weapons.

In fact, Scott Ritter, the former chief weapons inspector for the UN, had quit his post in 1998, in protest over the continuing sanctions against Iraq, and was making a documentary cataloguing the suffering U.S./UN policies were having on the children of Iraq.

At the time, I knew of Ritter only by reputation. The media had painted him as a hard-nosed ex-Marine officer who had pressured the Iraqis like a pit bull during weapons inspections. Following his resignation, he had become one of the more convincing speakers to appear before the Canadian Foreign Affairs parliamentary committee. It seemed Ritter's position on Iraq had suddenly undergone a tremendous transformation – from hawk to dove. Nevertheless, there was no one in the West better qualified to assess the threat posed by Saddam, and the former inspector's about-face spoke louder than words. Although I didn't get a chance to meet him during my trip, I did read about his planned documentary in the *Baghdad Observer.*

Despite growing vocal dissent in the international community, the UN Security Council, in December 1999, passed Resolution 1284, which outlined the mandate for yet another round of weapons inspections. While the U.S. was able to get the resolution passed, France, China and Russia – the three other permanent members – voiced their dissent but chose to abstain from the vote rather than exercise their vetoes.

In response, Iraqi officials vowed to refuse access to the new team of weapons inspectors. With international speculation that oil stocks were running low and driving up the price of crude to record highs, the economic fallout from maintaining a tight lock on Iraq's vast oil reserves made it even more difficult for countries to tow the U.S. line.

Russia's Foreign Minister, Igor Ivanov, sent a blunt letter to UN Security General Koffi Annan regarding the Iraqi sanctions on August 12, 2000. The letter outlined in detail how Russia had lost nearly $30 billion in trade and frozen debt payments as a result of complying with the 10-year embargo.

Ivanov wrote: "The issue of continued sanctions is now a hostage to the political objectives of some countries. The Russian Federal Council is under increasing pressure from social and industrial groups inside Russia in order for us to ease the sanctions for their benefit. By informing the UN of this issue, we count on your understanding. The time has come for a more accurate analysis on the effect of such sanctions – not only upon the catastrophic results in Iraq, but also on those other countries which are affected."

It was believed that Ivanov's letter was notice that Russia was about to invoke Article 50 of the UN embargo resolution, which would essentially allow her to trade freely with Iraq. Such a move by Russia would have signalled the collapse of the U.S. strategy and be heralded as a major victory for the long suffering Iraqi people and, in particular, Saddam Hussein.

"In 1993, our Leader (Saddam Hussein) told the Iraqi people that the UN sanctions would never be lifted by the Security Council," Dr. Al-Hashimi had told me. "Instead, [Saddam] predicted that the embargo would eventually collapse if the people continued to steel themselves to the U.S. aggression." (Official publications in Iraq still referred to the ongoing suffering as simply a new phase in the "Mother of all Battles.")

However, the allegation that the UN was unlikely to "lift" the sanctions "voluntarily" was not without some merit. For the once cash-strapped United Nations, the oil-for-food program had proven to be manna from heaven. It was the only UN mission in history that generated money – some $600 million U.S. alone had been deducted in "administrative compensation" for the mere 657 UN staffers assigned to the Iraq program.

However, with the solidarity necessary to enforce the embargo beginning to crumble, the days of the oil-for-food program appeared, at that time, to be numbered. Even the Pentagon had seemingly begun to soften its stance on Iraq. While continuing to insist on deploying new weapons inspectors, U.S. officials proclaimed in a statement issued in mid-August 2000, that Saddam Hussein was "no longer considered a threat to the Gulf region."

The American reversal suggested that this reduction in Iraq's ability to wage war was proof that their strategy of sanctions was effective. Over the next few months leading up to the U.S. presidential elections, it was expected that the international playmaking over Iraq would, yet again, come to a head.

On my final evening in Iraq, I was hastily summoned by my translator, Mohammed Hassan, to visit the Ministry of Information. After two weeks of fruitless endeavour, I had finally been granted an interview with a senior official. After receiving a long and eloquent background briefing from Dr. Humam Abdul-Ghafour, the Minister of Information, I was able to question him directly on the Canadian diplomatic position.

"I would hate to see Canada as part of this game," he replied. "We have no negative history with Canada, so why has Canada taken this negative stance towards us? We don't want the Canadian government as an ally, but we are confused when they consider us to be an enemy."

ABOVE: *Without the permission to import engineering equipment, Iraq's oil industry suffered a loss of production ability during 12 years of UN-imposed sanctions. (ALI HAIDER)*

OPPOSITE PAGE, TOP: *Iraqi women line up at a distribution centre to collect their rations. Under the 1996 UN oil-for-food program, Iraqis were provided with monthly allotments of food staples. (REIN KRAUSE, REUTERS)*

ABOVE, LEFT: Jabar Abu Marwan, an officer in the Mukhabarat (Iraqi Intelligence Service). He had been stationed at Iraq's embassy in Ottawa as a diplomat. (s. TAYLOR)

ABOVE, RIGHT: Talib Lamir Sahib displays the gash he received during the U.S. airstrike against Samawa in August 2000. The Pentagon claimed they had destroyed Iraqi air defence systems, but they had actually hit a food warehouse by mistake. (s.TAYLOR)

THIS PAGE: *Iraqi President Saddam Hussein wearing traditional Kurdish costume. By May 2001, Hussein's officials actually believed they had beaten the sanctions and were claiming victory in the Mother of all Battles.*

OPPOSITE PAGE: *Only weeks after he was sworn in as U.S. President, George W. Bush launched a series of airstrikes against Iraq. The international community protested the American aggression.* (U.S. DEPARTMENT OF DEFENCE)

CHAPTER FOUR:

Changing the [U.S.] Regime

NOVEMBER 7-13, 2000   After my original articles about the plight of Iraq under the sanctions were published in the *Ottawa Citizen*, they were put into much wider circulation by a number of international peace activist organizations. Largely in response to this, I received an invitation from Margarita Papandreou to participate in an 'embargo-busting' flight from Athens into Iraq.

Scheduled to take place in November 2000, the former First Lady of Greece intended to charter an Olympic Airways plane and fly into Baghdad in deliberate defiance of the U.S. blockade. Although Saddam Hussein had recently opened his airport and promised free fuel to any aircraft that would fly into the capital, the U.S. threat of military force had succeeded in keeping the embargo in place. However, Papandreou did not believe the Americans would actually shoot down an unarmed civilian plane in broad daylight – particularly if the passenger list included politicians and international journalists.

Although officially organizing this protest flight as a private citizen, in reality, Ms. Papandreou had the tacit support of the Greek government. Her eldest son, Foreign Minister George Papandreou Jr., was instrumental in arranging the state-owned airline's provision of a charter aircraft for his mother. During the 1999 NATO campaign against Yugoslavia, the Greeks had been singularly outraged at the U.S.-led aggression against the Serbs. Although a member of NATO, Greece did not participate in the airstrikes; instead, the country provided a military field hospital to help treat wounded Serbs.

In Athens, crowds had staged numerous violent demonstrations outside the British and American embassies during the 78-day bombing campaign. The following summer anti-American sentiment still ran high, and Ms. Papandreou's initiative to challenge the U.S. policy on Iraq was a popular one. Although the bulk of the passengers on this flight were Greek doctors, journalists and politicians, Margarita had also invited a small number of Americans, British and Canadians to join her.

I was pleased to learn that my old friend Rollie Keith would also be participating in this historic event. An ex-army officer, Keith had been serving as a UN observer in Kosovo when the airstrikes began in 1999. He was one of the few observers to break rank, quit his job and publicly state the Serbs had not been conducting a campaign of ethnic cleansing prior to the NATO attack, and that the refugee crisis was a direct result of the NATO bombing. Although Keith's voice went largely unheard in the jingoistic media barrage that supported the war, the former officer continued to speak out.

Keith and I met in March 2000, when we testified at a mock war crimes tribunal in New York City. Organized by former U.S. Attorney General Ramsey Clark, the tribunal was operating on a shoestring budget, so Rollie and I ended up sharing the same hotel room. Now, thanks to Clark's connection to Margarita Papandreou, Keith had also become involved in the embargo-busting flight to Iraq.

With several spaces still available on the plane, I recommended that Ms. Papandreou include Donn Lovett in her invitation. Although he had never been to Iraq, Lovett had been instrumental in organizing anti-sanction presentations to the parliamentary Foreign Affairs committee.

Given the purpose of the trip, I had initially thought it would be easy for me to obtain another Iraqi visa, but the powers that be in Baghdad were hesitant to grant me access. Apparently, the Iraqi leadership had been furious at my reports that painted the military's combat capability as a mere shadow of its former might. Although they didn't question my assessments, their collective pride had been bruised, and it took personal intervention on the part of Dr. Abdul Razzaq Al-Hashimi to get my entry visa approved.

The original date for Margarita's protest flight was November 10, with all the international participants gathering in Athens a few days earlier. It had been hoped that this protest would send a strong message to the newly elected U.S. presidential administration, to help shape a new Iraq policy before officially taking office the following January. However, the November 7 elections proved to be an un-precedented catastrophe. Although Republican George W. Bush was initially an-nounced the winner, electoral shambles in the state of Florida served to keep Demo-crat Al Gore's chances alive.

With the U.S. presidency in legal limbo, the American media became fixated on the outcome. Sitting in Athens, we realized that, with each day that passed without a binding decision, the chances a sanction-busting flight into Iraq would receive any attention at all in the U.S. decreased significantly. However, the ar-rangements were in place and the show would go on.

After linking up at the Athens airport, Rollie Keith and I once again shared a hotel room. For reasons unknown, Keith and I were the only international attendees to receive a summons to Margarita's suburban villa on November 9. Although a major strategy session was scheduled, when no details were forwarded to us, a majority of the participants had tired of waiting and, instead, went sightseeing in the Greek capital. This turn of events proved fortuitous as Keith and I were sud-denly elevated from merely fringe attendees to being an integral part of the plan-ning committee. As such, we were able to witness firsthand the cat-and-mouse game being played out by the U.S. State Department as they tried to thwart Ms. Papandreou.

Everything – from pressuring third party countries like Syria to deny the use of its airspace to direct threat of military force – was thrown up as obstacles. The State Department (via the UN) was desperate to get its hands on the passenger list. Although this was unquestionably a protest flight, a fair amount of medical supplies were also included in the cargo, courtesy of the Greek chapter of Médecins sans frontières.

Margarita remained steadfast in her refusal to co-operate with the Americans until they pulled a fast one. Directly contacting Lloyds of London, the U.S. State Department advised the insurance company of the intended "unauthorized" flight resulting in the prompt pulling of Olympic Airways' insurance coverage. This hurdle proved insurmountable. Although disappointed at the 24-hour delay this final tactic had caused, the consensus among those involved was that this was going to be a public protest anyway – covered by international media – so identity protection was, ultimately, a non-issue.

To minimize the impact this protest flight would have on the embargo, the UN suddenly granted consent – but not approval – for this humanitarian flight, but only after the passenger list had been faxed to the U.S. embassy in Greece. It was a petty, face-saving gesture, but it did little to diminish the fact that Margarita had held her ground.

Nevertheless, in what had become something of an international race into Baghdad, the delay had cost us the bragging rights of being the first plane to land in Iraq. A small twin-engine private plane had already touched down and the Russians had also successfully flown in a group of protestors. Our only claim to fame was being the first commercial planeload from the West to have successfully challenged the U.S. authority. Although none of us really expected to be shot out of the sky by American fighters, the very possibility made a valid argument for the Olympic Airways crew to keep the bar carts rolling throughout the flight.

The Iraqis, of course, maximized the arrival of our flight. Virtually the entire Baghdad press corps was in attendance to film the gaggle of the somewhat inebriated protesters that emerged from the plane.

Completely unused for over a decade, Saddam International airport was eerily deserted, except for the Iraqi media and a welcoming committee of senior officials. The bizarre interior décor – green '70s mod – was like something out of an Austin Powers movie. As our visas and immigration forms were processed, several people from our group moved into a VIP lounge. Iraq's Deputy Prime Minister, Tariq Aziz, was on hand to personally welcome Margarita Papandreou, and Dr. Al-Hashimi, who was also at the airport, greeted me like an old friend. Jabar Abu Marwan was also in attendance and was pleased to inform me that I would once again be subject to his services as 'guide.'

Although our actual stay in Iraq was limited to 48 hours, our hosts had set out quite a comprehensive program. Bus tours were arranged to the Amiriya shelter, the children's hospital and some of the UN oil-for-food depots. The Greek journalists and politicians in the group were able to make ample use of this rare opportunity to see inside Saddam's Iraq.

Having already seen these various locales, I was pleased to discover that Arthur Millholland, the Calgary oil executive, was also in Baghdad. Excusing ourselves from the main party, Donn Lovett and I linked up with Millholland's party at a downtown restaurant. Joseph Shamal, an American-Iraqi businessman, was Millholland's representative in Baghdad, and the restaurant we dined at that night belonged to his cousin. Shamal was obviously well connected to senior Iraqi officials and had thus been instrumental in arranging for Millholland's company to 'lift' oil under the oil-for-food program.

Just how connected Shamal was became evident during the course of our meal. A large, black Mercedes pulled up at the curb and a man identified only as Salim entered the restaurant with two bodyguards. Tall and slim and wearing a black leather coat, there was no question that this newcomer carried himself with a degree of authority. After exchanging cordial greetings with Shamal and Millholland,

Salim proceeded to ask me a barrage of questions about both my military and media backgrounds. What interested him most was how exactly I had become an acquaintance of Margarita Papandreou. At the end of his impromptu interrogation, and seemingly satisfied by my responses, Salim thanked Shamal and returned to his waiting car. Unbeknownst to me, I had just met Salim Said Khalaf al-Jumayli, one of Saddam Hussein's cousins, and the director of all North American intelligence operations for the Mukhabarat secret police.

The following day I was hosted by Enko Karabegovic at the Yugoslav embassy. Less than three weeks earlier, following a dramatic popular uprising, Yugoslav President Slobodan Milosevic had been forced to step down in favour of the opposition leader, Vojoslav Kostunica. The immediate future of this Balkan republic remained turbulent, and as I had just visited post-Milosevic Belgrade on my way to Greece, embassy officials posted in Iraq were anxious to hear of recent political developments in their country.

The ambassador was also keen to meet with Rollie Keith and to hear his accounts of the Kosovo crisis. During our discussions, Karabegovic impressed upon us the fact that the Americans and British had lost their bid to keep Iraq isolated.

"The sanctions are crumbling as more and more countries either openly or quietly ignore them," said the diplomat. "Saddam Hussein has already won a major victory in the eyes of not only Iraqis, but of the entire Arab world."

According to Karabegovic, nearly 60 diplomatic missions had re-opened in Baghdad and everyone was keen to get in on the ground floor of major trading deals they expected would soon materialize. "It will not matter whether Bush or Gore becomes the next president, the U.S. will have to concede to world opinion and let Saddam re-enter the world community," he said. "Now that these countries have their own representatives here in Iraq, they don't have to rely upon U.S. intelligence reports. They can see for themselves that Iraq no longer poses any military threat to the region."

On the afternoon of November 13, we departed Saddam International on our Olympic Airways jet. It would be another full month before Democratic candidate Al Gore was to exhaust all legal avenues and concede the U.S. presidency to Republican George W. Bush.

~ ~ ~ ~ ~ ~ ~ ~ ~ ~

BAGHDAD, MAY 7-15, 2001   Having spent most of the past six months reporting on the continued violence and bloodshed in the Balkans, I had not had the time or opportunity to return to Iraq. However, as a result of my new 'friend of Iraq' status, I had been invited to attend a conference at the Baytol Hikma Institute. Literally translated, Baytol Hikma means "house of wisdom" and, in keeping with this lofty title, the organization claimed to be an independent think tank. Of course, in reality, the institute was state-funded and staffed liberally with senior Baath party loyalists. However, as my invitation to attend did not require me to give a presentation and came with a pre-approved visa, I accepted.

The theme of the conference was the effect of U.S. sanctions on Iraq and it was to be attended by several hundred delegates from more than 70 countries. From an organizational standpoint, the affair was a complete fiasco. Although Royal Jordanian Airlines and Syrian Airways had established commercial service into Baghdad, there were only a handful of flights each week. Along with the majority of delegates, I had to make the arduous overland trek from Amman.

By the time Deputy Prime Minister Tariq Aziz gave the opening address, the registration process and primitive simultaneous translation system had broken down completely. Given its 11-year drought of hosting international delegates, the 2001 conference proved far too ambitious for Baytol Hikma's limited resources. Although foreign languages were still taught at the high school and university levels, few of the interpreters had ever had any practical experience. While the original program had been scheduled to last three days and feature some 60 presentations, halfway through day two – and after only a dozen speeches – the organizers admitted defeat and suddenly called an abrupt halt to the proceedings.

Nevertheless, from a purely propaganda point of view, the overall event would have to be considered a great success.

~ ~ ~ ~ ~ ~ ~ ~ ~ ~

The Iraqi media had made the most of the conference by focussing on the cosmopolitan composition of the attendees. While the claim that "the world was coming back to Iraq" was a little premature, there was definitely a newfound sense of optimism in Baghdad. On February 16, just four weeks after being sworn in as president, George W. Bush sent Saddam a message. In the largest series of air raids since the 1991 Gulf War, waves of American and British combat aircraft pounded over 35 targets in central Iraq.

Pentagon sources claimed the airstrikes were intended to "seriously downgrade Iraq's air defence system." Unlike the ongoing sorties flown over the imposed no-fly zones, this massive raid focussed on radar sites, anti-aircraft artillery and surface-to-air batteries between the 35th and 36th parallel. Under the terms of the 1991 cease-fire agreement, such weaponry was not prohibited – and Iraq was still authorized to exercise sovereignty over this airspace.

The casualties were not limited to Iraqi soldiers; a large number of civilians were among the dead and wounded. With many countries now maintaining embassies in Iraq, independent confirmation of the death toll had been quick, and condemnation of the American-British bombing strike followed swiftly. Declaring them to be an unprovoked aggression, the international community denounced the airstrikes. Despite protestations from the Pentagon and the British Ministry of Defence that the attacks had been necessary to protect the lives of their pilots, only Canada, Mexico and Poland gave the allies a vote of confidence. (After a series of public protests, the Polish government subsequently rescinded its support.) With only America's two continental neighbours claiming the attacks were 'justified,' Prime Minister Jean Chrétien came under domestic pressure to explain taking a stance so out of line with the world community.

Chrétien simply re-iterated the standard response lines being issued by the U.S. State Department, even going so far as to proclaim Saddam posed a regional threat and was in possession of weapons of mass destruction. As Canada's embassy in Baghdad had remained closed since 1991, and since it was without an independent intelligence agency in Iraq, Canada was forced to make decisions based entirely on second-hand CIA or British intelligence reports.

Although not made public at the time, U.S. President George Bush first confided to staffers his intentions toward Iraq in February 2001. In his book *The Right Man*, former presidential speechwriter David Frum detailed his first meeting with Bush. During a conversation with his new speechwriting team, the U.S. president declared it was his aim to "dig out Saddam" during his first term in the White House.

However, if the message that Bush had intended to send Saddam was in the form of airstrikes, the world community subsequently replied overwhelmingly with its own message: unilateral military action against Iraq, without due cause, would not be tolerated.

Instead of shoring up the crumbling sanctions against Saddam, the February 2001 aerial assault had actually hastened their collapse. In just six months appreciable changes had become evident on the streets of Baghdad. A fleet of brand-new double-decked buses, delivered from the People's Republic of China, were now plying their trade on the clogged roadways of the Iraqi capital. Electronic goods and modern luxury goods had appeared in the shops along Al-Sadoon Street in the main commercial district. Although still rare, more foreign visitors – mostly businessmen and delegations of peace activists – were filling up the long-vacant

Baghdad hotels.

As for the Iraqi authorities, they seemed to have developed a renewed confidence – almost arrogance – and they now looked optimistically to the future. As expected, Jabar Abu Marwan had been waiting for me upon my arrival in Baghdad. He told me I would have a new guide and that his boss, Salim Said Khalaf al-Jumayli, would be personally visiting me that evening at my hotel. After keeping me waiting for nearly two hours, Salim entered the Sheraton lobby, accompanied by two bodyguards.

Introduced only as Sami and Muhammad, I would later learn these two secret service agents held the respective ranks of lieutenant colonel and major in the Mukhabarat. During my subsequent visits to Iraq, this duo (not Jabar) would monitor my every move. That evening Salim was in an expansive mood, and he explained he wanted to send his own message to Canada. Tell your government that its "support of the recent U.S. airstrikes and ongoing sanctions against Iraq will prove very costly. Not only in economic terms, but also with reciprocal meddling in [Canada's] internal affairs. Prime Minister Chrétien should have been wise enough to realize that his country is not immune from interference," he warned.

The Iraqi regime had been quick to respond to Canada's position; within days of the February airstrikes, Iraq had cancelled more than $2 billion worth of current and future wheat purchases from Canada and ordered a boycott on all Canadian goods.

"Canada's loss was Australia's gain as we transferred our contracts to those who do not condemn us," said Salim. He went on to explain that Canada was now the only country to receive a "double X" boycott rating from the Iraqi government. "Even the U.S. and UK only have a single X as we recognise that we have past issues with these nations which formulate their present policy," he told me. "Canada's actions, on the other hand, are unprovoked and completely out of step with the rest of the world community."

According to Salim, Saddam Hussein hoped to open independent political and economic ties with Quebec as a measure of "reciprocal meddling."

"The people of Quebec have Saddam's sympathies in their quest for independence, and a direct trade agreement with them would be welcomed," he said. "We have the world's largest reserve of oil and Quebec is a potential supplier of goods required for the massive rebuilding of Iraq's infrastructure." Smiling mischievously, Salim admitted that the Iraqi proposal to offer highly discounted oil and major purchasing contracts was "deliberately aimed at straining Quebec's relations with the federal government and Jean Chrétien's U.S.-driven foreign policy."

While it seemed a little premature for the Iraqi intelligence director to be trying to use economic pressure to destabilize North America, Salim's sense of optimism was reflected in Baghdad's diplomatic community. Over a quick lunch at his residence, Enko Karabegovic explained:

"Everyone has realized that the U.S. objective of deposing Saddam Hussein can no longer be achieved through either the sanctions or these limited military measures. One by one, nations are beginning to ignore the embargo; the Americans are desperately trying to save face and some measure of control over their crumbling coalition."

Many Middle East analysts felt that the deteriorating situation in Palestine had also forced the U.S. to soften their hard line on Iraq. "Saddam Hussein's defiance of the U.S. over the past 10 years has made him a powerful force throughout the entire Arab world," said Toby Dodge, a research fellow at England's Royal Institute of International Affairs.

Dodge also attended the Baytol Hikma conference and was doing research for a book about Iraq's complex society. Far from being the stereotypical dry, academic type, the youthful Dodge joined the informal drinking parties hosted by the Western participants of the conference. Over shots of the local *Monika* brand of whisky, he shared his insight and research with the rest of us.

"In Palestine they are flying the Iraqi flag, and posters of Saddam are everywhere. The U.S. State Department fears a wholesale defection of their Arab allies, including the Saudis and Kuwaitis if they continue to pressure Iraq," he said.

Canada's Foreign Affairs Minister, John Manley, and Louise Frechette, the Deputy UN Secretary General, also discovered how closely linked the Palestine-Iraq issues were during a conference in Amman, Jordan. Although the two-day annual meeting of the UN's Human Security Network was to focus on the Israeli-Palestine situation, a special session was conducted to address the suffering of Iraqi children under the embargo.

Rather than being praised for their objectivity, the attendance of Manley and Frechette at this conference was sharply criticized by some of Saddam Hussein's top officials. "For Canadian politicians to support bombing attacks and sanctions, and then to shed crocodile tears for the victims is absolute hypocrisy," said Dr. Al-Hashimi.

When I visited him at the Organization for Friendship, Peace and Solidarity, the director had been incredibly busy. There were numerous international delegations in Baghdad, and trying to lodge and co-ordinate these hundreds of peace activists was proving to be as easy as herding cats.

"The world is once again coming to Iraq and, in doing so, ignoring the will of the U.S. State Department," gloated Al-Hashimi. "It was superiority of modern weapons which defeated our army on the battlefield, but it was the courage of the entire Iraqi people that has proven itself to be unconquerable. However, it has come at an enormous cost. We have won the mother-of-all-wars, but we will not easily forget those who opposed us."

Al-Hashimi was referring to the death toll of Iraqi children, whose numbers increased with each year of sanctions. Although black market luxury items were available in limited quantities in Baghdad markets, the medical shortfalls of the oil-for-food program had not been properly addressed.

I had not intended to revisit Baghdad's children hospital during this trip, but I had met a Hungarian journalist at the conference, Lazlo Zoldil (Laci to his friends), who persuaded me otherwise. A dead ringer for a young Donny Osmond, he had arrived at the Baytol Hikma conference just as the proceedings were called off. Having never been to Iraq before, Laci admitted he had accepted the invitation because he thought he would be able to gain information about the effect of the sanctions for some stories he wanted to file.

Knowing the Iraqi Ministry of Information's approval process was going to take too long, given the short time Laci had left in Iraq, I volunteered to help him out. Without any handlers, or prior permission, we took a taxi out to the children's hospital. Luckily for us, Dr. Abili was not only on duty, but he also remembered me from my previous visit.

My second trip to the leukemia ward proved no easier than my first. As Abili explained to Laci that all of the children on that ward were dying, I approached one pretty young girl who looked desperately weak. Her mother, at the head of the bed, seemed nervous about my presence.

Through an interpreter, I learned that the tiny patient was six years old. I rummaged through my wallet to show them a photo of my son, who was the same age. This seemed to reassure the mother and I asked if I could photograph her daughter. She spoke a few words and, from her demeanour, I was sure she was going to refuse my request. However, the interpreter explained that she only wanted a few minutes to make her daughter look her best. As the mother combed her daughter's hair and adjusted the buttons on her dress, I could see the bruising caused by the pools of blood in her eyelids and on her arms. Underneath the child I could see a drip bag that was half filled with blood.

I will never forget how that dying little girl, at her mother's instruction, tried to manage a smile for the photo. As we left the ward, Dr. Abili shook his head and told us that she probably wouldn't see morning.

Farther down the hall we watched two orderlies gently trying to pry the body of a premature baby from his inconsolable mother. With tears streaming down his cheeks, Laci photographed the woman as her dead child was finally taken from her, and she collapsed into a sobbing heap on the hospital floor.

Visibly shaken, Laci said, "This is genocide."

The sanctions may have been slowly unraveling, but the dying continued unabated.

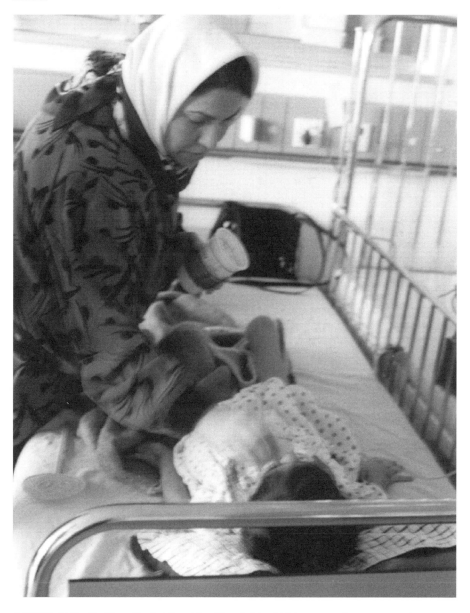

ABOVE: *At the Saddam Central Teaching Hospital for Children, a mother prepares her daughter, who was in the last stages of leukemia, before having her picture taken.* (S.TAYLOR)

ABOVE AND FACING: *Scenes of devastation in New York City as terrorists crashed into the twin towers of the World Trade Centre on September 11, 2001.* (ABOVE: CARMEN TAYLOR/AP/WIDE WORLD; OPPOSITE: THOMAS NOEPKERS/MAGNUM)

CHAPTER FIVE:

9/11: The Countdown Begins

SEPTEMBER 11, 2001   It could be argued that the final stage of the U.S. campaign to effect a regime change in Iraq was set in motion at 8:45 a.m. on September 11, 2001. It was at that moment that American Airlines Flight 11 – a Boeing 767 en route from Boston to Los Angeles – was deliberately plunged into the North Tower of the World Trade Center in New York.

In the initial chaos and confusion it was believed that this was simply a horrible tragedy. However, at 9:03 a.m., with television crews already on the scene, the image of United Airlines Flight 175 crashing into the South Tower was broadcast live to a stunned global audience.

Unbelievably, continental America was under attack. The U.S. Federal Aviation Administration took the unprecedented step of shutting down all air traffic across the United States at 9:40 a.m., but three minutes later a Boeing 757 was piloted into the Pentagon.

By 10:30 a.m., television viewers around the world had witnessed the fiery collapse of both World Trade Center towers and had learned that a fourth hijacked airliner had crashed near Pittsburgh. All airborne traffic was directed to land immediately at the nearest airport and overseas flights heading for the USA were redirected to Canada or Mexico. Border checkpoints were put on highest alert.

Visibly shaken, U.S. President George Bush spoke briefly to the media at an air force base in Louisiana before boarding Air Force One. Bush would spend the remainder of the day in a bunker at the Offit Air Force Base in Nebraska, head-quarters of the U.S. Strategic Air Command.

By early afternoon, American security forces had been deployed. Aircraft car-riers and destroyers took up station off the East Coast, missile batteries and air defence units assembled in New York City and Washington, DC. The only thing flying in the skies were roving patrols of Air National Guard F-16 fighter jets.

Although the attacks were apparently over, confusion and fear remained. It was soon discovered the airliners had been hijacked by suicidal terrorists, although no group claimed responsibility and the identity and motive of the attackers were unknown. Every military and intelligence pundit interviewed seemed to suggest a list of possible suspects, but topping them all was Osama bin Laden's al-Qaeda network.

Despite a lack of any proof of bin Laden's complicity, the Bush administration did not hesitate. With the majority of the al-Qaeda based in Afghanistan under the protection of the Taliban regime, the Afghan capital was targeted. At approxi-mately 6:00 p.m. EDT, air defences in Kabul opened fire followed by several mas-sive explosions – presumably caused by U.S. ship-launched Tomahawk cruise missiles. Two and a half hours later, President Bush again took to the airwaves. This time, he vowed to punish "evil acts."

The national desire for revenge, fuelled by the reverberating fear and shock at having America's sense of invulnerability destroyed, had severely challenged Bush's senior military leadership. "For the first week after the (World Trade Center) attacks there was a 50-50 split among the senior planning staff," Chuck Spinney, a former Pentagon advisor, told me in a phone conversation. "The hawks were ad-vocating a nuclear retaliatory strike against Afghanistan. It was unbelievably close, until cooler heads prevailed."

Around the world, that fear and rage were sensed, prompting an immediate outpouring of loyalty to America and condolences for the victims and their fami-lies. Even world leaders who had been frequently at odds with U.S. foreign policy were quick to offer support. Who can forget the sight of Palestinian leader Yasser Arafat giving blood to be sent to New York, while outside in the streets his people danced in celebration and burned American flags?

Saddam Hussein was the singular exception. The official statement issued by the Iraqi president offered sympathy for the innocent victims, but also warned the U.S. administration that they were "reaping what they had sown." In response, Bush immediately put the Iraqi leader on notice and publicly warned him to "watch his step."

On September 20, with British Prime Minister Tony Blair in attendance, George Bush addressed the U.S. Congress and declared a war against terror. Although no one could define the parameters of such a general declaration, virtually every country pledged to join Bush's coalition. The U.S. had given the Taliban regime an October 6 deadline to hand over Osama bin Laden and all of his lieutenants, or face the consequences. On October 7, British and American aircraft launched airstrikes against targets inside Afghanistan and the U.S. coalition launched a whirlwind campaign to overthrow the Taliban. A combination of air attacks, Special Forces raids and an offensive by anti-Taliban Afghan warlords quickly accomplished their goal. By December 7, the last of the Taliban resistance had retreated from their stronghold in Khandahar. Unfortunately for the U.S., their original aim – the bringing of Osama bin Laden to justice – had not been achieved. Although a number of his operatives had been killed, the elusive senior leadership of al-Qaeda remained at large.

Nearly $40 billion had been spent mounting the American campaign, and virtually nothing had been accomplished. The Taliban had been ousted from power, but in its place were now equally brutal warlords. The Americans supported Hamid Karzai as interim president of Afghanistan, even though his leadership was not widely accepted. Protected by a 5000-strong international peacekeeping force, Karzai's authority did not extend beyond Kabul. It was estimated that at least $20 billion would be required to rebuild Afghanistan's war-ravaged infrastructure. Just 90 days into the war on terror, Bush's campaign had become a costly failure. More important, the mighty American war machine had suddenly been deprived of a tangible target.

Prior to his January 2002 State of the Union address, President Bush met with his senior speechwriters. According to David Frum's personal account in *The Right Man*, it was during this meeting that staff were instructed to include Iraq, Iran and North Korea as potentially threatening states. Although the three countries were not linked by economics, religion or even political philosophy, Frum imaginatively labeled them the "axis of hatred." In subsequent drafts of the speech, Frum thought that is was Bush himself that scratched out the word 'hatred' and replaced it with 'evil.' When George Bush spoke to America this became the sound bite that captured the media's attention. Frum had deliberately chosen the phrase to evoke memories of World War II when the Allies battled the German-Italian-Japanese axis.

Although military analysts were quick to label Iran and North Korea's nuclear programs threatening, it was clear from the outset that Iraq was the first axis member that would be targeted. As early as the previous October, when the first cases of anthrax poisoning were diagnosed and the ensuing 'powder panic' gripped America, Saddam had been singled out as a likely culprit.

The only link offered to support this theory was the knowledge that Iraqis had stockpiled biological weapons, including anthrax, during the Iran-Iraq War in the 1980s. Saddam's suspected guilt in the anthrax scare continued to linger even after evidence pointed to the likelihood that it was homegrown American psychopaths that had stolen the spores from a U.S. laboratory. Over the ensuing months, the Iraqi president even found himself accused by some U.S. pundits of creating weather disturbances that resulted in a particularly harsh hurricane season.

Chicago-based Middle East analyst Emmanuel A. Winston went one step further when he suggested Iraqi secret service agents could be responsible for the spread of the West Nile virus. While Winston admitted he had no proof, he also rightly contended there was no evidence to disprove his theory. Perhaps the most imaginative plot attributed to Saddam's evil genius, however, was the report that Iraq had recruited and trained a secret squad of belly-dancing assassins. According to the British tabloids, more than a dozen of these Arabian beauties were roaming European cabarets just waiting for the opportunity to seduce then kill senior coalition officials.

These same London-based papers had erroneously begun reporting Saddam was fatally ill in the fall of 2000 and, by December of that year, they had pronounced him dead of cancer. The following May, a very much alive and fit Saddam celebrated his birthday by staging a major military parade. As each of the more than 100 regiments marched past his reviewing stand in central Baghdad, the Iraqi dictator loaded and fired a rifle in the air. In addition to saluting his loyal troops, the repeated firing was meant to demonstrate to the Iraqi people that their 64-year-old president was in superb physical condition.

When Saddam marked an earlier birthday by swimming across the Tigris River, Iraqi opposition leaders in exile had suggested to the British media that a stunt double must have performed this feat. The following week, Saddam swam across the Tigris twice. He jokingly claimed that proved his identity "because my double could never swim so far."

On the more serious issue of cataloguing Iraq's purported weapons of mass destruction, the London-based, CIA-funded Iraqi opposition informants had proven themselves to be equally unreliable. For nearly 8 years, UN chief weapons inspector Scott Ritter had diligently followed every lead provided to him by this group of exiled Iraqis. In 1998, Ritter had demanded access to Saddam's palaces, because "reliable sources" had reported chemical and biological weapons were being produced and stored in the vast underground chambers. After endless rounds of heated discussions, an outraged Baghdad regime eventually acquiesced to Ritter's demands. However, when the UN inspection teams descended into the palatial depths, "all we found were sewage pipes and septic tanks," said Ritter.

~ ~ ~ ~ ~ ~ ~ ~ ~

BAGHDAD, APRIL 2002   With the world's attention shifting from the aftermath of war in Afghanistan to the prospect of war in Iraq, I gladly accepted an invitation to attend the Baytol Hikma's 2002 annual conference. Although the theme was Globalization and its Effect on World Economies – something outside my normal field of study – it was an opportunity to return to Iraq.

With Royal Jordanian Airlines now operating regular flights into Baghdad, I no longer had to make the gruelling desert drive. Despite the arrival of few aircraft – rarely more than one a day – at Saddam International airport, the long-dormant customs facilities had difficulty coping with the sudden surge of passengers.

Upon arrival, one had to fill out a number of declarations to clear the various levels of Iraqi bureaucracy. Health officials needed to either administer or formally waive an AIDS test. Immigration personnel laboriously processed passports and visas. Customs officers inspected all luggage, including cameras. And prior to exiting into the arrival hall, passengers also had to make a foreign currency declaration.

Only if you were designated an invited guest – in handwritten script alongside your entry visa – would you be spared the bribery gauntlet. Health officials would ask for up to $50 U.S. to forego the 'mandatory' AIDS test, while the remainder of the Iraqi authorities would deliberately slow inspections until baksheesh was produced. If the amount offered was insufficient, the search would continue.

As for the Ministry of Interior officers, they were far more concerned with the value of satellite phones and laptop computers than anything else. The more expensive the gear, the greater the bribe that had to be paid for its quick release. Luckily for me, my Baytol Hikma passport authorization spared me from a shakedown on this trip. It was also helpful that Sami and Mohammed, the Mukhabarat agents assigned to me on former trips, were both present and had greeted me as an old friend.

While there was no doubt the 2002 conference was much better organized than the previous year's, a surprise lay in store for me when I arrived. Despite previous assurances to the contrary, as soon as I entered the conference room I was informed I would be giving a presentation. Handing me a copy of the program, Sami, beaming, said, "You are to make your presentation right after Tariq Aziz gives the opening address."

While this was obviously supposed to be an honour, the truth is that I'm petrified of public speaking, particularly when I have had no time to prepare – and I'm following the deputy prime minister. Rather than offend my hosts by declining to speak, I quickly scribbled a few notes down. Not being familiar with the conference's theme, I stumbled through my presentation by talking vaguely about the concept of a military industrial complex.

Most of the delegates were academics and economists from South American countries. In discussions aimed at reversing the U.S. domination of global markets, a strategy often advocated was for countries to begin trading commodities in the new Euro rather than in the traditional U.S. dollar. Obviously, vital commodities such as oil would be the key to success, and this idea had already been discussed when Venezuelan President Hugo Chavez met with Saddam Hussein in 2000.

Presenting economists made the convincing argument that should all OPEC countries switch to trading in Euros, the U.S. dollar would collapse. With only one cent of gold retained in the American Treasury for every dollar in circulation, the U.S. currency is highly exposed. International banking regulations specify that a minimum 10 cents of gold per dollar printed should be kept in reserve. But since oil and other vital commodities are all purchased by importing countries in U.S. dollars, this over-circulation is considered safe by the U.S.

With so many treasuries keeping American dollars to pay for goods, it was in everyone's interest to keep the dollar high and the price of oil low. However, should OPEC nations be convinced to collectively switch the oil trade into Euros, even the U.S. would have to begin stockpiling the new currency. And every other oil-importing nation would hastily dump their American dollars back on the U.S. Treasury.

That night, after the conference ended, the British Broadcasting Corp. reported that an abortive coup attempt had been made against President Chavez in Venezuela. Gathering in the hotel hallways, the South American economists began animatedly discussing various conspiracy theories. The one thing they all agreed on was that the CIA was likely the driving force behind the attempted regime change. After hearing their presentations about the possible impact Chavez's switch to Euros could have on the U.S. economy, their ideas no longer sounded so far-fetched.

One of the more colorful guests at this impromptu hall party was none other than Sam Bockarie. Leader of the Sierra Leone rebel forces, Bockarie was now living in exile in Liberia. Conducting a cross-border guerrilla war in West Africa, Bockarie had a notorious reputation and was an indicted war criminal. In spite of his reputation, he was still welcomed by Saddam's regime as a 'friend.' Wearing their traditional, colourful African dress, Bockarie's entourage of young women and bodyguards attracted a lot of attention at the conference.

"Mr. Bockarie wants to see you," said one of the guards, ushering me into an adjoining suite. The rebel leader was surprisingly youthful and very charismatic. "I understand you have military connections," said Bockarie, "and I wish to make you a proposal." Bockarie explained how the Sierra Leone government was employing mercenaries to pilot its new helicopter gunships and his Revolutionary United Front (RUF) soldiers had begun taking a lot of casualties as a result. "We need to find trained air defence gunners and some missiles – and we are willing to pay heavily for this service." To emphasize his point he had emptied a small bag of diamonds on the bedspread. "As you can see, I'm a man of means."

The proposal was intriguing and I certainly knew a lot of former Serbian soldiers that might have been interested in such lucrative employment. I nevertheless turned down his offer. "I'm a journalist," I explained, "not a mercenary." But when Bockarie invited me to visit Monrovia, saying, "You can join my troops on their next hunting trip into Sierra Leone," I told him I'd consider it.

THE FOLLOWING MORNING, I dropped by the Rasheed Street office of the Organization for Friendship, Peace and Solidarity. My friend Abdul Razzaq Al-Hashimi was in a fluster, the confidence he exhibited six months earlier now replaced by anxiety.

"America will soon discover – to its peril – that Iraq is not Afghanistan," said Al-Hashimi. "The U.S. threat of using military force to remove Saddam Hussein will backfire on them."

Since September 11, Iraq had been bracing for an escalation of U.S. military attacks. Key government offices were relocated throughout the capital's suburbs, and additional anti-aircraft defences were deployed around presidential palaces.

According to Iraqi press reports, an elite squadron of suicide pilots had been formed to retaliate should the U.S. launch an offensive. Equipped with an assortment of old MiGs and Mirage fighter jets, this martyr squadron would target Israel and the oil producing capability of Arab Gulf states. The Iraqi military also claimed it no longer possessed a missile threat and it was believed there were only three serviceable Scud missiles left out of a pre-Gulf War inventory of nearly a thousand.

Without a sophisticated air-control system, the Iraqi air force knew it could not penetrate U.S. military air defences, so it vowed to aim its missiles at unprotected regional targets instead.

Following President George W. Bush's January proclamation of an Iraqi, Iranian and North Korean "axis of evil," Saddam Hussein had hurriedly begun assembling an "axis of defence." Over the past two years, Iraq had been slowly making amends to previous enemies, Syria and Iran. Prompted by the threat of U.S. military attacks, the peace-making process was shifted into high gear.

Although Iran had reportedly threatened to destroy oil wells in U.S.-friendly Gulf states if it came under attack, no other Arab country had agreed to join Saddam Hussein's call for a complete oil embargo against the U.S. On April 8, Iraq had taken the unprecedented step of ceasing all oil exports – nearly two million barrels a day – for 30 days or until Israel withdrew from the occupied West Bank.

In April, U.S. Secretary of State Colin Powell had been sent on a whirlwind round of shuttle diplomacy in the Middle East. An intensified campaign of suicide bombings by Palestinian militants had prompted a massive Israeli military offensive into the West Bank. Attempting to up the stakes in the already volatile crisis, Saddam Hussein publicly voiced his support of the Palestinian cause.

In response to the April 8 oil cutoff, U.S. National Security Advisor Condoleezza Rice called Iraq's bluff: "They're going to have a hard time eating their oil."

"We will drink it if we have to," said Al-Hashimi, adding, "Let's see if Americans are willing to burn their furniture for fuel!"

Al-Hashimi recognized that unless other Arab nations joined the embargo, Iraq's output could easily be replaced without creating a shortage in the world market. "However, as a symbolic gesture, Hussein's gamble is already paying off in terms of creating widespread regional unrest," said Al-Hashimi.

Throughout the Arab world, Iraq's singular support for the Palestinians in the West Bank had driven an increasingly violent wedge between popular opinion and moderate governments. In countries such as Lebanon, Jordan and even Saudi Arabia, pro-Palestinian protests were mounting and Saddam Hussein was emerging as a figurehead of the pan-Arab movement.

Although they believed their actions would hurt the U.S. and Israel, Iraqi officials denied accusations they were inciting violence. "If certain people are blaming terrorism and terrorists for these developments, the majority of countries and their people will blame America in the medium- and long-term because it failed to deal with the September 11 attacks with wisdom and to search for its root causes," said Tariq Aziz, Iraq's deputy prime minister, during his address at the Baytol Hikma conference. "Those who choose to die in order to harm America and Israel do not have the same fear of the U.S. aggressive military force which terrorizes wealthy regimes."

Aziz also believed that the United States' ability to form a coalition for military intervention in Afghanistan would not be repeated if an offensive campaign was mounted against Iraq. "That (post-September 11) influence will fade with time and the U.S. will be unable to blackmail and pressure those countries into further participation in its war on terror," he said.

Iraqi officials were pleased with Prime Minister Jean Chrétien's position and believed Canada had so far shown "a reasonable response in the face of tremendous U.S. pressure to commit to action against Iraq," said Aziz.

Earlier that year, Canada had announced that it would not support any U.S. military action against Iraq without proof of weapons of mass destruction. In Baghdad, foreign diplomats agreed with Aziz and suggested it would be difficult for Bush to form a strong coalition against Iraq.

In spite of relentless pressure from the U.S., more than 60 foreign diplomatic missions had re-opened in the Iraqi capital. Most were arranging trade negotiations with Iraqi purchasing agents. Some of these transactions were authorized under the oil-for-food program, but it seemed that many countries were simply ignoring the UN sanctions or were trading on the black market.

"Iraq has the largest oil reserves in the world, and we are in desperate need of nearly every commodity," said Al-Hashimi. "Everyone is anxious to trade with us – with or without the U.S.'s blessing."

Nevertheless, no one was ignoring the threat of a U.S. military strike. Although Yugoslav Ambassador Enko Karabegovic had returned to Belgrade for health reasons, his first consul agreed to meet me for lunch at the embassy to discuss recent events. Having held diplomatic postings in Iran and Libya prior to Iraq, Jelko Gajic had the added advantage of speaking Arabic fluently.

"Most of us in the diplomatic community believe that no major ground strike is imminent," said Gajic. "However, everyone believes that a major airstrike could happen at any moment."

It was believed that the hot summer months, with temperatures soaring to 60° Celsius would prohibit a major ground offensive until at least the fall. "It may even take until the fall of 2003 before the U.S. is ready," said Gajic. "But everyone senses that with or without a coalition, Bush is going to go after Saddam Hussein before his re-election campaign begins in 2004."

~ ~ ~ ~ ~ ~ ~ ~ ~ ~

While I had not seen either Sami or Mohammed since my arrival, on the third day of the conference another Mukhabarat agent sought me out. "Your interview with Naji Sabri (the Foreign Minister) has been cancelled," Ahmed said. "You are to come with me instead."

Unwilling to leave the conference with this complete stranger, I insisted on being told our destination. "You are to dine with General Hasan, the head of the Mukhabarat, and we are already late."

Still a little perturbed , I asked, "Do I have a choice?" Ahmed looked me in the eye and said flatly, "No."

Lunch had been arranged in a private room at the prestigious Hunting Club. General Hasan arrived in the company of a nervous-looking Sami, clearly uncomfortable in the presence of his boss. Hasan, on the other hand, seemed relaxed. Wearing a brightly coloured Hawaiian print shirt, a gold necklace, and sporting the typical Iraqi jet-black hair and moustache dye jobs, Hasan appeared harmless, even comical. Short and rather stout, the fifty-something head of intelligence had spent time in Washington, and his English was excellent.

Throughout the four-course meal, only the general and I spoke, while Ahmed and Sami silently took notes. Surprisingly, Hasan seemed to have a good grasp of the Canadian political scene and asked a number of questions about newly appointed Foreign Affairs Minister Bill Graham.

After the table had been cleared, Hasan lit up a cigar, sat back in his chair and said matter-of-factly, "Iraq's army is fucked if the Americans attack. There is no way we can stop them. You have seen our troops, so you know what I'm saying is true."

While I understood perfectly, I could not believe the general's candor, particularly in front of subordinates who solemnly nodded in agreement. All of the Iraqi officials I had met to date had sputtered the party line that ultimate victory would be attained through loyal sacrifice, etc. However, when I asked Hasan if he would be prepared to go on the record with his comments, he smiled and said, "I will deny I ever met you."

I soon learned, however, that the purpose of our meeting was for Hasan to convey to me Iraq's novel plan for victory through defeat. The idea was to create a humanitarian crisis of such magnitude that the world would be compelled to intervene, bringing any U.S. military intervention to a halt. Hasan proudly described the tactic as a copycat of the Albanian strategy in Kosovo.

"There are nearly 8 million inhabitants in Baghdad. If we keep only males of military age inside the city limits, we could push 6 million non-combatant refugees into the path of the Americans," Hasan explained. "Even the U.S. military could not supply enough food and shelter for so many and still feed their own soldiers."

The Iraqis believed Saddam Hussein could keep the moral high ground by claiming that the exodus was initiated to prevent civilians from becoming collateral damage. As the Americans struggled to feed so many displaced persons, the presence of foreign journalists would make the plight known the world over, further fuelling anti-war sentiment.

This plan to deliberately jeopardize the lives of so many of their own people indicated just how desperate the situation had become. However, as a strategic manoeuvre, I could not imagine how the U.S. could cope with the massive flow of refugees or how they could possibly ignore the global backlash.

Throughout our discussion, Hasan had occasionally directed his underlings to pass along certain orders to various cabinet ministers, including Tariq Aziz and Naji Sabri. Curious to learn where exactly he fit into the command structure, I asked Hasan to explain his level of authority. Amused by the question, Ahmed and Sami listened as the general replied, "Let's just say I can get things accomplished."

From then on I could easily identify Hasan in the televised images of Saddam's Revolutionary Command Council: more often than not, the head of Iraqi intelligence sat right next to the president.

~ ~ ~ ~ ~ ~ ~ ~ ~ ~

On my first night in Baghdad I had stopped by the lobby of the Palestine Hotel and watched as several busloads of European peace activists disembarked. A small group of journalists separated from the main party and began setting up cameras and recording equipment in a first-floor banquet room. My curiosity peaked when one of the German reporters told me the speakers would be a pair of coalition soldiers.

Representatives from British and French Gulf War veterans' associations, the men were touring Iraq, visiting old battlefields and meeting former foes. The delegation hoped to initiate cooperation and discussion between Western and Iraqi health officials in studying the effects of depleted uranium (DU).

"We may have been enemies in 1991, but now we're all suffering the same fate," said Bernard McPhillips, a spokesman for the Scottish chapter of the British Gulf War Veterans Association. "If our governments are serious about caring for their sick soldiers, they'll follow our lead and start working with the Iraqis to find an answer to the DU problem."

During the Gulf War, Leading Seaman McPhillips had been a member of the British Fleet Air Arm, serving aboard HMS *Ark Royal*. He maintained Sea Harrier fighter jets, which pulverized Iraqi frontline positions, and Sea King helicopters, which transported SAS commando detachments deep inside Iraq. By October 1991, McPhillips had developed a loss of strength in his limbs, the first symptom of what he calls Gulf War syndrome.

Discharged from the navy in April 1992, his condition steadily worsened. Now, he looked much older than his 34 years, and suffered from crippling arthritis, chronic fatigue, gastrointestinal disorders, and frequent blackouts. Making matters worse, all three of his post-Gulf War children suffered a variety of congenital anomalies.

Still, McPhillips considered himself one of the lucky ones. "We've had 600 British servicemembers die since returning from the Gulf. Of the 56,000 troops who served in theatre, over 11,000 have reported disabilities. At least I'm still alive and able to help the others," he said.

Norbert Simion served with the French division that swept into Iraq from Saudi Arabia during *Operation Desert Storm*. His unit engaged and destroyed an Iraqi armoured force outside the desert village of As-Salman. In the immediate aftermath, French and Iraqi soldiers alike were exposed to a lingering depleted uranium aerosol created by exploding tank shells.

American scientists first developed DU munitions in the 1980s, when they realized the density of this nuclear waste had armour-piercing capabilities. Far cheaper than other dense metals such as tungsten, DU had the additional property of igniting on impact, thereby transforming the interior of an enemy tank into a skin-removing fireball of radioactive particles.

Although depleted uranium itself contains only low levels of radiation, leading DU experts believe that after it explodes into tiny ceramic particles, it is easily inhaled. Once lodged in the victim's lungs or lymph nodes, the DU particles continue to emit radiation..

"When our troops first began developing strange illnesses, our military doctors told us it was all in our heads," said Simion. "As the casualty figures rise and independent scientists continue revealing the dangers of DU, the French government keeps telling us there is no proof."

McPhillips and Simion believe that the proof can only be found through a major scientific survey conducted at ground zero – namely, the most DU-impacted areas inside Iraq. "While U.S. and coalition troops were briefly exposed to small amounts of DU for a short time, we dropped over 300 metric tones of the stuff into southern Iraq," said McPhillips. "It's been part of their lives, including their food chain, for the past 11 years, and the results have been horrific."

Following McPhillips' and Simion's opening addresses, a number of Iraqi scientists gave short presentations to the journalists based on their own published reports and statistics compiled on the impact of DU. However, even their top officials admitted that they were not trained or equipped to properly study the long-term effects. "This is completely new science for everyone," said Dr. Baha Marouf. "The previous examinations of DU (as a nuclear waste product) were conducted on its inert state. Nobody looked at the dangers posed by exploding it and inhaling it."

Dr. Marouf, a specialist in radioecology, received a Ph.D. in biochemistry from the University of Texas. Part of Iraq's scientific team, he was dedicated to testing DU and studying its effects on the population. Although, like Marouf, most Iraqi researchers had been educated in the West, their initial DU findings were ignored by the international scientific community. However, "the one thing which they cannot continue to ignore is the growing number of DU victims," said Marouf.

The Iraqis have experienced a significant increase in the prevalence of cancer, particularly leukemia, over the past 11 years as well as an alarming number of premature births and deformities in newborns, as I had witnessed firsthand at the children's hospital. Health Minister Dr. Umeed Medhat Mubarak was keen on having international experts peer review the findings of his researchers. In particular, Dr. Mubarak hoped to attract the interest of the Canadian-American team known as the Uranium Metal Project. Directed by Dr. Asaf Durakovic and based at Memorial University in Newfoundland, the Uranium Metal Project has been instrumental in proving the existence of depleted uranium in the bodies of deceased Gulf War veterans.

"We would welcome all cooperation with Dr. Durakovic's team," said Mubarak.

"The British Gulf veterans have independently financed DU testing at Dundee, Lincoln and Nottingham universities, all of which gave us positive results, which ran contrary to the Ministry of Defence's denials," said Bernard McPhillips. "The problem is we need to centrally coordinate all these efforts."

Michel Collon, a Brussels-based investigative journalist, was instrumental in bringing the hazards posed by DU to the world's attention. Collon brought McPhillips and Simion to Baghdad as part of a ten-member international commission on depleted uranium in the hopes of raising international awareness. Collon was disappointed that more scientific heavyweights did not join his commission in Iraq. He remained hopeful, however, that the meeting would highlight the need for cooperation between Western and Iraqi scientists and that a major, independent scientific study on DU would be established around the southern Iraqi city of

Basra, the area heaviest hit during the Gulf War.

In 1991, U.S. and coalition jets ravaged the retreating Iraqi army, leaving smoldering wrecks of thousands of vehicles in their wake. The preponderance of congenital anomalies among the children born over the past decade in this region, dubbed the Highway of Death, defies explanation. "The only medical precedent we could compare Basra to was post-World War II results from Hiroshima and Nagasaki," said Dr. Marouf.

As part of the Iraqi DU research team, geneticist Dr. Selma Taher studied the phenomenon. Her research showed that birth deformities appearing in other parts of Iraq, which at first seemed unrelated, could often be traced back to Basra and exposure to DU. In the northern village of Dilayah, where three babies were born a short time apart with similar congenital anomalies, Dr. Taher discovered all three fathers had served in the same regiment and had survived the bombing on the Highway of Death.

For Dr. Taher, the visit by McPhillips and Simion offered an opportunity to widen her research to include allied Gulf War veterans who had experienced similar birth defects in their own children.

The reception they received from Iraqi officials and former enemy soldiers took the veterans by surprise. "I must admit I was apprehensive about coming here, after all the destruction we'd caused," said McPhillips. "But they've welcomed us with open arms."

~ ~ ~ ~ ~ ~ ~ ~ ~ ~

BAGHDAD, SEPTEMBER 6-12, 2002   In early August, the U.S. Joint Chiefs of Staff announced they had formally approved a war plan for intervention in Iraq. Discussion in the Western media shifted decisively from "if" to "when" a second Gulf War would begin and President Bush made it clear his administration was intent on enforcing a regime change in Iraq. In fact, he said, the buildup of U.S. forces in the Persian Gulf was already underway.

World opinion, it seemed, mattered little to the Bush administration. When the U.S. failed to put forward a strong enough case for intervention, France, China and Russia all said they would use their Security Council vetoes to prevent the U.S. and Britain from obtaining a UN mandate for the attack.

To give the appearance of continued diplomacy, the U.S. and Britain publicly maintained that, by refusing to readmit the UN weapons inspectors, Iraq was in violation of the 1991 cease-fire agreement. The two superpowers urged a new resolution be passed that would authorize the use of military force.

Neither the European Union nor NATO would lend their support to a U.S.-led attack on Iraq. Even Arab countries long considered staunch supporters of America, such as Saudi Arabia, were unwilling to back Bush. This limited the buildup of U.S. forces in the Persian Gulf to Kuwait and Qatar. Nevertheless, Bush was determined to wage war on Iraq – with or without allies.

Although I knew September would be too hot to launch a ground invasion in Iraq, I had a hunch Bush might use the first anniversary of 9/11 to send Saddam a message. While many journalists headed to New York City to cover commemorative ceremonies, I booked a flight to Baghdad.

By the pool at the Al-Rasheed Hotel, I bumped into Toby Dodge, the British academic expert on Middle East affairs I had met at the previous year's Baytol Hikma conference. He was finalizing research for his book and hoped my premonition of a September 11 air attack would prove false.

However, at 10:30 that evening, as Iraqi air defences began pounding tracer fire into the air in the western suburbs of Baghdad, it appeared as though the U.S. would beat the anniversary by four days. Hearing the distant thumping of cannons, Dodge brought a bottle of whisky to my room and invited me to "enjoy the fireworks."

Over the next 30 minutes, the gunners concentrated their fire on one unseen target after another. But there were no explosions or bomb blasts indicating the Iraqi capital had actually come under attack. Since air raid sirens had not sounded in the downtown core of the city, most residents appeared unperturbed.

From my balcony, Dodge and I watched four bikini-clad Russian prostitutes cavorting in the pool below as rockets and tracers arced skyward in the distance. The women were part of a rotating harem kept by Saddam Hussein's eldest son, Uday, and their regular semi-clad poolside antics had become the gossip du jour for foreign correspondents staying at the Al-Rasheed.

As for the half-hour of anti-aircraft fire, either jittery gunners were shooting at shadows or, more likely, the U.S. was conducting a test of the Iraqi air defence system by using unarmed drone aircraft. Whatever was going on in the airspace over Baghdad, it was not the first raid in George Bush's promised war.

On that same night, up to 100 American and British warplanes pounded Iraqi military installations in the isolated village of Rutba, 60 kilometers southwest of Baghdad. There were reports of serious damage and an undisclosed number of casualties.

With the war of words mounting between Washington and Baghdad, allied airstrikes inside the southern no-fly zone had become an almost daily occurrence. The number of planes involved in this raid, however, was said to be the largest in a single attack since *Operation Desert Storm.*

Rutba is close to the Jordanian border, where a large number of American ground troops were conducting desert warfare training. Although the Jordanian government maintained U.S. maneuvers were a routine annual exercise and not part of a buildup to an invasion of Iraq, Sami and Mohammed claimed to have proof the Americans were using this deployment to conduct reconnaissance and to establish Special Forces bases inside western Iraq.

As the military action intensified, it seemed Iraqi efforts to resolve the crisis diplomatically were floundering. A hoped-for intervention by Russia at the end of August failed to materialize. A crucial summit between British Prime Minister Tony Blair and U.S. President George Bush took place a few days after the Rutba attack. At this meeting, Blair brought forward the British intelligence's dossier on Iraq's weapons programs while Bush shared the CIA's files. Despite this deliberate showboating for the public, it seemed only the timing of the intervention was still in question. Nevertheless, some Iraqi officials remained optimistic that armed conflict could be avoided.

"I don't believe that the Iraqis understand the urgency of the matter and don't realize how high the stakes have gotten," said Toby Dodge, who had spent the previous week conducting frustrating discussions with top officials from Iraq's Ministry of Foreign Affairs. "The time for diplomacy has almost expired. This is no time for Iraq to begin bargaining for a better position."

Tariq Aziz, Iraq's deputy prime minister, had just tabled a new proposal with UN Secretary General Koffi Annan. Iraq's position was that it would submit to further weapons inspections, but only after 19 pre-conditions had been met by the UN. In addition to lifting the 11-year-old economic sanctions and setting a finite time limit on inspections, Iraq demanded financial compensation for the war damage it had suffered in 1991.

As one of several top European academics in Baghdad, Dodge was trying to help broker a peaceful resolution while there was still time.

"In my opinion, the only option is for Iraq to submit to weapons inspections with a security guarantee from a third party, such as Russia or France," said Dodge. "Unfortunately, no one seems to be listening."

The Iraqi media and government spokesmen had played up reports of international anti-war protests and, in particular, anti-U.S. protests. Unfortunately, those responsible for broadcasting the propaganda had apparently started believing their own fabrications.

"The people of the world are not so stupid," said Director General Uday Al-Tai, the Iraqi government's senior press relations officer. "They know that the U.S.

is not justified in attacking Iraq, and that is why you see so many American flags being burned and trampled all over the globe."

Tall, thin and immaculately dressed, Al-Tai cut a dapper figure. And, he was eager to conduct interviews with the foreign press. There were some 40 international journalists registered in Iraq, but when you discounted camera crews and producers, only a dozen reporters were in place. Officials from the Ministry of Information had deluded themselves into believing their messages were being heard around the world. When I spoke privately with Al-Tai later, I didn't have the heart to tell him more than 3,000 journalists were converging on New York City to commemorate the first anniversary of 9/11.

A number of international delegations had also come to Baghdad in early September to help boost morale. One of the most politically significant was a contingent of Turkish politicians. Bringing their own entourage of journalists, the Turks wanted to publicly demonstrate their opposition to a U.S.-led war. This was significant, not only because Turkey is a member of NATO, but because this country's shared border with Iraq was considered one of the few 'friendly' invasion routes for coalition troops into Iraq.

The same weekend Bush and Blair were to conduct their summit meeting in Washington, maverick British Labour Party MP George Galloway, long an outspoken critic of the sanctions, was expected to arrive in Baghdad with his own group of high-profile protesters from the U.K. Austrian Vice Chancellor Jorg Haider's decision to publicly ally himself with Saddam caused a sensation in the Austrian press. Widely viewed as a right-wing nationalist, Haider's support for Iraq probably had more to do with trade than ideology.

Should this wave of international support fail to achieve a last-minute diplomatic solution, Baghdad authorities were now more willing than ever to fight. In a public address, Saddam Hussein said, "While we pray that war will never happen… if the U.S. attacks Iraq, then the Iraqis will fight in an extraordinary manner to ensure their defeat."

Uday Al-Tai told any reporter who would listen that Iraq could bolster its army of 500,000 troops to a fighting force of 8 million volunteers, insisting, "Everyone of fighting age can be called upon to resist a U.S. invasion."

In a short interview conducted in my hotel room at the Al-Rasheed, General Hasan offered a more realistic assessment. This time, he would allow me to publish his comments, but only on the condition of anonymity. Allowing for the U.S.'s vast technological superiority and the questionable loyalty of the Shiite majority in southern Iraq, Hasan said, U.S. forces would make substantial initial gains in any war.

"We cannot hope to match a superpower in the desert. They will destroy us from the air and at ranges from which we cannot return fire," said Hasan. That is why Iraq announced it would pull its troops back from he desert and fight in the cities. While admitting Iraq would once again suffer "catastrophic" losses, Hasan said his men "would welcome the chance to finally be able to kill Americans. They slaughtered us during the Gulf War and we could do nothing. For the past 11 years they have bombed us whenever they wanted, and we could do nothing. Now if the Americans come into Baghdad, they will learn what war really is."

As for the humanitarian crisis idea floated during our last conversation, the general said the president himself had vetoed this idea. Apparently, Saddam believed his people would not want to participate in such a plan because "every one of them would rather volunteer to fight."

Not all Iraqi authorities believed the Pentagon would pursue the risky strategy of pushing straight into Baghdad, however. Some senior officials feared U.S. forces would simply lay siege to major Iraqi cities, thereby causing widespread suffering and hardship among the civilian population.

"During the last Gulf War and the initial years of the embargo there was rampant civil disobedience and disorder," said Dr. Asmaa Alawai, a senior physician at Baghdad's second largest medical facility. "My fear is that the U.S. will simply cordon us off and starve us into barbaric acts of inhumanity against each other."

Alawai had good reason to be concerned. She was part of the planning team that drafted a contingency medical plan for various scenarios should war become a reality. Despite her pessimism, Alawai had no doubts that the Iraqi army would put up a stiff fight. She believed her soldiers "would die bravely so long as their leader (Saddam Hussein) remains alive and is able to communicate orders to them."

~ ~ ~ ~ ~ ~ ~ ~ ~ ~

As American and British governments tried to convince the world Saddam's weapons programs posed "a clear and present danger" to global security, the last thing they needed was former UN weapons inspector Scott Ritter undermining their arguments.

Since resigning in protest from his UN position in 1998, the former Marine lieutenant colonel had embarked on a one-man international crusade to educate the world about the suffering of Iraqis under the sanctions. Although he had returned to Baghdad on several occasions, this trip was special: It would be the first time a foreigner had ever made a presentation to the Iraqi National Assembly.

Although we had spoken on the phone and exchanged e-mails, our first meeting was in the lobby of the Al-Rasheed Hotel. Ritter was on his way to the parliamentary building to deliver his speech and, tall and muscular, he still looked the part of the all-American Marine. His comments, however, were bluntly critical of the Bush administration's push for war.

"Given the situation today, it is impossible to conjure up any scenario that would justify military action against Iraq," Ritter said in his opening remarks. "The United States' case for a war is based on fear and rhetoric, rather than facts and truth."

In addition to the 200-plus Iraqi politicians in attendance, all the Baghdad-based journalists, including the Turkish contingent, were on hand to record Ritter's comments.

Ritter made it clear he was making his address to the Iraqi assembly as a private citizen and not as a formal representative of the U.S. Despite his harsh criticism of the American policy toward Iraq, Ritter made it clear he was proud of his country's Bill of Rights, which allowed him to make such public statements.

Ritter told parliamentary officials that the Iraqi flag and a poster of Saddam would have to be removed from behind the podium where he would speak. At first, the Iraqis refused, but when the assembled press corps pressed for an explanation of the delay, they acquiesced. From the outset, Ritter made it evident that although he disagreed with U.S. policy, he was not in Baghdad to side with the Iraqi leadership.

Convinced the U.S. was "poised on the brink of making an historical mistake," Ritter said he could not sit idly by "as my country behaves in this fashion."

Noting the first anniversary of 9/11 was just days away, Ritter asked the Iraqi leaders to understand how fear was clouding the average American's judgement. "This fear has fuelled a war fever, and it has been exploited by those with a dangerous agenda."

Acknowledging his inspection team had conducted the "most intrusive" searches ever performed on a country, Ritter stated Iraq's weapons programs had been "90 to 95 per cent decommissioned" when the inspectors were withdrawn in December 1998. Of the remaining capacity, Ritter explained the material was strictly "technical, and in no way posed a threat."

"Since there is no proof that Iraq possesses weapons of mass destruction, and because there is no evidence linking Iraq to terror attacks against America," he continued, "the rationale behind a U.S. military strike remains based purely on speculation. And there is no basis in international law for a country to go to war based on speculation."

The former Marine added that should evidence be subsequently uncovered that showed Iraq posed "a clear and present danger to America, [he] would volunteer [his] services to counter that threat."

On issues of the past, Ritter said there "was blame enough for everyone – including the Iraqis." Such previous violations as the gassing of Kurdish rebels and the 1990 invasion of Kuwait made it easy for "the average American to now believe every allegation they hear pertaining to Iraq, whether or not it can be backed up by hard fact."

The loudest objections expressed by the Iraqi assembly came when Ritter tabled his recommendation for resolving the current crisis by having Iraq "submit itself immediately to unconditional and unfettered resumption of the UN weapons inspections." This was the only way Iraq could "eliminate the remaining doubts of Americans, which the fear mongers are manipulating," he noted.

Ritter's second recommendation was that the Iraqis should "embrace the U.S. suffering [from 9/11] and make it clear to the world that, although they are a Muslim country, Iraq in no way sponsors such terrorist activity." Acknowledging Iraq had suffered the loss of 1.5 million people over the past decade, Ritter urged Iraqis, nonetheless, to extend their empathy to the families of the 3,000 Americans who perished in the World Trade Center attack.

Noting they had long since been engaged in suppressing the very same Islamic fundamentalists that attacked the U.S., Ritter urged the assembly to let the world know "that Iraq stands shoulder to shoulder with them in the fight against terror."

Adopting a defensive posture and preparing for a possible war, Ritter advised the Iraqis, allowed "U.S. warmongers to distort [this] defiance into aggressive intent."

Ritter's most controversial remark was that Iraq must be prepared to accept a negotiated solution to the Palestinian question. (Saddam had remained a steadfast supporter of the Palestinian cause, and Iraq still refused to recognize the state of Israel.) "It is time that you stop being more Palestinian than the Palestinians," he said. This statement, once translated, brought a chorus of disapproval from the assembly. Ritter also admitted for the first time that his weapons inspectors had been used to spy on Iraq. He told the Iraqi parliamentarians they were justified in their concern about re-admitting inspection teams because, in the past, the access they granted had been used to violate the UN mandate.

Ritter said his former supervisor, Richard Butler, had ordered him to "provoke an incident with the Iraqis" in December 1998. When Ritter refused, Butler had personally ordered the inspection teams withdrawn from Iraq. Subsequently, American and British forces launched airstrikes against more than 100 targets purported to be Iraqi weapon stores. According to Ritter, however, "the majority of the sites targeted had been, in fact, directed against the Iraqi leadership, not their weapons capability." Moreover, "acquiring those specific targets had been assisted by the inspection teams."

While the U.S. had always maintained that Saddam had kicked the inspectors out of Iraq, the facts support Ritter's version of events. In October 1998, the U.S. Congress passed the Iraqi Liberation Act (HR4655), which was reluctantly signed by President Bill Clinton. The reason for the hesitation is that, while previously working in conjunction with Iraqi opposition groups, the CIA suffered a number of embarrassing reversals in Iraq. The most notable occurred in 1996.

At that time, the CIA was heavily supporting Jalal Talabani's Patriotic Union of Kurdistan (PUK) against rival warlord Massoud Barzani's Kurdistan Democratic Party (KDP). Not wanting to be pushed out, Barzani made a separate deal with Saddam Hussein. In a surprise strike north, Saddam's tanks assisted the KDP's peshmerga fighters in pushing into PUK territory.

Unable to use air power in the no-fly zone to support one Kurdish faction against another, the U.S. could not intervene. As a result, Saddam's agents had successfully dismantled the CIA's operation in northern Iraq. Without their own sources in place, additional pressure had been put on Ritter to use his UN access to gather intelligence on the Iraqi president's whereabouts.

Despite this startling admission, Ritter believed Iraq could trust a new set of inspectors. "The world knows about the abuse of access which occurred and they would be carefully monitoring the situation," he said. "In this case they would not tolerate similar action."

~ ~ ~ ~ ~ ~ ~ ~ ~ ~

Despite official calls to convert Iraqi cities into fortresses, no real defensive preparations seemed to be taking place. The few measures underway seemed aimed more at boosting civilian morale than providing any real military defence.

Dr. Hameed Saeed, the director of the Baytol Hikma Institute, was a prominent academic and a respected writer. Gray-haired with a hefty paunch, the sixty-one-year now had to spend three hours every morning doing military training, basic drills and rudimentary weapons practice.

With the U.S. threatening war, Iraq had begun recalling its nearly 3 million reservists to active duty. All men of military service, aged between 18 and 65, were required to begin refresher training at local military depots. The reservists in Saeed's unit were of all ages and included his son. "I'm a pacifist by nature, not a soldier," explained Saeed. "If Iraq was declaring war on the United States, I would be the first one in the streets to hold a peace protest. But this is something different. If Iraq is attacked, then everyone must fight."

Iraqi border posts had been reinforced in response to increasing U.S. demands for a regime change, and manpower had been mobilized from the reserves. One call-up was Mohammed Noori, a 42-year-old father of four who had spent the previous twenty years working for the Iraqi Ministry of Information. Noori had been recalled briefly to active duty during the Gulf War in the air defence of Baghdad. A week ago, he had received his latest orders: Noori would spend the next two months bolstering border patrols along the Kurdish-controlled provinces of northern Iraq. In the event of war, this was considered to be one of the most likely U.S. invasion routes.

"I have not been in uniform in 12 years," said Noori. "The Americans are professional soldiers and they have the best equipment in the world." Noori's voice trailed off before he nervously added, "nevertheless, this is our country and we will fight them if necessary."

After years of embargo, the Iraqi army was forced to cannibalize many of its tanks just to keep others serviceable. The shortage of replacement parts also prohibited them from conducting large-scale training exercises. While the best of Iraq's equipment was issued to the elite Republican Guard units, even they were hit hard by the shortages. With tightened security in effect throughout Baghdad, Republican Guard units, distinct in their desert camouflage, could often be seen patrolling the main streets in civilian pickup trucks mounted with light machine guns.

Although regular conscripts guarded most of the government buildings in Baghdad, key facilities were protected by select units of Saddam's elite regiments. I had discovered this firsthand while out for my daily run. Normally, my passing would elicit friendly waves and mocking laughter from bored guards at various facilities along the route. But one morning I decided to run in a different part of the city. Approaching the massive Monument of the Unknown Soldier with my Sony Walkman at full volume, I didn't hear a Republican Guard sergeant shout at me to stop. Seconds later, a squad of soldiers converged from behind a gate, blocking my path with their Kalashnikov rifles at the port. From their demeanor, I knew something – or someone – very important was housed in the vicinity. Saying "Asaf (Sorry)" with my hands raised above my head, I quickly turned and continued running in the opposite direction.

Some foreign journalists posted in Baghdad chafed at the close scrutiny. Taking photographs was now severely limited and almost everything was prohibited without prior permission. Even photographing such landmarks as the crossed swords gateways around Baghdad's central government district required official permission. "Before we used to prohibit journalists only from filming military installations," explained an official with the Ministry of Information. "Now, with the possibility that Baghdad itself could soon become a battlefield, everything must be considered of military importance."

If you really wanted a picture of an Iraqi landmark, however, all you had to do was buy a postcard of it in the market.

~ ~ ~ ~ ~ ~ ~ ~ ~ ~

Following the summit meeting at Camp David, it was clear British Prime Minister Tony Blair was fully aboard President George Bush's war wagon. For their part, Iraqi information officials were doing their best to undermine American efforts to drum up a coalition force.

When Pentagon officials released a satellite photo of a 60-truck convoy purportedly leaving a chemical weapons plant, the Iraqi Ministry of Information moved quickly to squelch the allegation. Rounding up the tiny cadre of foreign journalists still in Baghdad on September 10, they drove us out to the site in question.

While the Iraqis openly admitted there had been a 60-truck convoy at the site, we were able to report firsthand that the building was, in fact, a warehouse containing nothing more than tea, sugar and flour. The vehicles in the satellite photo had been delivering rations under the direction of the United Nations oil-for-food relief program. Given the time difference, the sluggish Iraqi bureaucracy and the increased security measures in effect in Baghdad, however, the news was already 48 hours old by the time the Pentagon claim was convincingly refuted. Needless to say, the correction made barely a ripple in the press.

In the interim, a second, more damaging satellite photo had been released. This one was attributed to British intelligence and purported to show Iraq was resurrecting its nuclear arms project. According to U.S. officials, Iraqis had rebuilt a research facility at the bombed out Tamuze nuclear site. It was here that the Israeli air force had struck in 1981, on the eve of the Iraqis making the reactor operational. The Tamuze I reactor was destroyed in that raid, but Iraq contrived to continue developing nuclear technology.

When the Gulf War began in 1991, the Iraqis had had a much smaller reactor, the Tamuze II, in full operation. During the *Operation Desert Storm* air raids, the Iraqi nuclear plant was targeted and destroyed. Recognizing they could not let these new allegations stand unchallenged, the Iraqis again rounded up foreign journalists and arranged a visit to the site.

Over the course of a three-hour visit, they opened all the buildings shown in the Pentagon's satellite photo to media inspection. From the display of fertilizers and medicinal products, the facilities appeared to be used for agricultural and pharmaceutical research. The buildings contained none of the sophisticated hardware one would expect to find at a nuclear arms development site. In fact, the conditions were so primitive, we questioned whether the nuclear waste from the previously destroyed reactors was not creating an environmental hazard. In the bathrooms, signs posted in English and Arabic explained how to flush the toilets – hardly the sort of direction one would expect top-level rocket scientists to require.

For the reporters who visited the Tamuze site, the openness of the Iraqi officials and the evidence provided brought the Pentagon's allegations into question. But then, as one of the British journalists quipped, "Not being scientists, we wouldn't recognize anthrax from applesauce." We could report what we had witnessed, but contrary to the Iraqis' intent, we could not conclude no nuclear research was being conducted at the site.

Many of the officials at the Ministry of Information were disappointed that our reports reflected this doubt. "What more can we do to prove this point to you?" asked an exasperated Uday Al-Tai. In response, I said that, in my opinion, the only way to prevent a war at this eleventh hour was for Iraq to convince the world it had nothing to hide. Such reassurance, I said, could be provided only by qualified weapons inspectors, not by a bumbling bunch of journalists.

~ ~ ~ ~ ~ ~ ~ ~ ~ ~

Although President Bush would not use the 9/11 anniversary to launch a punitive attack against Iraq, a group of commonwealth reporters staying in Baghdad decided to have a party that night – just in case. As a matter of courtesy, the British, Australian and Canadian journalists invited their Turkish colleagues to attend.

We had presumed that since they were Muslims, the Turks would be teetotalers. To our surprise, they made a serious dent in our whisky stock beneath a dense pall of acrid blue cigarette smoke. Toby Dodge arrived late as he had been summoned to a meeting with Tariq Aziz. He excitedly told us about his 90-minute tête-à-tête with the deputy prime minister.

"They finally get it," he said. Over cigars and brandy, Aziz had confided to the

British academic that Iraq was going to waive its demands and allow the weapons inspectors to return unconditionally.

On September 9, Aziz had returned from a meeting with Koffi Annan in Johannesburg, while Foreign Affairs Minister Naji Sabri had flown back from an Arab summit in Cairo. Both ministers had brought back some bitter truths for Saddam. Apparently, the British had met with Jacques Chirac and had convinced the French to support a framework agreement that would be in place by the 20th of September. Under the terms of this proposal, Iraq would be given a three-week ultimatum to comply with weapons inspections.

This about-turn by the French had shocked the Iraqis, particularly since it came on the heels of the Russian pullout. Over the previous few months, the Russians had signed nearly $40 billion worth of trade agreements with Iraq. The Iraqis had naively believed this would buy them Russia's protection at the UN. Instead, the Russians had used the hefty price tag as a bargaining chip with the Americans, effectively putting a price tag on their Security Council veto.

Since it was generally agreed the Chinese would never stand alone on the issue, the betting was the Americans and British would be cleared to obtain a UN resolution. Sabri had equally sobering news from the Arab council. While publicly denouncing the American intervention, the consensus had been that Iraq must submit to new inspections.

Dodge went on to explain the only card the Iraqis could play would be relenting at the eleventh hour, thereby taking the wind out of Bush's sails. After months of international arm twisting, Bush had finally sold the world on the need to resume weapons inspections.

The battle cry for weapons inspections quickly replaced the battle cry for regime change. With no concrete evidence of weapons of mass destruction to offer, America's strongest card became Saddam's refusal to accept inspections. If Saddam has nothing to hide, then why is he hiding it, spokesmen for the U.S. State Department asked at every opportunity. By agreeing to weapons inspections, Aziz and his colleagues knew that they would at least pull the rug out from under the American rhetoric.

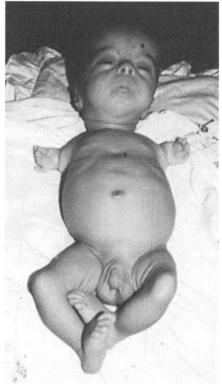

ABOVE, LEFT and RIGHT: Deformed babies born to U.S. Gulf War veterans bore a remarkable resemblance to post-war Iraqi infants born with congenital anomalies. An increasing number of medical scientists believe that the allied use of depleted uranium munitions may have been the cause of this tragedy. (DEREK HUDSON; INSIDE EDGE)

LEFT: The author speaking at the April 2002 conference organized by the Baytol Hikma Institute in Baghdad. The topic of the conference was globalization and one of the main themes was how the U.S. economy could be undermined by exporting oil in the new Euro currency rather than in U.S. dollars.

(INSTITUTE PHOTO, COURTESY THE AUTHOR)

TOP: *Iraqi soldiers killed following combat with the British "Desert Rats" Brigade during Operation Desert Storm. The British commander warned his colleagues not to draw any tactical conclusions based on such a one-sided affair. (RICHARD KEMP)*

ABOVE: *In the immediate aftermath of the first Gulf War, allied troops climbed aboard shattered Iraqi vehicles in search of souvenirs and to spray-paint them with graffiti. No one was warned of the possible long-term health hazards posed by lingering depleted uranium residue. (SCOTT TAYLOR)*

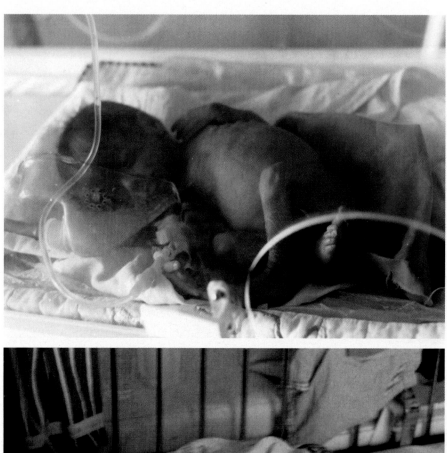

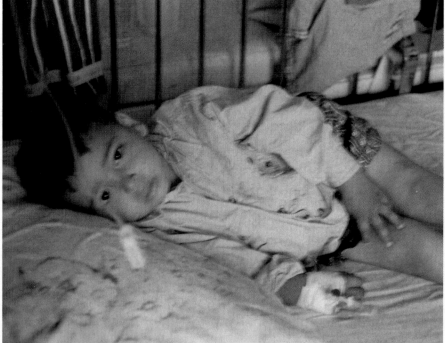

TOP AND ABOVE: *The instance rate of leukemia among infants, as well as premature births and congenital anomalies, soared in post-war Iraq. One common link appeared to be parental exposure to depleted uranium. (SCOTT TAYLOR)*

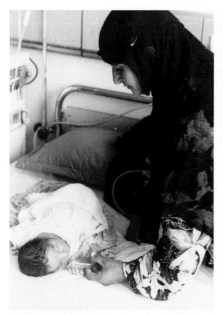 

TOP LEFT: *With a shortage of trained nurses, Iraqi mothers cared for their own infants' non-medical needs at Saddam Central Teaching Hospital for Children. (SCOTT TAYLOR)*

TOP RIGHT: *Youthful vendors were a common sight on Baghdad's streets. While Iraq's pre-war literacy rate had been the envy of the region, the country's economic collapse forced children on to the street to seek employment to help feed their families. (SCOTT TAYLOR)*

ABOVE: *On Basra's waterways, the young and elderly sought means to survive. Boats could be chartered for as little as $2 U.S. a day. (SCOTT TAYLOR)*

TOP LEFT: *Baghdad's markets revealed the measure of ingenuity that had been forced upon the once-affluent Iraqi society. Everything and anything had a value in a country where imports were barred by the UN-enforced embargo. (SCOTT TAYLOR)*

BOTTOM: *This scene of downtown Baghdad reveals the one-time splendour of the Iraqi capital during its heyday. (SCOTT TAYLOR)*

PREVIOUS PAGE, TOP RIGHT: *Shiite beggars lived a far different lifestyle than Baghdad's social elite. (SCOTT TAYLOR)*

THIS PAGE, BOTH PHOTOS: *While the poor and middle classes suffered, decadent pleasures were still available to the rich and powerful. The two Russian girls sunning themselves poolside at the Al-Rasheed Hotel were part of Uday Hussein's private harem. Under Saddam's rule, Iraq was a secular Muslim country and many of the young upper class enjoyed Western-style entertainment. (OSMAN TUGRUL)*

TOP LEFT: *U.S. instructors train Iraqi volunteers at a training base in Taszar, Hungary. The CIA-sponsored project failed to attract the expected number of recruits.* (*U.S. ARMY*)

TOP RIGHT: *At Saddam's October 15, 2002 presidential referendum, one of the common themes was demonstrations by young Iraqis, often dressed in camouflage clothing, chanting slogans supportive of the Palestinian cause.* (*AFP*)

ABOVE: *One of America's most effective propaganda weapons was the fact that Saddam Hussein had gassed his own people. Pictured is one of the 5,000 Kurdish victims of the 1988 chemical weapons attack in Halabja, northern Iraq.* (*IRAN PHOTO FOUNDATION*)

TOP LEFT: *The main organiser of the human shields initiative was Ken O'Keefe, an ex-Marine and a veteran of the first Gulf War. Following much bickering between his volunteers, O'Keefe was asked to leave Iraq; after refusing, he was deported.* (SCOTT TAYLOR)

TOP RIGHT: *Just prior to the U.S. attack, the Baath party issued weapons to all of its members in the hopes they would resist the Americans. In reality, most planned to use the weapons to defend their homes from the expected looting.* (AP PHOTO/JEROME DELAY)

ABOVE: *Shortly before the war, international human shields staged a demonstration at the Baghdad oil refinery. Their slogan was "no blood for oil".* (SCOTT TAYLOR)

TOP: U.S. carrier-borne fighter jets were part of the first wave of attacks against Iraq on March 20, 2003. Their target was intended to "rid Iraq of its leadership." (U.S. AIR FORCE)

ABOVE: The massive explosions of U.S. Secretary of Defense Donald Rumsfeld's "shock and awe" campaign did not force Iraqi authorities into early capitulation. (AP/JEROME DELAY)

LEFT: *U.S. Tomahawk cruise missiles played a significant role in the United States' precision-guided aerial bombardments. Despite the Tomahawk's satellite global positioning system (GPS), a number of the missiles nevertheless went astray, killing a large number of innocent Iraqi civilians. (GETTY IMAGES / RICHARD MOORE)*

BELOW: *The U.S. armoured thrust north from Kuwait into Iraq met with only relatively light opposition from the Iraqi army. Rather than confront the superior coalition force tanks in the desert, the Iraqis fell back into the urban centres. (U.S. ARMY)*

TOP: *For those Iraqis unable to pull back, there was little option but to surrender to the advancing Americans. (U.S. ARMY)*

ABOVE: *When U.S. forces entered Baghdad, some of the key prizes to be seized were Saddam's numerous palaces. For propaganda purposes, U.S. personnel posed in a deliberately disrespectful manner in order to show Iraqis that their president was now powerless. (AP/JOHN MOORE)*

TOP LEFT: A Marine places a U.S. flag over Saddam's likeness for only a brief moment prior to toppling the statue in Firdos Square. The Pentagon feared that the use of the American flag in this manner would symbolise "occupation" to the Iraqi people, rather than "liberation." (AFP/KARIM SAHIB) / **TOP RIGHT and ABOVE:** *As soon as the Iraqi police lost control and the Iraqi army deserted, looting broke out across the entire country. Communities organized vigilante groups to protect their homes and families from armed looters.* (AP/ANJA NIEDRINGHAUS)

Kurdish peshmerga militiamen quickly moved southwards following the Iraqi army's collapse. After seizing Kirkuk and Mosul, many Kurds continued straight down to Baghdad and took part in the looting.

OPPOSITE PAGE, BOTTOM:
A former Iraqi policeman enters the U.S. administrative headquarters in Kirkuk in order to apply for his old job. The U.S. soldiers guarding the premises appear impatient to terminate their occupational duties. (SCOTT TAYLOR)

BOTH PHOTOS, THIS PAGE: The U.S. forces wasted no time and quickly seized Iraq's entire petroleum industry, including the refineries used for producing domestic fuel. For the first time in memory, gasoline was in short supply in Iraq and strictly rationed. (SCOTT TAYLOR)

TOP LEFT: *A U.S. Abrahams tank sits outside a Mujahadeen Khalq compound north of Baghdad. The Iranians residing there had fought for Saddam and against the Ayatollah Khomenei. Following the U.S. intervention, however, these Mujahadeen have become virtually stateless.* (SCOTT TAYLOR)

TOP RIGHT: *U.S. soldiers secure Saddam Hussein's main palace in central Baghdad. The heat and exhaustion had already taken a toll on the Americans in May 2003.* (SCOTT TAYLOR)

ABOVE: *The headquarters of the Mukhabarat (Iraq's secret service) in Baghdad. This compound was heavily bombed in the first days of the war, despite the fact the offices were known to be empty.* (SCOTT TAYLOR)

TOP: *Despite a shortage of troops on the ground, particularly in the north, the U.S. made the protection of Iraq's oil industry infrastructure from looters a top priority.* (SCOTT TAYLOR)

ABOVE LEFT: *Baghdad continued to burn even six weeks after Saddam's and his Baath party regime's collapse. Looting and arson were commonplace in the post-war anarchy.* (SCOTT TAYLOR)

ABOVE RIGHT: *In an attempt to convince the locals this was a "liberation," the U.S. started mounting joint police patrols with rehired Iraqi security officers. Unfortunately, the optics of unarmed Iraqis sitting in a vehicle with heavily armed U.S. soldiers only reinforced the appearance of an occupying army.* (SCOTT TAYLOR)

ABOVE: *By August 28, 2003, the U.S. had lost more soldiers "losing the peace" than they had in "winning the war". (U.S. ARMY)*

TOP and LEFT: *The Iraqi death toll also continued to climb. The U.S. must establish a secure environment and develop a sound exit strategy from Iraq before it becomes bloodily embroiled in a generational quagmire of anti-American hatred. (STEPHEN HIRD/REUTERS / SPENCER PLATT/GETTY IMAGES)*

ABOVE: *While British and U.S. officials continued to claim a diplomatic solution was still possible, the troop buildup in the Persian Gulf continued unabated. (COMBAT CAMERA)*
LEFT: *As a last resort, Saddam Hussein allowed UN weapons inspector back into Baghdad. The first teams began operations on November 27, 2002. (AP)*

THIS PAGE: *By early October 2002, the U.S. Third Division had already deployed into Kuwait and its soldiers were conducting training exercises along the Iraqi border.* (U.S. DOD)

OPPOSITE PAGE: *In an effort to demonstrate to the world that he maintained popular domestic support for his presidency, Saddam Hussein staged a referendum on October 15, 2002.* (JASSIM MOHAMMED, ASSOCIATED PRESS)

CHAPTER SIX:
Postponing the Inevitable

BAGHDAD, OCTOBER 14, 2002   Billed by Baghdad officials as a "demonstration of honest democracy," there could be no doubt Saddam would be re-elected for another seven-year term in office: he was the only candidate on the ballot.

Nevertheless, Baath party officials staged large-scale political rallies across the country, and the main thoroughfares of Baghdad were adorned with gaudy, multicoloured election banners. Although portraits and statues of Saddam Hussein had always been prominently displayed in public areas, photos of the president could now be seen on every corner and storefront window. Large hand-painted signs, many written in English, proclaimed "Yes, Yes to President Saddam Hussein" and "We love The Leader," and songs and poems paying tribute to the glory of Iraq and the virtues of Saddam were played repeatedly over public loudspeakers.

To witness the presidential referendum, nearly 1000 international observers and media had been invited to visit polling stations throughout the country. Although I had received a personalized invitation from Vice-President Taha Yassin Ramadan, I doubted he remembered me from our previous encounter, when I had interrupted his parliamentary speech.

Once again, Sami and Mohammad greeted me when I arrived at the airport. They apologized for General Hasan who, they said, would be unable to meet with me during this visit because, as head of Iraqi intelligence, he would be preoccupied with monitoring the elections.

While the majority of the foreign observers invited were from neighbouring Arab countries, a large number of Western journalists also took advantage of the referendum to obtain an entry visa into Iraq. Since the U.S. had stepped up its calls for a regime change in Iraq, security in the capital had been tightened and the issuance of visas to media was severely restricted. The sudden influx of foreigners overtaxed Iraq's unwieldy bureaucracy. With as many as four fully loaded, wide-bodied aircraft arriving daily at Saddam International from Syria and Jordan, there were interminable delays at customs and immigration checkpoints. The airport had been restored to only marginal capacity, and airport staff were accustomed to no more than a dozen flights a week. As a result, some travellers had to spend up to 4 hours just to have their documents processed.

In the days leading up to the referendum, Saddam Hussein was committed to staging a demonstration aimed at convincing the international community he maintained a popular mandate, thereby undermining support for the U.S. campaign to oust him. Many Middle East experts attending the referendum were skeptical.

Yoshiaki Sasaki, a senior research fellow with a Tokyo foundation that specializes in Iraqi studies, had been invited to participate in the referendum as an official observer. We had first met on the flight from Amman and, due to the backlog at the airport in Baghdad, we had discussed the Iraqi situation at length.

"The Iraqis claim that Saddam Hussein is not a dictator," said Sasaki. "Unfortunately, they don't understand the basic tenets upon which Western democracies are based."

Under the terms of the referendum, Saddam's nomination was first put forward by the members of his Revolutionary Command Council. This group was largely comprised of Saddam's closest associates and was, in fact, the Cabinet that ruled Iraq. Following his nomination, Saddam's presidency was approved in a unanimous vote by the Iraqi National Assembly, all members of the ruling Baath party. Under Iraq's constitution, the presidential candidacy must be upheld by a public referendum within 60 days.

On the Royal Jordanian flight, I had been fortunate enough to be seated next to a surprisingly outspoken resident of Baghdad. "For me, I wish that he would step down from power immediately, but tomorrow I will go and cast a vote for Saddam Hussein," Wahab Hindi, a 40-year-old former pilot turned merchant, told me. "This is not an exercise in democracy; it is simply a matter of Iraqis impressing the authorities. With the U.S. policy, the only way we can avoid complete destruction is if the current regime capitulates, but that will never happen. In the meantime we must somehow survive."

Having worked for Iraqi Airways, Hindi had been forced to seek an alternate career when the Americans imposed their post-1991 no-fly zones over Iraq. Despite the sanctions and without any Baath party loyalty to fall back on, Hindi managed to build a tannery business and a poultry farm. His English was excellent and he invited me to visit his home anytime I was in Baghdad.

At a pre-election press conference, Mohammed Saeed Al-Sahaf, Iraq's Minister of Information, made the first of many classic denials to assembled Western media. He categorically denied the leadership vote was being held to undermine President Bush's push for regime change. "We do not submit to outside pressures, that would be stupid," said Al-Sahaf. "The people of Iraq will send their message of support for Saddam whether or not there is a threat of war. Whether this will be accepted in the West is irrelevant." However, when asked to explain why the majority of the election banners were in English and displayed in front of hotels housing foreigners, the minister refused to answer.

Handouts provided by the government showed 11,798,000 eligible voters, all residing in the 15 southern provinces still under the central authority of Baghdad. Although technically part of sovereign Iraq, the three northern provinces – populated by an ethnic Kurdish majority – were under UN protection.

The nearly 3 million Kurds residing in the northern provinces had broken all ties with Baghdad in 1991. The two rival warlords, Massoud Barzani, leader of the Kurdistan Democratic Party (KDP) and Jalal Talabani, leader of the Patriotic Union of Kurdistan (PUK), who controlled this territory still aspired to establish an independent Kurdistan. When asked about the omission of these provinces from the voter list, Al-Sahaf replied: "The Kurdish voters who wish to support Saddam Hussein will be welcomed at polling stations across Iraq." As for the number of votes he expected to be cast, Al-Sahaf made a prophetic prediction: "There is no need for estimations. You will see the positive results."

~ ~ ~ ~ ~ ~ ~ ~ ~ ~

BAGHDAD, OCTOBER 15, 2002   Although the official results would not be made public until the end of the day, local papers mirrored Al-Sahaf's optimism by proclaiming Saddam's overwhelming victory in front-page headlines before the voting had even begun. As nearly 11.5 million Iraqis headed to polling stations to participate in the referendum, Nasra Al-Sadoon, editor of the *Baghdad Observer*, Iraq's only English-language daily newspaper, announced that Saddam's vote share "will be almost 100 per cent." Al-Sadoon's editorial also assured her readers that this vote would reflect "the free choice of Iraqis, their legitimate right and patriotic duty."

The only Canadian government representative attending as a monitor to the election was Windsor-St Clair MP Joseph Comartin. Visiting Baghdad at his own expense, Comartin made it clear to me he was not in Baghdad in any official capacity and that he was representing neither the House of Commons nor his NDP caucus. "A large number of my constituents are of ethnic-Arabic origin, and a potential U.S.-Iraq crisis has been of great concern to them," he said.

After spending the day touring four separate polling stations, Comartin reported he had seen no evidence of threats or pressure to coerce voter turnout. "There were no gun-toting goons forcing people to cast ballots," said Comartin. Although "with only one candidate in the running, you have to question the validity of the democratic process. But there was definitely real sentiment being expressed. The U.S. will of course portray this whole election as a farce or a show, but if this didn't represent democracy, the referendum certainly illustrated that deep-rooted anti-Bush and anti-U.S. sentiments exist throughout Iraq."

Political rallies and festivities had started the night before, with many of the larger ceremonies taking place in front of hotels housing international monitors and journalists. A national holiday having been declared in honor of the referendum, streets normally clogged with pedestrians and merchants were nearly deserted. Most vehicles on the road were brightly decorated buses and taxis ferrying voters – free of charge – to the polls.

At the ballot centers, local officials had organized day-long concerts and demonstrations. Although the legal voting age in Iraq is 18, many of those at the rallies were school children. Giving his name only as Mahmoud, one 12-year-old boy stated he would "proudly give his blood to defend his glorious Leader." Like his classmates, Mahmoud was dressed in combat fatigues and took part in a demonstration of Iraqi-Palestinian solidarity against U.S.-Israeli aggression.

A common theme in banner slogans and at demonstrations was Iraq's continuing support for the Palestinian cause. Iraqi officials believed Saddam's pan-Arab popularity, particularly among Palestinians, would pose a real threat of a wider Middle East war should the U.S. launch military action against their country.

For Joseph Comartin, on his first visit to the Middle East, the sight of children celebrating violence was particularly disturbing. "You realize that if a crisis cannot be averted between the U.S. and Iraq, many of these children will be killed in the conflict. Bush can blame Saddam for the tragedy and Saddam can blame Bush, but in the end it's the children that will suffer."

After the journalists and monitors left the polling stations, organized political presentations were replaced by folklore and dance troupes. The mood was festive and people stayed for hours, enjoying free refreshments and mingling with neighbours and friends.

"It is important to be seen at these events by Baath party officials," explained Mohammed Yahya, a 24-year-old merchant, as he exited a polling booth. "The authorities have the voter registry so they will know exactly who did or did not vote. But even people who are reluctant to vote don't want to be singled out for retribution."

When asked whether he had supported Saddam on his ballot, Yahya replied, "This is not about choosing a leader. It is simply to send a message of solidarity to the United States, and, yes, I added to that message."

Throughout the day, local television stations had been steadily broadcasting glorious images of Saddam Hussein's 22 years in power. Saddam himself, however, had become a leader in hiding. His last public appearance had been at a tribute to the troops on his birthday in May 2001. Since then, Saddam had communicated only through recorded messages from inside his palaces and bunkers. Not even the occasion of the leadership referendum could justify a risky public appearance. In his stead, Revolutionary Command Council members gave press statements and hosted victory celebrations in downtown hotel lobbies.

The imminent threat of an attack had increasingly put Iraq on a war footing, and many reserve soldiers had been called up for 60 days of service. As a precaution against early airstrikes, many of the military headquarters had been temporarily relocated outside the sprawling Ministry of Defence complex. At Baghdad's central district HQ, now housed in a nondescript office tower above several shops, even soldiers on duty were given two-hour rotating breaks to vote.

I discovered one such military facility purely by chance when I walked away from the organized tour that shuttled journalists and monitors between voting centers. Without a personal minder on this day, I took the opportunity to shoot footage with my digital camera of some Iraqi air defence positions and sandbagged bunkers that had been recently constructed near many government buildings. My intent was to contrast the jubilant election events with the more somber war preparations. I was filming a bus full of celebrating voters en route to a polling station when I felt a heavy tap on my shoulder. I turned and was surprised to see seven disheveled Iraqi conscripts, all leveling their assault rifles at me. They appeared to have emerged from the doorway of a disused theatre – large movie posters were plastered over the front of the boarded-up building.

Unable to speak any English, the soldiers made their meaning clear through hand signals. I was to follow them into the building. As I disassembled my tripod, one nervous-looking young soldier, standing only a few feet away, trained the barrel of his Kalashnikov squarely on me. Not trusting the young man's proficiency with a rifle, I pushed the barrel aside and said sternly in English, "There's no need for that. I'm coming peacefully." Although he had not understood what I said, my authoritative tone did the trick for he quickly apologized, saying, "Asaf (I'm sorry)." The tension now defused, his companions good-naturedly offered to help carry my gear as they lead me away.

Once inside the eight-story building, I was taken on an extensive guided tour, apparently because nobody quite knew what to do with me. Roused from their cots, several officers repeatedly chastised my seven-man entourage for disrupting them and ordered the soldiers to take me to another commander. As they directed me down several different hallways, I noticed that, in the Spartan offices, portraits of Saddam Hussein had been gaudily decorated with colored paper and balloons.

I was finally brought before a colonel, who turned out to be the district commander. He summoned a captain to translate. Having left my passport at my hotel, I had no identification on me, no handler, and no way of contacting either of my Mukhabarat guides. It was not a good situation to be in, particularly when the commander insisted on reviewing the footage I had shot.

Luckily, they did not know how to operate the digital camera so I was able to fast-forward and rewind past the images of the military installations to innocuous pictures of the polling stations I had recorded earlier. Marveling at the camera's technology, everyone in the tiny room wanted a turn at the viewfinder. The seven soldiers who had detained me had stayed to watch my interrogation and several of the commander's staff were now also crammed into the office's doorway. Fearing they might eventually find damning footage, I explained through the translator that I had to conserve the batteries. The Iraqi officer nodded knowingly and handed back my equipment.

Not wanting to make the issue bigger by involving other security agencies, the colonel declared that I was "not a spy" and ordered tea, Pepsi, cigarettes and a meal of bread and chicken livers be brought for me. He also apologized for any inconveniences the soldiers' detaining me might have caused. I told him it was a rare opportunity for me to speak to 'real' soldiers. He seemed pleased by the compliment.

For the next three hours, we chatted about politics and the state of the Iraqi military. When we got around to the subject of the referendum, the commander suddenly remembered he not yet cast his vote and the meeting was hastily concluded. My original 'captors' insisted on hailing a taxi – and paying my fare to the Sheraton Hotel.

When I walked into the hotel lobby, Tariq Aziz was leading the crowd in one of many parties being hosted by the victorious Baath party. Amid pounding drums, blaring trumpets and twirling dancers, everyone chanted "Nam, nam, Saddam" in jubilant support of their president.

~ ~ ~ ~ ~ ~ ~ ~ ~ ~

BASRA, OCTOBER 16-17, 2002   The celebrations in Baghdad continued into the next day. In anticipation of Saddam's win with a 100 per cent landslide majority, a state holiday had been declared so that all Iraqis could celebrate the "joyous triumph of honest democracy in Iraq."

In flood-lit stadiums in central Baghdad, thousands of revelers were televised chanting praise to Saddam and dancing to the music of top-name Iraqi pop singers. In the rest of the country, however, such festivities were uncommon. In the southern city of Basra, for example, there were no demonstrations at all of patriotic fervor.

Since arriving in Iraq, I had repeatedly asked Sami and Mohammad for authorization to visit Basra again, and they always assured me this would not be a problem. Taking that to mean I was cleared to proceed, I booked myself on a ridiculously cheap ($20 U.S.) Iraqi Airways flight and headed off to the airport in the early morning hours. I knew that traveling without a handler – and without express permission to leave the capital – would be pushing the Mukhabarat's patience, and I fully intended to beg forgiveness upon my return.

Although technically still within the U.S.-enforced southern no-fly zone, Iraqi Airways had started running daily flights to Basra about 12 months earlier. Twice a day, the U.S. Air Force and the Iraqi pilots played out the same ritual.

"As soon as we cross into the no-fly zone, we are contacted by a U.S. AWACS radio operator," said Abid Ali Abud, a 47-year-old captain with Iraqi Airways. "They tell us that we are illegally entering U.S. airspace and should turn around immediately. We reply that this is sovereign Iraqi airspace and continue to Basra." Although U.S. F-16 fighters stationed in Kuwait are frequently scrambled to escort passenger planes, to date no aggressive action had been taken. "The Americans will not dare shoot down a plane full of civilians," said Ali Abud. However, U.S. airplanes had already launched several major airstrikes against the airport at Basra, completely destroying its radar system.

On entering Basra, one of the first things I noticed was that there was little evidence of the pre-election banners and portraits of Saddam that had adorned Baghdad's main streets. And the few posters that proclaimed "We love Saddam" were displayed only on federal buildings and only in Arabic. Knowing none of the international delegates and journalists would be invited to Basra to monitor the referendum, Saddam's Baath party had targeted their campaign messages to the capital.

Although the previous day's official poll results showed no dip in regional support for Saddam, many of the Iraqi officials I spoke to secretly admitted that there was little love for the Baghdad regime in Basra. As General Hasan had acknowledged in our earlier conversation, in the event of an invasion by the United States, "the Iraqi army could not expect to hold the ground south of Baghdad itself, as local conscript soldiers are unlikely to put up much of a fight."

These sentiments were openly voiced by many residents of Basra. Nabil Al-Gorani, a 36-year-old photojournalist, told me that "the people of Basra are simply tired of war. It seems that we are always at the centre of these conflicts and, as a result, we suffer the most."

Al-Gorani could barely recall a time in his life when his hometown was not subject to regular airstrikes. During the decade-long Iran-Iraq War of the 1980s, Basra was the most contested battleground. Strategically located on the Shatt-al-Arab waterway, Basra was also the major logistic staging area for Saddam's ill-fated 1990 invasion of Kuwait. During the airstrikes of *Operation Desert Storm*, Basra was regularly pounded by allied bombers. When the defeated Iraqi army fled north out of Kuwait, the coalition ground forces followed them to the outskirts of Basra, leaving behind a trail of death and destruction.

In response to the U.S. threat of regime change in Baghdad, Saddam Hussein inevitably issued brave statements about Iraqis resisting American aggression until "the last drop of blood." And many of the younger generation, those who had not experienced, or were too young to remember the last Gulf War, professed to embrace this defiance.

For the residents of Basra, however, daily reminders of Iraq's human sacrifice in recent wars are a fact of life. Along the highway to Kuwait, thousands of destroyed armoured vehicles stand as grim testimony to the lethality of allied air power. And along the banks of the Shatt-al-Arab lie rusting hulks of half-sunken tankers and warships – some from the Iran-Iraq War; a few actually dating back to World War I.

Another reason for resentment toward Baghdad is the comparative poverty endured by southern Iraqis. The Shiite Muslim majority of this region had never been particularly loyal to Saddam Hussein's primarily Sunni Muslim regime. At the end of the first Gulf War, Iran-backed Shiite rebels had staged a bloody revolt in Basra. During the few days extremists held Basra, they exercised a terrible and violent vengeance on Saddam's captured Baath party officials. Many prisoners were reportedly tied between two cars, then ripped in half by the accelerating vehicles to the cheers of fanatic onlookers.

After Baghdad re-established its authority in Basra, many residents felt they had been deliberately shortchanged in the national oil revenue distribution. "Admittedly, the 12 years of sanctions have severely hurt all of Iraq. However, we don't see the same number of palaces, public buildings or federal investment projects as Baghdad," said Al-Gorani. "The people here in Basra feel cut off completely from the televised images we see of Baghdad."

Things were even worse for the Marsh-Arab tribes that had joined in the revolt. Following the return of Saddam's troops, Iraqi engineering efforts intensified to complete the drainage of the marshes – first begun by the British in the early 1950s – where the Euphrates and Tigris rivers meet at the Shatt-al-Arab delta. This effectively took away much of the natural habitat the primitive Marsh-Arabs need to exist.

Although only 600 kilometers from the capital, Basra had remained relatively isolated from central Baghdad control. The national telephone system, largely destroyed during *Desert Storm*, had not yet been repaired and few lines were available between the two cities. Since my last trip to Basra, things had not improved: Most senior Basra bureaucrats still had no way of calling Baghdad.

As a result, when I tried to visit the children's hospital, the director would not allow me to enter the facility without express permission from his superiors. Unable to phone Baghdad, he explained he would have to draft a letter and wait for a reply. Although local government officials were still willing to rely on Saddam's regime for direction, I got the distinct impression Baghdad's iron grip on the local population was starting to slip.

With U.S. ground forces already building up in Kuwait and President Bush armed with congressional approval for a military strike, most residents of Basra believed the next bloody round of fighting was only weeks away.

Ali, a manager at the Sheraton Hotel in Basra, was nonplussed. "Everyone in Baghdad is yelling 'Nam, nam, Saddam' for the referendum," he said, "but they would be just as enthusiastically shouting 'Nam, nam, Tommy Franks' if the U.S. launched an attack."

Most Iraqis were well informed of America's proposal to establish a military command structure within an occupied Iraq. U.S. Middle East Commander Tommy Franks had been named as the most likely candidate for this post. With his hotel occupancy down below 20 per cent, Ali said he would gladly open his doors to American soldiers. "Chanting slogans and professing a love for Saddam does not put food on my hungry family's table."

That evening, during my return flight to Baghdad, the tiny Iraqi Airways 727 encountered terrible turbulence and we landed at the airport in a full-blown desert storm. Throughout the night, gusting winds ripped at the shutters of my window while, in the streets below, merchants' kiosks were knocked flat. Swirling dust filled the air like a dense fog, giving the moonlit sky a strange orange glow.

When the winds abated in the morning, remnants of election banners and posters of Saddam were hanging in shredded tatters from branches and lampposts. For the superstitious doorman at the Sheraton, a desert storm blowing in to tear down Saddam Hussein's proclamations of a continued presidency was a singularly bad omen.

"This was Allah's will," whispered a bellhop as he surveyed the garbage littering the streets. "Saddam has angered even God."

I didn't know it, but I was about to face my own personal storm, one brought on by the Mukhabarat. When I filed my story about the mood in Basra, I titled it 'Iraqis weary of war' and had deliberately buried a quote about Iraqis being just as willing to chant "nam, nam General Tommy Franks" as they were to shout out support for Saddam at the bottom of it. *Ottawa Citizen* editor Bruce Garvey, however, decided to play up that part of the article. The published headline read 'No love for Saddam in Basra: Unhappy residents debunk claims of 100 per cent voter support.'

Upon reading the "offensive article," the Iraqi chargé d'affaires in Ottawa immediately faxed a copy of it to the Ministry of Information in Baghdad. Mohammed Al-Sahaf, himself, had demanded an explanation from my handlers as to how I came to be in Basra without his department's knowing about it, let alone approving it.

Following Al-Sahaf's dressing down, Sami and Mohammad did not waste any time in tracking me down at the Sheraton. A prolonged shouting match that lasted several hours, erupted in my room. The Mukhabarat agents accused me of fabricating quotes while in the same breath demanding I provide them with my sources' identities. I reminded them their own general had acknowledged that my assessment of Basra's questionable loyalty was correct.

In the mistaken belief that I was threatening to reveal Hasan's private admission publicly, Mohammad went berserk. We came close to exchanging blows but, in the end, calmer heads prevailed and we managed to come up with a face-saving solution.

To appease Al-Sahaf's anger, we agreed they should expel me from Iraq immediately. As I had already booked my return flight to Amman for the following morning, the expulsion was purely symbolic.

~ ~ ~ ~ ~ ~ ~ ~ ~ ~

BAGHDAD, DECEMBER 7-11, 2002   Late in the afternoon, tempers flared as the foreign press corps jostled for position outside the Iraqi National Monitoring Directorate. Believing those in front were actually filming Iraq's much-anticipated weapons dossier, the cameramen in the back pressed closer and hoisted their cameras higher in the vain hope of getting some lucky footage. The crush of bodies actually jammed the doorway, making it impossible for anyone to either enter or leave the exhibition room. At the front of the melee, a British journalist repeatedly screamed for everyone to "get the fuck back," while a score of others shouted their own expletives. The chorus of panicked voices reached a crescendo when a plate glass window was smashed. Unable to restore order, the Iraqis suspended the entire press conference.

The exasperated organizer, Uday Al-Tai, Iraq's normally dapper and composed Director General of Information, then proceeded to reprimand the journalists for their "shameful behaviour." When the official briefing finally resumed, Iraq's formal declaration of its weapons programs proved to be anticlimactic.

As they had maintained since the United Nations Security Council approved Resolution 1441 on November 8, the Iraqis again denied being in possession of nuclear, biological or chemical arsenals. "We don't have any of these weapons now, and we have no intention of acquiring any in the future," said General Hussam Mohammad Amin, the head of Iraq's National Monitoring Directorate. "Iraq has no weapons of mass destruction – absolutely."

General Amin did admit that the 11,807 pages of material that had been handed over to the United Nations included some items that had previously been withheld from weapons inspectors in 1998. When asked whether the United States could use this prior non-compliance to justify a military intervention against Iraq, Amin told reporters that this possibility had been discussed in advance with the UN inspectors and the International Atomic Energy Agency (IAEA).

"If the U.S. allows the minimum of fairness and demonstrates the minimum of courage, then they will accept this report as proof of Iraq's disarmament," Amin said.

Even before copies of the declaration could be delivered to the IAEA in Vienna and to the UN Security Council in New York City, the U.S. administration began denouncing the documents as "incomplete." When it was learned in Baghdad that the Americans had obtained an advance copy of their dossier from the Colombian Security Council delegation, Iraqi officials were furious.

"If the U.S. claims to have proof of any violation, I call upon them to present such evidence forthwith," said General Amer Al-Saadi, the science advisor for Armament Affairs and one of the authors of Iraq's declaration. "The Americans can present their material to the UN inspectors here [in Baghdad] immediately to either prove or disprove the claims, so why are they playing these games?"

Since their arrival in Baghdad on November 27, the UN inspection teams had proven to be a valuable public relations tool for the Iraqi government. Throughout the first week of their operations, the greatly increased foreign press corps and Iraqi monitors closely followed the inspectors. Every morning at 8:30 a.m., the UN vehicles rolled out of their hotel compound and raced toward undisclosed inspection sites. Iraqi authorities and a veritable media circus followed in hot pursuit through congested city streets.

The UN inspectors denied media access and remained tight-lipped about the results of their searches. However, Iraqi officials, anxious to convince the international community of their compliance with the UN resolution, permitted journalists to conduct their own inspections after the UN teams departed.

The biggest challenge to the inspection process occurred on the morning of December 3, when two UN teams suddenly arrived at one of Saddam Hussein's palaces. Although there was some confusion among the guards, after only an eight-minute delay the gates were swung open. While the search revealed no evidence of any weapons program, the Iraqis were quick to capitalize on the incident as proof of their willingness to co-operate. They were also quick to point out to reporters that the inspectors had not worn their chemical protection suits when they inspected the palace.

"They knew they would not find any weapons cache here," Sami said to me as we drove away. While he had seemed genuinely pleased to see me at the airport, his partner, Mohammad, still smoldering from our last exchange, now petulantly pretended to speak only Spanish.

"Saddam Hussein has shown the world that he is prepared to open his own palaces, and that we have nothing to hide," continued Sami. "What more can Iraq do?"

President Saddam Hussein had answered that very question on December 7 with a startling apology to the citizens of Kuwait for his 1990 invasion. Although the official statement claimed this sudden goodwill gesture had not been prompted by the current crisis, few Iraqis believed it.

"This is the first time that I believe our President is truly afraid," said Anmar Saadi, a 42-year-old taxi driver. "However, the people realize that he is doing this for our sakes – to save Iraq from further bloodshed."

I had met Anmar as a random fare outside the Al-Rasheed Hotel. He spoke only passable English, but was eager to practice. Although I had initially assumed his attempts to converse were designed to land a bigger tip, I soon realized otherwise. To my surprise, at the end of the day he invited me to have dinner with him and his family. Over a meal of roast chicken and bottles of arak – alcohol made locally from grapes or dates – Anmar discussed his wartime experiences as a former commando.

Later that evening, one of Anmar's neighbours stopped by for an unexpected visit. In a remarkable coincidence, the neighbour turned out to be Wahib Hindi, the former Iraqi Airways pilot I had met on an earlier flight from Amman. Hindi was as outspoken in his contempt for Saddam as I remembered. He was extremely concerned about the safety of his family and had begun making arrangements to ship his children to Jordan. When our impromptu party broke up, I promised to visit the Hindi household before the family separated. I also agreed to contract Anmar's services whenever possible as I believed his military experience and insight would prove invaluable.

Even with the desperate concessions being made by the Iraqi president, there were indications the Iraqis' fear of an imminent invasion was justified: More than 60,000 American troops were conducting large-scale military exercises in Kuwait; U.S. and British jets had stepped up their attacks in the no-fly zones; and Iraqi naval vessels had recently engaged a Kuwaiti coast guard vessel in the Persian Gulf.

~ ~ ~ ~ ~ ~ ~ ~ ~ ~

MOSUL, DECEMBER 12-13, 2002   With more than 200 foreign journalists now registered in Baghdad, officials with the Ministry of Information had experienced something akin to a gold rush. As with any supply-and-demand situation, the fact that visas for journalists were tightly controlled had led to massive bribes. The relative shortage of translators (i.e., handlers) and drivers meant rates had more than quadrupled since my last trip. The Ministry also wanted to cash in on the action and had started charging a $100 U.S. daily fee just to work in Iraq; for television crews, the charge was $500 a day. As I was technically considered a guest of the Mukhabarat, however, I did not have to pay.

When I had officially obtained permission to fly north to Mosul, the only stipulation from Sami had been that I travel with one of Al-Sahaf's handlers. Not wanting a repeat of the Basra episode, I reluctantly agreed. The only additional costs I had to cover were those of my guide, Alla.

Of all the translators the Ministry could have foisted on me, Alla was possibly the most repugnant. From other media outlets he had pocketed up to $400 a day in "tips" and was quick to display his newfound wealth by wearing expensive jewelry and suits. Used to being tipped, he was upset when I would not pay the extra $4 per ticket to fly business class. However, once we arrived in Mosul, Alla's confidence seemed to evaporate. And as we drove further north toward the Kurdish border, Alla looked decidedly uncomfortable.

WHEN WE REACHED THE last checkpoint, seven young Iraqi conscripts were huddled in the back of a battered Nissan pick-up truck, their parka hoods drawn tight to ward off the cold morning air. The section commander, the only one issued with a helmet, manned a light machine gun balanced atop the Nissan's cab. Orders were shouted to the guardhouse before the overloaded little truck rumbled off northwards to patrol the boundary with the Kurdish-controlled zone, an area of barren foothills that had been bandit country for centuries, and which remained a smuggler's paradise.

There was no love lost between the soldiers and the peshmerga militia just across the border. Saddam Hussein's regiments had fought a series of bloody guerrilla wars against the Kurdish separatists for decades. After the post-Gulf War Kurdish rebellion was suppressed in 1991, the United Nations brokered the ceasefire agreement that gave virtual autonomy to the three Kurdish-populated provinces of northern Iraq. To ensure that Saddam's forces did not attempt to re-enter this region, British and United States aircraft continually patrol this no-fly zone in support of the lightly armed Kurdish militia.

Troops stationed along the border feared a new threat could come from the north at any time. "We have been advised that U.S. Special Forces are already operating in our sector," said Sergeant Ahmed Noori. At 38 years of age, the grizzled Noori already had 20 years of military service and plenty of combat experience.

"When we fought the Kurdish rebels and the Iranian army, they fought with courage," said Noori. "However, when we fought the Americans in Kuwait, it was different – we never saw an American. They killed us without us being able to fight back."

Offering to share their lunch of roast chicken and rice, Noori and Sergeant Major Khalid Hammad did their best to extend a measure of generous hospitality in their Spartan guardhouse. The unheated, windowless cinderblock shelter was littered with filthy bedrolls. There was one table and the only chair was of the plastic patio-style variety and was missing a leg. It was interesting to note that, in this front-line outpost, no photograph of their president hung on the wall. Despite the limited amenities, the food was excellent and helpings were generous. Patting Noori's hefty paunch, the equally robust Hammad proudly proclaimed, "We eat good."

Despite the short time we spent there, it was readily apparent that the two veterans had little regard for Alla. They openly mocked his leather dress shoes, which were totally unsuited for the thick mud that surrounded the border post. Later, they made him translate an insult: "They say to tell you 'I am a dandy.'" The two sergeants laughed heartily at their own joke. And it was obvious that Alla was shit-scared of them.

THIS VISIT TO THE FRONTLINES provided me with an even clearer perspective on Saddam's military preparedness. Although there were professional soldiers like Noori and Hammad in the army, the majority of the troops were half-starved, skinny conscripts. There was, however, no shortage of uniforms for these frontline troops. These northern units wore a green camouflage pattern to blend in with the relatively lush landscape, whereas soldiers in southern sectors wore a tan desert camouflage. Helmets and boots were in short supply and protective body armour items were non-existent. Communication equipment was primitive at best; the outposts still used hand-crank field telephones to contact each other.

In downtown Mosul, I saw a convoy of construction dump trucks being used to shuttle soldiers between their barracks and the frontline. And the few air-defence weapons visible were antiquated, manually aimed 23-mm cannons which, because of their limited range, were completely useless against jet aircraft.

At the nearby airport, about a dozen old MiG fighter jets lay abandoned beside the runway. These aircraft had not been destroyed in combat; they had been cannibalised for spare parts. A large number of reinforced concrete aircraft hangars stood empty. The fighters they once housed now sat on an airstrip in Iran, where they had been impounded after the Iraqi air force flew them there for sanctuary during *Operation Desert Storm*. As for the Soviet-style helicopter gunships that had once been stationed in Mosul to combat Kurdish guerrillas, they had long since been destroyed or moved out of the no-fly zone.

South of Mosul, relic military bases were enclosed by a low sand berm (wall), around the perimeter, with a guardhouse atop each corner. Visible inside was a collection of primitive barracks, a sports field, parade square and vehicle park.

"The young soldiers find it difficult to deal with the boredom on these postings," Hammad, a 42-year-old father of four, told me. "However, they will soon learn that if a war comes, there are things more terrible than boredom."

~ ~ ~ ~ ~ ~ ~ ~ ~ ~

In addition to venturing north to get a rare glimpse of the remote border posts, I had a more personal reason for being there. I wanted to visit the St. George Chaldean Christian Monastery and pay my respects. Najeeb and Sami Shallal's eldest brother, Vadri, had passed away only weeks before and had been interred in the monastery's cemetery.

I had met Faleh and Fatin, Vadri's sons, at Najeeb's restaurant in Ottawa, where they worked. However, because they feared being forced into military service, the brothers had made the difficult decision of not returning to Iraq to attend the funeral.

But there was another familial connection to this sacred site. St. George's bishop, Hermes Shallal, who at 87 years of age was still an imposing figure, was also Najeeb's uncle. I had brought letters and photos from his nephew in Ottawa as well as a cash donation to help the monastery. After speaking with me for some time, the elderly gentleman excused himself so he could take a nap. Father Fadi Hanna, the director of St. George, offered to take me on a tour of the 300-year-old monastery.

"As a minority, we are often overlooked when people discuss the current U.S.-Iraq crisis," said Father Hanna. The estimated one million Christian Iraqis are mostly located in the north, and many of their communities had been divided by the administrative boundary with the Kurdish provinces. The Christians were also further divided into two major denominations: Chaldean and Assyrian.

"Under Saddam Hussein's regime, Christians do not suffer from any religious oppression in Iraq. However, if America changes the balance of power, this may not remain the case."

Father Hanna continued to explain how many Christians privately feared the consequences should the fundamentalist Shiite Moslem majority seize control of a post-Saddam Iraq. Upon hearing this, Alla immediately protested against Father Hanna's comments about Saddam's continued presidency. Although Alla appeared satisfied with the placating apology Father Hanna offered him, the priest then turned and winked at me in a conspiratorial manner.

When we arrived, an Iraqi army unit had been in the process of setting up a temporary fuel dump next to the monastery walls. "The local commander thinks that George Bush would never let his air force bomb a Christian holy site," Father Hanna had said. "And I pray to God that he is right."

TOP: *The 300-year-old St. George Chaldean Christian Monastery in Mosul. The often-overlooked Christian minority of Iraq are located mainly in the country's northern provinces.*

ABOVE: *U.S. Special Forces troops had been operating in northern Iraq in support of Kurdish peshmerga fighters for months prior to the actual war. (U.S. DOD)*

ABOVE: *Britain and Australia were the only two countries that provided significant military clout to George Bush's "coalition of the willing."* (U.S. DOD)

OPPOSITE PAGE: *With the diplomatic efforts seemingly stalled, Iraqis stepped up demonstrations in Baghdad.* (GORDON TOMASEVIC/REUTERS)

CHAPTER SEVEN:
On The Brink

As the countdown to war entered its final stages and all eyes were focussed on the Middle East, a bizarre sideshow was developing in Eastern Europe. Laci Zoldi, the Budapest-based reporter that I had met in Baghdad in May 2001, sent me an e-mail outlining how the U.S. was going to use a Hungarian military base to train an Iraqi army-in-exile.

In the face of tremendous public opposition, Hungarian officials insisted the Iraqis would be trained only as "civil administrators." As many of them were being recruited in Turkey, I forwarded this information to Osman Tugrul. (I had first met Tugrul, who works for the Ankara daily newspaper *Sabah*, at the Al-Rasheed Hotel during one of the journalists' social nights.) Through contacts Tugrul provided for the Iraqi Turkmen Front – an international organization which represents the Turkmen population in Iraq and abroad – I was able to confirm not only that the volunteers were undergoing military training, but that some had actually been recruited in Canada.

Before heading back to Baghdad, I arranged to fly to Budapest and accompany Laci to the remote training camp. To help us root out the story, a couple of my old Balkan compatriots, American Chris Deliso and Australian Sasha Uzonov, headed north from Skopje, Macedonia, and joined us in Taszar.

Taszar, January 21-25, 2003   Security was extremely tight at this NATO base in southwest Hungary as the first Iraqi volunteers had begun arriving. It was expected that, over the next six months, nearly 3000 expatriates would be organized into the nucleus of a post-Saddam Iraqi army. As conceptualized (and equipped) by the CIA, this 'liberation' force would be composed largely of members of the Iraqi National Congress (INC), a seven-party anti-Saddam coalition in exile.

Contrary to initial reports, Pentagon officials reluctantly admitted the Iraqi "volunteers" would wear uniforms and carry weapons. "This group will include former Kurdish opposition fighters as well as many Iraqis who served their basic national conscription," said Dan Hetlidge, a Pentagon spokesperson. "Depending on their capability and experience, they will be tasked as guides for U.S. ground troops. Who better than those who know the territory? [They will also be tasked with] prisoners-of-war handling and rear-area security."

The fact that Iraqi Canadians were also recruited for this covert military force raised serious questions about the Canadian government's involvement. "Unless this is sanctioned by our government, we can't permit covert military recruiting in Canada, even if 'friendlies' are doing the recruiting," said David Harris, former Chief of Strategic Planning at CSIS. "Within our frontiers, the Canadian State must always have a monopoly on the recruiting and control of any armed force, however loosely described."

While there was no official word of Canada's participation in this program, Harris believed that such co-ordination could be facilitated only at the highest levels. "Formally, this would be up to Foreign Affairs to initiate and then hand over the operational aspect to other departments, such as National Defence," said Harris. "However, realistically, official co-operation in such a fast-moving context would see more PMO [Prime Minister's Office] and less Foreign Affairs involvement."

The short timetable and ambitious recruiting objectives for this Iraqi 'liberation army' program precluded the United States from conducting thorough background security checks on the volunteers. Although the INC had first been asked to provide the CIA with a list of available candidates the previous October, many of the groups did not forward their initial applicant roster until early January 2003. When asked how the U.S. could possibly screen such a large number of volunteers from countries around the world on such short notice, Pentagon spokesman Dan Hetlidge declined to comment.

Mustafa Ziya, head of the Turkmen Front's Ankara chapter and one of the primary recruiters for this program, confirmed the tight deadlines. "I forwarded the first 200 names to the U.S. embassy [in Ankara] on January 15, and our people were to be en route [to Taszar] within the week," said Ziya. The Turkmen Front was to supply an additional 200 recruits to fulfil its quota of the overall force objective.

Sources close to the Pentagon admitted that the response had been below expectations. "We are certainly short of our predictions at this point," said Ben Works, director of the Strategic Intelligence Research Institute of the United States (SIRIUS), "but we're still ahead of where we were at this stage in the Afghanistan operation."

The Iraqi volunteers reportedly received a $3,000 U.S. "signing bonus" and CIA and State Department officials at American embassies around the world were directed to process all travel arrangements for the recruits. In order to qualify, applicants had to be between 20 and 40 years of age, have prior military service and speak at least two languages. (Although English was preferred, Iraqi volunteers had to have a basic understanding of a European language, in addition to their own dialect.)

One factor negatively affecting recruiting was the confusion surrounding the force's purported role. "The Americans don't need any military assistance to topple Saddam Hussein. They have the overwhelming means to do this all on their own," said Asif Sertturkmen, the co-ordinator of the Toronto-based Turkmen Canadian Cultural Centre. "Our community was canvassed, but even those interested were not clear on what the U.S. had in mind," Sertturkmen stated. "We believe in regime change, but only through peaceful means."

Mustafa Ziya had no such qualms. "We were told to recruit soldiers," he said. Among those recruited was 28-year-old Gaan Latis, a former anti-Saddam Turkmen guerrilla fighter. Following the failure of the 1991 Gulf War uprising in Iraq, Latis and many of his comrades had fled to Turkey. Since his defection, Latis worked at Radio Free Iraq Liberation in Istanbul, which he readily admitted was operated by "DOT… the CIA." On January 17, just two days after Mustafa Ziya submitted his name as a recruit, Latis was told to head to the American embassy in Ankara.

Since the story of the secret U.S. training base in Hungary was first broken by John Nadler in the *Ottawa Citizen* on January 2, 2003, a number of contradictory official statements had been made regarding the true nature of this program. Originally, the U.S. position was that these individuals would be trained simply as "translators"; however, as details were revealed about the weapons, uniforms, and training by U.S. Special Forces, an angry backlash from concerned Hungarians began to be heard.

"The original U.S. explanation that Iraqi ex-soldiers would be at desks while an American sergeant taught them the basics of English grammar was beyond believability," said Karoly Szita, mayor of Kaposvar, the small town located just outside the Taszar military compound. "When I heard this story, I laughed my head off," he said.

Hungarians, and in particular the citizens of Kaposvar, were concerned that the presence of this Iraqi training camp would make them a potential target for terrorists.

Knowing the nature of soldiers, we deliberately staked out one of the local striptease bars. The only other patrons at the club were a table full of Americans. Although they were incredibly suspicious at first, Deliso's New England accent worked like a charm. Within an hour, the soldiers admitted they were Special Forces personnel who had been sent to Taszar to "train a bunch of fucking Iraqis."

At the time, the Americans had at least five public affairs officers dedicated to this program and had established a media operations centre on the base; however, no press conferences were held and media were denied all access.

Since George Bush and Tony Blair were still insisting that they were seeking a diplomatic solution, it wasn't in their best interest to publicise the fact that they were already recruiting and training a *new* Iraqi army.

~ ~ ~ ~ ~ ~ ~ ~ ~ ~

BAGHDAD, JANUARY 26-FEBRUARY 1, 2003   Incredibly, as the clouds of war continued to gather and the U.S. military buildup continued unabated in the Persian Gulf, the people of Iraq appeared fatalistic.

"They've simply had it. Both mentally and physically, the Iraqis are not prepared to suffer another war," said Denis Halliday, the former United Nations humanitarian co-ordinator in Iraq. "They will look you in the eye and say that 'if it is Allah's wish for me to die, then so be it.' The Iraqi people, after two decades of conflict and twelve years of economic sanctions, are beyond worrying about their future."

Like Scott Ritter, Halliday had also resigned in protest from his UN post in 1998 and had since become an outspoken critic of "the genocidal nature of UN sanctions vis-à-vis Iraq." He was in Baghdad to meet with other prominent peace activists, trying to find some way to avert a U.S. military intervention. "Basically, we are looking for a last-minute miracle," he said.

While in Baghdad, Halliday had visited a number of families to verify the claim that Saddam Hussein had distributed an additional three months' worth of rations to his people. Under the terms of the oil-for-food program, each Iraqi household received a basic allotment of such staples as wheat, rice, flour, cooking oil, and tea. However, in December, anticipating a possible war, Saddam had issued a 90-day supply in advance and announced that in early February he would distribute an additional two-month supply.

"Although the United States has always accused Saddam of diverting the food program proceeds to ulterior sources, this was never the case," said Halliday. "With 150 UN inspectors conducting random spot checks over the past seven years, not a single case of diversion was ever uncovered."

The former UN co-ordinator believed that Saddam's own political survival played a major role in his willingness to support the food program. "If there is one thing that would force the people of Iraq to rise up and overthrow the government, it would be starvation."

Iraq's water supply was another major consideration. During the 1991 Gulf War, water treatment plants, sewage facilities, and pumping stations had been destroyed by airstrikes. Without access to potable water, desperate Iraqis resorted to using water directly from the Tigris River. As a result, it was estimated that nearly one million Iraqis died of dysentery or other water-borne diseases. To prevent such a tragedy from recurring, the Iraqi government launched an initiative to encourage those with property around their homes to sink wells. Even some government parking lots in the centre of Baghdad were drilled for such a purpose.

"The well water will still need to be boiled before it is potable," said Halliday, "but it will be far more sanitary than river water." Iraqi officials admit, however, that no study has been conducted into what the long-term effects of sinking tens of thousands of wells would have on the local water table.

In late January, Baghdad hosted its annual Euro Med exhibition at the Al-Rasheed Hotel. With a macabre sense of timing, European medical suppliers displayed such items as artificial limbs, blood transfusion machines and incubators to eager Iraqi health officials.

"Admittedly, the timing is unfortunate, on the eve of a possible war," said Stefan Ohletz, the German trade delegation's organiser at Euro Med. "However, this is all part of the authorized oil-for-food program. The Iraqi health ministry needs everything, but they are only allowed to purchase certain basic items, subject to approval by the UN sanction committee. The only thing they do have an abundance of is money."

When asked whether or not the Euro Med exhibitors felt uneasy about signing contracts with the Iraqi government at this uncertain time, Ohletz replied, "We are confident that Bush is not so mad as to ignore the will of the world. However, if there is a war, Iraq will still need medical supplies, possibly even more so."

Most Iraqis shared the view that Bush would not dare endure "the wrath of the world" as a result of Iraq's internal propaganda campaign, which steadily played up international opposition to a U.S.-led intervention. The newspapers were full of coverage of the anti-war protests taking place around the world; and visits by foreign delegates were hailed as "proof" that Iraq was not alone.

In a front-page story, the *Baghdad Observer* hailed "Jan Critian (sic) ... the Canadian Premier (sic)" for joining France and Germany in rejecting war. In the same edition, some of Tariq Aziz's comments were quoted: "Colleen Beaumier, Liberal MP for Brampton-West Mississauga, was in Baghdad to deliver an unofficial message that "without a UN resolution, Canada will not participate in a war against Iraq."

Beaumier was accompanied by her assistant, Natalie Jewett, and consultant Donn Lovett. Calgary oilman Arthur Millholland and Lovett had desperately tried to put together a full-scale parliamentary delegation to visit Iraq at this eleventh hour; at the last minute, however, several politicians, who had agreed in principle, backed out.

Despite her long and honourable efforts on behalf of the Iraqi people, Colleen Beaumier found herself viciously attacked by the very media outlets that had previously praised her. Dubbed "Baghdad Beaumier" by pro-war columnists and the Canadian Alliance, her visit to Iraq was denounced as "anti-American." (To be fair, the *Calgary Herald* had dispatched Linda Slobodian and Global TV sent Gary Bobrovitz to accompany Beaumier and report on her visit.)

The Iraqi authorities, meanwhile, continued to present a one-sided perspective on the crisis by staging daily 'spontaneous' demonstrations of anti-U.S. defiance. The drill was always the same: Baath Party officials rallying several hundred protesters in front of a UN office or embassy. The rhythmic Arabic chants were well choreographed and some of the more colourful participants, such as children wearing combat clothing, turned up at all the protests. The fact that many of the chants such as "Down, down U.S.A." were yelled in phonetic English made it obvious these events were being staged for the benefit of the international press corps.

In the few short weeks that I'd been away from Iraq, the number of foreign journalists in Baghdad had nearly tripled. Drivers, handlers, and translators, many of whom could hardly understand English, were now demanding up to $500 U.S. a day to 'assist' reporters. Given the depressed state of the economy – 30 cents can buy a decent lunch or a cross-town cab ride – these fees, paid in foreign currency, were astronomical. Meanwhile, protestors were trying to convince reporters that all Iraqis, regardless of age or culture, were willing to give their lives for their country. One protest staged by expatriate Palestinians living in Baghdad was targeted at the Qatari embassy. Their message was that no Arab land should be used to launch strikes against Iraq.

Fadhle Daud Assadi, the organiser of this protest, was a 58-year-old school headmaster and father of six. "We want George Bush to start behaving like a gentleman," said Assadi. "But if there is to be a war, Palestinian-Iraqis will fight for Saddam."

~ ~ ~ ~ ~ ~ ~ ~ ~ ~

Immediately following the presentation by Executive Chairman of the UN Monitoring, Verification and Inspection Commission (UNMOVIC), Hans Blix and the release of his weapons inspection report to the Security Council on January 27, Iraqi President Saddam Hussein issued a morale-boosting message to his senior leadership. Praising his loyal commanders for their "persistence," Saddam stressed that "real men should not panic, because they have national burdens."

Panicked, however, would appear to be the word best suited to Iraq's senior leaders. Seemingly caught unaware by Blix's position that seemed to leave the door open for a possible U.S. intervention, the Iraqis were unable to co-ordinate a press conference to present a response of their own. Even top Baghdad government officials, such as Mohammed Al-Sahaf and Uday Al-Tai, who were normally available for media comment were suddenly inaccessible. Despite the lack of an official response, however, the average Baghdad resident appeared to understand the implications.

Televised late Monday night, most Iraqis tuned in, hoping that Blix would provide a strong enough statement to deter any military action. However, his assessment that Iraq was being "less than fully compliant" left the decision for war entirely in the hands of U.S. President George Bush.

"The State of the Union address will determine our fate," said Walid, a 60-year-old waiter at a chicken restaurant. "If Bush says tonight 'Iraq is good,' there will be no war. However, if he says 'Iraq is bad,' then it is a declaration of war."

On Tuesday night, U.S. President George Bush removed all hope for a diplomatic resolution when he gave his much-anticipated address:

"The dictator of Iraq is not disarming. To the contrary, he is deceiving… Trusting in the sanity and restraint of Saddam Hussein is not a strategy and it is not an option. …Tonight I have a message for the brave and oppressed people of Iraq: Your enemy is not surrounding your country. Your enemy is ruling your country. And the day he and his regime are removed from power will be the day of your liberation."

War had been declared. Only the start date had to be determined.

~ ~ ~ ~ ~ ~ ~ ~ ~ ~

Ironically, it was inside the suburb that bore his name that one was most hard-pressed to find either a statue or portrait of Saddam Hussein. Unlike the rest of the capital, where the Iraqi president's likeness was omnipresent, few tributes were visible in the poverty-stricken streets of Saddam City.

This sprawling slum on the eastern outskirts of Baghdad is home to nearly 3 million Shiite-Iraqis. On filthy boulevards, gangs of barefooted children sift through piles of rotting garbage, looking for anything of potential value – paper clips, rubber bands, even bottle caps. Herds of goats rummage through the same stinking mounds, adding their dung to Saddam City's filth.

This is the Baghdad that officials try hard to keep hidden from foreigners and international media. To arrange an official visit to this neighbourhood, journalists were required to submit formal requests, which could take up to two days to approve, and even then, access was permitted only if a handler, who would pre-arrange 'spontaneous' interviews, was present.

I had originally tried to get official clearance from my Mukhabarat contacts, but despite repeated requests, I could not get an audience with Sami or Mohammad. Eventually I had teamed up with fellow Canadian journalists Linda Slobodian and Gary Bobrovitz and had arranged for Anmar Saadi to drive us there.

Although there was no formal checkpoint or police barrier to mark the beginning of Saddam City, the abject poverty made the boundary immediately apparent. Also apparent was the virtual absence of Iraqi security forces, either police or military. Throughout Baghdad, uniformed personnel were now positioned at every intersection and guards were stationed outside every government office building. But in Saddam City, the only group of soldiers we spotted during a two-hour tour was a ragged-looking section manning a light machine gun mounted on a battered Toyota pickup truck. Although the soldiers seemed uninterested in our presence – they kept sharp watch over a crowded fruit market in the centre of the district – the same could not be said of the local inhabitants.

Every time our taxi stopped, we were swarmed by crowds of mostly young, curious children, yelling, chanting, and trying to get in front of our cameras. Even elderly people pressed in close to stare at us or to join in the chorus of songs. These spontaneous eruptions of emotion had no political overtones. In fact, the most often-repeated chant was from an Iraqi children's verse, which reminded me of "Ring Around the Rosie." No anti-American sentiments were expressed and certainly no cries of "Nam, nam Saddam" – the staple refrain chanted at most of the political rallies organized by the Baath party.

The impoverished inhabitants of Saddam City would undoubtedly prove to be a strategic wild card in a war. Although it is widely recognized that the Shiite majority has little love for Saddam's predominantly Sunni Muslim Baath party, their loyalty to Iraq would be a key factor in the overall equation.

Nzer Hadami, a 38-year-old private in Saddam's Republican Guard, was on leave at his home in Saddam City. His crisp Airborne camouflage uniform and maroon beret stood out in the crowd of urchins that followed him down the street. "My unit is composed of both Sunni Muslims and Shiite," he said. When asked if he would fight for Saddam Hussein, the veteran replied warily, "I will fight for Iraq. And right now, Iraq *is* Saddam Hussein."

Originally called Revolution City, this Baghdad suburb was conceived in 1961 by former Iraqi President Abdul Karim Kassem. Built as a government housing project designed for 500,000, President Kassem had wanted to lure unemployed Shiites from southern Iraq. When he rose to power, Saddam Hussein bestowed his name on the ghetto. Through two decades of war and 12 years of economic sanctions, the population of Saddam City has multiplied sixfold. While the upper middle class of Baghdad has suffered hardship, the working poor Shiites struggle just to survive.

Having received their three months' worth of advance rations, the residents of Saddam City had plenty of basic foodstuffs. However, in case of war, any disruption in food distribution could prove disastrous.

"Unlike other Baghdad residents, these people don't have enough storage space or the resources to stockpile emergency rations," explained Anmar, who acted as our tour guide. "During the last Gulf War, when they were starving, there was much violence. People committed robbery just to feed their families."

Echoing Anmar's fears, many of Baghdad's citizens expressed their concerns over possible domestic unrest. Haider Hindi, the night manager at the Sheraton Hotel and the father of three young daughters, was anxious to obtain exit visas so his family could flee Iraq to safety in the coming weeks.

"It is the possibility of a civil war being unleashed that I fear the most," said Haider. "The Americans have no idea how much hatred exists between the various factions. Under Saddam's control, at least we are all safe."

Civil disobedience and localized violence were expected to pose the biggest threats to the diplomatic corps and Western expatriates living in Iraq. Most of the 60-plus foreign missions operating in Baghdad were still working at a feverish pace, trying to forge a peaceful solution. However, those same embassies were also making contingency evacuation plans.

"Many diplomats took their families home for the Christmas holidays and then returned alone to Baghdad," said Jelko Gajic, a Yugoslav embassy official. For those families remaining, the international school in Baghdad has intensified its curriculum in order to shorten the school year. Although no formal arrangement had been made for a diplomatic convoy to leave Iraq, most embassy officials already had emergency suitcases packed in advance.

"We have not given up all hope of avoiding war," said Gajic. "In fact, the position taken by Germany, France, and Canada has given us all renewed hope for success. However, we also recognize that the window for peace is very small. And we, too, have to prepare to survive as well."

~ ~ ~ ~ ~ ~ ~ ~ ~ ~

NORTHERN IRAQ, FEBRUARY 2-6, 2003   I was still about 20 metres from the border outpost when an Iraqi soldier yelled out the first warning. By the time I reached a spiked metal barricade, two more soldiers were racing from a bunker to take up firing positions. The first soldier was now screaming hysterically at me.

Anmar Saadi, my guide, was several paces behind me on the roadway, trying to shout instructions to me in English. "The briefcase! They are terrified of the briefcase!"

When I placed my briefcase on the ground and started to advance toward them, the Iraqi soldiers stopped shouting and cocked their Kalashnikov assault rifles. The metallic sound of bullets being chambered stopped me cold.

With hands raised in the air, I began to slowly back up, kicking my briefcase behind me along the road rather than risk further alarm. At the barricade, Anmar was shaking in fear, his hands above his head.

"They gave the order to shoot you! Do you realise how close a call you just had?"

After several tense minutes, an Iraqi officer appeared and ordered his soldiers to put down their rifles. "Sahafi Kanadi? (Canadian journalist?)" he asked. When I said yes, he told Anmar they had been expecting us, but we were late and the border had just closed. Faced with the prospect of having to turn around and recross the 400-metre bridge that separated northern Iraq from the south and wait out the night at a Kurdish gatehouse, we pleaded with the officer to make an exception and let us pass.

"You have amused my troops — they have never seen two people so frightened," he said. "Plus my dinner is getting cold, so I will allow you passage."

This border crossing drama marked the climax of an adventurous four-day trip into northern Iraq. Buoyed by our success at entering Saddam City without repercussion and with still no sign of the Mukhabarat, Anmar and I had decided to go for broke and take our chances by simply driving out of Baghdad. Admittedly, many things could have gone wrong since our plan had been hatched after several drinks and only minimal preparation. Given the number of checkpoints on the major highways, not to mention the actual border crossing, we never actually believed that we would get as far as the Kurdish-controlled sector.

We had soon discovered, however, that the bigger the bluff the less likely the Iraqi security forces were to challenge you. As soon as we departed Baghdad shortly after dark, Anmar and I began imbibing from our provisions: Anmar had brought a two-litre bottle filled with a 50/50 mixture of arak and water, whereas my poison of choice was whisky and cola.

As a former commando, Anmar understood the Iraqi soldier's mindset. As we approached a checkpoint, Anmar would roll down his windows and, in a very authoritative voice, tell the guards that this was an official delegation, then quickly ask them a simple question such as, "Is this the road to Mosul?" Believing us to be in some position of authority and relieved to be able to easily answer Anmar's query, we were invariably waved through. Incredibly, this gimmick continued to work even when Anmar was so inebriated he could barely drive the car. Although my Arabic was limited to a few words, even I knew Anmar's speech had become heavily slurred, yet not once were we stopped or even questioned at any of the roadblocks.

When we finally arrived in Kirkuk some six hours later, it was 3:00 a.m. On entering the Palace, the only hotel in Kirkuk open to foreigners, we could see from the special glass shrine erected in his lobby as a tribute to Saddam that the hotel proprietor was an ardent Baath party loyalist. The manager demanded to see our travel authorization. Tired, irritable, and roaring drunk, Anmar flatly refused and in no uncertain terms reminded the "fat little bastard" that he was a hotel clerk, not a policeman.

A hung-over Anmar was much more sheepish when he awoke. Having seated ourselves in the hotel's breakfast room, this same manager wasted no time in approaching our table, accompanied by two Mukhabarat agents. "Now, I think you will provide me with your authorizations," one of them said. Unable to produce any documents, we were escorted to the local intelligence service headquarters, which just happened to be right across the street from our hotel. Our presence this far north without permission posed a conundrum for the Mukhabarat. Techni-

cally, we could not have possibly come this far, so there was no bureaucratic pro-
cedure for them to authorize our return to Baghdad. Not wanting to make a decision, the chief intelligence officer simply instructed us to make our own way back
to the capital. As he had not specified a particular route or time limit, we decided
to continue heading north and take a roundabout route via Mosul.

As we drove along the major highways, no checkpoint guard challenged us,
even though Anmar's battered old Volkswagen Passat hardly looked like the type
of vehicle one would associate with an official delegation. When we were stopped
by soldiers, it was to request a few dinars so they could eat or a lift into the next
town.

As we drove across the countryside I was amazed to see the army's commanders had actually deployed combat forces out in the open. Contrary to claims made
by Baghdad press officials that the Iraqi army would fight in the streets, the bulk
of Saddam's tanks, artillery, and heavy weapons appeared to have been ordered
out of their casernes and onto the barren desert plains. Although there were some
earthwork structures for protection, no camouflage nets had been erected and I
couldn't help but think that thousands of poor conscripts were going to be sitting
ducks for the U.S. air force.

"It makes it more difficult for them to desert," said Anmar. "If they were in the
cities, these soldiers would have already melted away back to their homes."

~ ~ ~ ~ ~ ~ ~ ~ ~ ~

When we arrived in Mosul, we were told by taxi drivers that permission could
probably be obtained locally to cross the Kurdish boundary. However, the office
administering these visas had already closed for the day. With time to kill, Anmar
suggested we set off to find some local "devil worshippers" who lived in a nearby
village.

Without prior notice of our arrival, the inhabitants of Bachiqa were fearful and
reluctant to talk. As we began filming the distinct conical temples and ancient
grave markers of this unique Iraqi society, small crowds gathered to gawk at Anmar
and me. When approached directly, the children fled while the adults protested
they spoke neither Arabic nor English.

Eventually, a Christian villager came and spoke to us. "These are very tense
times, and the Yazidi don't know whether you are CIA or Iraqi intelligence," said
Mariam Wadir. "The only person you can talk to is the temple servant."

When we arrived at the Sher (Great) Mohammad temple, the sunset ceremony
was underway. Emerging from a small, dark crawl space in the centre of a simple

altar, Khalid, the temple servant, began to chant and swing a smoking pannier of incense. Before each of the seven pillars erected within the marble courtyard, Khalid paused briefly to kiss the masonry before resuming his rhythmic singing of prayers. Each pillar represents one of the seven angels worshipped by the Yazidi, and this ritual is performed nightly to ward off the evil spirits of the dark.

Many in Iraq, both Christian and Muslim, believe that members of the reclusive Yazidi sect are "devil worshippers." However, to Khalid, this oft-repeated denigration hits a nerve. "We only worship one God – our single creator," he says. "We recognise that evil exists, but we do not pay homage to it."

It is believed there are about 300,000 Yazidi living in northern Iraq (about one million worldwide), their only indigenous homeland. Although not significant in terms of numbers, their strategic location – astride the Kurdish-Iraqi boundary – means they cannot be ignored. With U.S. Special Forces openly training in the Kurd-controlled northern provinces, the loyalty of Iraq's various minorities was becoming an important consideration.

In the past, the Yazidi had proven to be fiercely loyal to Saddam Hussein. Yazidi recruits had proudly served in the ranks of the Iraqi army during the war with Iran and in the Gulf War. "Our cemeteries are full of brave soldiers who died for their leader," said U'Day Jallal Hassan, a 24-year-old medical student and head of the area's Baath party. "In 1991, when the Kurds staged their uprising, we fought right here in our village," he said. "It is only because of our fierce fighting that this area remains under the control of Saddam."

A few kilometres north of Bachiqa, the Kurdish peshmerga of Massoud Barzani's Kurdistan Democratic Party (KDP) patrolled the territory. "When the Iraqi army fell back in the face of the Kurdish guerrillas, the Yazidi defended their own homes," said Hassan.

Now, with U.S. troops already assembling in the village of Zibar, just 60 kilometres from Bachiqa, Hassan affirmed his people's fearlessness. "We look forward to them trying to occupy this village. The Americans will learn what the Kurds already learned, at the cost of their blood. The Yazidi will not give up their homes."

Although not pushed from their villages, the 1991 Kurdish rebellion resulted in the Yazidi being separated from their most sacred religious site of Lalish by a demilitarized boundary.

"To the Yazidi, this burial ground of Saint Shaykh Adii (who co-operates with Malak Ta'us, the messenger of God), is like Mecca to the Muslims," said Khalid. "We must make two pilgrimages there each year, and it is difficult now to accept that this site is under Kurdish control."

The Yazidi religion originated in this barren region of rolling foothills about 2,000 years before the birth of Christ. Over the centuries, despite numerous occupations by conquering empires, the Yazidi remained a solitary, independent entity. Although their dialect resembles Arabic, it is distinct. In fact, during the Gulf War, when the U.S. jammed communications, the Iraqi army resorted to using Yazidi soldiers as signallers to transmit sensitive messages in their own dialect.

The loyalty of the Yazidi toward Saddam has not gone unrewarded. "We are very proud to include Yazidi as senior commanders in the army – even one general – and we have many top spots in the Baath party," said Hassan proudly. "Under the rule of Saddam, we are free to practise our customs and religion without fear of oppression or discrimination."

In Bachiqa, a town of 30,000, the Yazidi lived in harmony with Chaldean and Protestant Christians, as well as with a small minority of Sunni Muslims. In addition to the Sher Mohammad temple, a church and mosque are also present in the village of Bachiqa.

"We (Christians) have lived as neighbours to the Yazidi all of our lives," said Mariam Wadir. "Unlike those who are ignorant of their culture, we do not fear them as 'devil worshippers.' The only difference between us here in Bachiqa right now is that they are prepared to fight to maintain their freedom, while we only pray for peace."

~ ~ ~ ~ ~ ~ ~ ~ ~ ~

Although we knew we were pushing the limits, we were blessed by a tremendous stroke of luck when we visited the Mukhabarat office in Mosul. As the final step in making our application for a visa into the Kurdish zone, I was interviewed by a senior agent. Unwilling to admit he spoke no English and too embarrassed to ask for Anmar's assistance in translation, he had simply sat across from me pretending to read the various international stamps in my passport. The only thing he could read were the hand-written Arabic notations beside my Iraqi visas. Recognizing the invitations for the referendum from Vice President Ramadan and the conferences sponsored by the Baytol Hikma Institute, he overestimated my authority and was seemingly afraid to deny me access. Much to our surprise, Anmar and I were officially cleared to cross into Kurdish territory.

Although things had gone smoothly on the Iraqi side of the border, it was a different story once we reached the Kurdish side of the bridge. What the checkpoint commander had originally described as just a short delay turned into a four-hour detention. Only when we told the guards that we were out of time and were going to head back to the Iraqi side did we realize that we were not free to go. A Kurdish secret service driver eventually arrived. He summarily dismissed Mazen Ziya, the taxi driver we had hired in Mosul, and ushered us into the backseat of a black Mercedes. My original intention had been to meet with some of the opposition leaders, however, as the car continued past the last of Erbil's city outskirts, we realized our program had been altered.

Atop the rocky plateau known as the Salahudin Massif sits the mountain stronghold of Massoud Barzani, the leader of the Kurdistan Democratic Party (KDP). Although the Kurdistan parliament buildings are located 33 kilometres away in the city of Erbil, Barzani and his KDP peshmerga fighters are the sole power in this region of Iraq. Although media access to this remote region was all but impossible at this time, the KDP had recently constructed a brand new public relations office at their headquarters in Salahudin.

"We are anticipating a flood of Western journalists to arrive here in the coming weeks," explained Maraan Mirkhan, official spokesman for the KDP. "We provide access to Internet, telephones, coffee — anything you like."

As for the role the KDP would play in the event of war, Mirkhan emphasized that no commitment had yet been made. "Our provision of assistance to the United States depends entirely upon the guarantees which we receive," he said. "Massoud Barzani is willing to commit his forces to oust Saddam Hussein, but we have very bitter memories of U.S. betrayal. The Americans sold out the Kurds in the 1975 Algeria agreement and in 1991 they abandoned our uprising as well."

A major strategic consideration in the north for any post-Saddam Iraq is the issue of an independent Kurdistan. At that moment, KDP leader Barzani had complete autonomy in the provinces of Dohuk and Erbil, while rival Kurdish leader Jalal Talabani and his Patriotic Union of Kurdistan (PUK) party controlled the province of Sulaimaniyah.

"We fly our own flag and patrol our own borders at present, but ultimately we are still Iraqi citizens," said Mirkhan. "We fight to someday unify Iraq, but under a form of federation which protects us from discrimination and oppression."

While members of Barzani's KDP are regarded as moderates, those of Talabani's PUK are considered Kurdish nationalists, openly advocating independence.

Syria, Iran, and especially Turkey, a vital U.S. ally in this crisis, were concerned that an independent state for Iraq's 3.5 million Kurds would only increase separatist sentiment in their own sizeable Kurdish minorities. Already, pro-Kurdistan rebels in these neighbouring countries had begun to use the autonomous northern Iraqi provinces as support bases for their operations.

In newly constructed military barracks in the village of Salahudin, large numbers of new peshmerga recruits were undergoing basic training. In traditional baggy pantaloons and checkered headscarves, the Kurdish militiamen also wore an assortment of U.S. combat clothing. Although they possessed few heavy weapons or armoured vehicles, the peshmergas were equipped with new assault rifles and light machine guns.

"Our army is not very powerful in the sense of weaponry, but we have skill and experience as guerrillas," said Mirkhan. "If we do assist the Americans, it will not be only as guides and translators. We will fight to liberate the people of Iraq from Saddam Hussein."

On the road from the border, our driver had proven very talkative for an intelligence officer. Prior to joining the Kurdish secret service, 24-year-old Gilman Haja fought both as a soldier in the Iraqi army and as a peshmerga. "In 1991, during the Kurdish rebellion, I was a conscript in Saddam's forces," said Haja. "When we were sent into the lines opposite the peshmerga, my Kurdish comrades and I took the first opportunity to discard our uniforms and switch sides."

Asked to predict the probability of a U.S.-led intervention into Iraq, Haja appeared surprised: "It is 100 per cent that the Americans will proceed — in March."

Given that both Bush and Blair were insisting a diplomatic solution was still possible, Haja's certainty was surprising. He told us U.S. troops had been conducting training exercises in northern Iraq, in the vicinity of Zibar, and operating a major airbase in Sulaimaniyah. He also said that between Erbil and the Iraqi-controlled border, Kurdish workers were hastily widening the highway, turning it into four lanes, "so the Americans can move quickly into Iraq."

Although officially the KDP maintained that "there are no U.S. soldiers on any Kurdish-controlled land," privately Mirkhan had confirmed their presence. "Every night there is footage of the Americans training in Zibar shown on Turkish television. But I am to sit here and tell you that, officially, this is not true."

Despite the imminence of war, many Kurds expressed no fear of Iraqi reprisals in response to assisting the American buildup. "Saddam's troops are too respectful of American and British air power to risk attacking us," said Mirkhan. "The only thing which we fear is that Saddam would unleash a chemical attack on us in a final doomsday scenario."

In anticipation of a joint American-Kurdish offensive from the north, we had seen for ourselves how Saddam's forces had been deployed out of their casernes and into frontline trenches. We stopped at one of the camouflaged bunkers outside of Mosul for a nature break. Amused by our circumstances, the Iraqi soldiers were anxious to chat with us. The oldest of the three-man gun crew was 38-year-old paratrooper Anmar Ibrahim.

Proud of his maroon beret and 22 years of loyal service to Saddam, Ibrahim explained with a gap-toothed smile that he was still a private because of his love for arak. Patting the barrels of his twin 23-mm guns, Private Ibrahim explained: "These are useless against American warplanes. But if the Kurds attack us on the ground, we will slaughter them with these guns."

From what I could see, the many defences had been established to defend the approaches to Kirkuk. Outside this ancient city lies the Baba Gurgur oil field, the oldest and richest deposit in northern Iraq. This is the strategic crown jewel of the region, and would mean economic independence for whichever faction gained control of it. With no oil reserves inside their present territory, both Barzani and Talabani were eager to wrest control of Kirkuk from Saddam's forces.

Added to the equation were the aspirations of the local Turkmen population. Estimated to be nearly 2 million in number, these descendants of ancient Turkey are the second-largest ethnic minority in Iraq, after the Kurds. Split between the Kurdish-controlled city of Erbil and Saddam-held Kirkuk, the loyalty of the Turkmen would be a major factor in the event of war.

"Under both the Kurds and the Baghdad regime, the Turkmen presently have no civil rights," explained Mazen Ziya. Following the incident when we tried to cross back into Iraqi territory at dusk, Ziya's taxi had fortunately still been waiting for us at the guardhouse. Not wanting to lose his fare back to Mosul, Ziya had hedged his bets that we'd be coming back across the border that day, so he waited for us. Otherwise, Anmar and I would have had an awfully long walk back to Mosul.

Originally from Kirkuk, Ziya had fled to Erbil after the Kurdish rebellion of 1991. "I thought that things would be better (for Turkmen) under the Kurds. But nothing changed." In order to make ends meet, taxi drivers operating in the north worked both sides of the border, securing fares wherever possible.

Ziya was now an active member of the Turkmen Front, a political party with a hard-line nationalist platform. It was in fact Sanan Ahmat Aga, the Turkmen Front leader, that I had originally hoped to interview in Erbil. Independent of Berizani's KDP, the Turkmen Front was working in conjunction with the U.S. to assist in the war effort. This group had supplied a number of individuals for the CIA-sponsored Iraqi opposition military training camp at the NATO airbase in Taszar, Hungary.

"I wanted to volunteer to fight, but I did not have any prior service in the army," Ziya told me. "If we help the Americans by fighting Saddam, the Turkmen will be rewarded with increased autonomy — and some of Kirkuk's oil riches."

~ ~ ~ ~ ~ ~ ~ ~ ~ ~

BAGHDAD, MARCH 5-12, 2003   Having just returned to Iraq, I was fortunate to be on hand to witness what would be Saddam Hussein's last massive rally of his security troops. Immediately following the March 5 parade, the forces assembled – equipped with machine guns, helmets and combat webbing – deployed to take up positions around key installations throughout Baghdad. At likely airstrike targets – such as the bridges over the Tigris and the Ministry of Interior (police) headquarters – Iraqi forces had assembled a collection of fire trucks and other emergency vehicles.

"When I saw the soldiers on the streets, I cried," said Nadia Hassan, a 37-year-old schoolteacher. "For the first time in this crisis, I now believe that there will be a war. And I'm very afraid for Iraq."

Although intended as a show of force to boost civilian morale, Saddam's security demonstration inspired little confidence. The primary combat vehicles in evidence were just civilian pick-up trucks that had been mounted with light machine guns. And the policemen, sweating in their dress uniforms and combat gear, looked decidedly unmartial.

"I feel sorry for those men," said Hassan. "So many will soon become martyrs."

The Iraqi army had issued yet another call-up of reservists. Outside a temporary military depot in central Baghdad, I watched a group of about 50 young reservists as they waited patiently beyond the compound fence. Clad in a variety of uniforms – and many of them without boots – the soldiers passed their identity cards to a clerk and, in exchange, received deployment orders.

Mustafa Khalid, a 27-year-old baker by profession, was one of the lucky ones. "I will be attached to an air defence unit close to Baghdad," he said, "so I will be able to visit my family on a regular basis."

Another reservist, Adeep, was not as pleased with his assignment. "I will be going to the south," he said. In recent weeks, the U.S. and Britain had stepped up their airstrikes in the imposed no-fly zone where, particularly in the south, warplanes had been deliberately targeting what was left of Iraq's air defences. "We are not afraid to die," explained Khalid, "but we only have limited training and we have never experienced war."

When the draft was complete, a battered little Nissan minibus, hauling an open trailer, pulled up to the curb. All those who could fit inside climbed aboard the bus, while the remainder piled onto the overloaded trailer. Only one mother, Fadia, had come to see her teenage son off, her tears and sorrow causing her son to turn his head in embarrassment as the vehicle pulled away.

"His father was killed in the first Gulf War," explained Fadia. "He is all I have left and I fear this war will take him too."

Although it had not yet become a flood of humanity, a significant exodus out of Iraq had already begun. In December 2002, as part of sweeping reforms to Iraq's constitution, President Saddam Hussein abolished the $400 U.S. exit visa tariff that had been in place. Given that the average monthly salary in Iraq is less than $30 U.S., only the privileged few could afford to emigrate or travel abroad.

However, with war imminent, there was a tremendous increase in the demand for passports. Hundreds of people lined up daily in front of Foreign Ministry offices throughout Baghdad to get the necessary documentation. But this overwhelmed official process spawned a lucrative sub-industry of passport brokers.

"You can line up every day for a month and never get near the front of the queue," explained Anmar. "I paid the broker 100,000 dinars (about $50 U.S.) to speed up the process." Although he now worked as a taxi driver, Anmar's family owned a number of properties in Baghdad, so he could afford the large bribe. "I need the passport for my six-month-old son, Adeep," he said. "And then I will try to take my family to safety in Lebanon."

As tens of thousands of Iraqis made preparations to flee their country, hundreds of international peace activists poured into Baghdad. The most numerous of these – and certainly the ones with the highest profile – were the human shields. Organized through Dr. Abdul Al-Hashimi's Organization for Friendship, Peace and Solidarity, the volunteers were to live at various strategic facilities located outside Baghdad that would likely be bombed should war begin. However, when the Iraqi authorities took control of where the volunteers would be stationed, it created a serious schism within the group.

"The Iraqis wanted us to occupy strategic locations like power stations and water treatment plants, the destruction of which will cause suffering for millions," explained Ken O'Keefe, one of the primary spokespersons for the human shields. "Unfortunately, many of our volunteers thought they could place themselves atop schools or hospitals of their choice. When they learned they would have to comply with the Iraqi authorities, many decided to head home."

With his spiked, punk haircut, unkempt beard and facial tattoos, the 33-year-old O'Keefe bore little resemblance to the young Marine who had seen combat in Kuwait 12 years ago during the first Gulf War. Describing himself as "stateless," O'Keefe was prepared to face "whatever consequences occur" in his effort to deter U.S. coalition attacks.

Following their initial deployment, the human shields held a press conference to announce they had informed President Bush, by letter, of their whereabouts.

"Now that they know where we are, if the U.S. attacks us it will not be collateral damage. It will be murder," shouted O'Keefe to the thunderous applause of the peace volunteers.

"We Iraqis appreciate the gesture and all the sympathetic emotion that these [human shields] express," said Shahta al-Azzawi, a 27-year-old reporter for the *Baghdad Observer*, Iraq's daily English-language newspaper. "However, I think that this idealism will fade at the sound of the first air raid siren – and disappear altogether when the first bombs fall."

The human shields were definitely an odd assortment of people, representing a wide variety of cultures, religions, and age groups. There were many young Europeans, including a Balkan peace team from Slovenia, while the oldest member, at 75 years of age, hailed from Britain. Many of the younger ones were dressed in punk chic or '60s retro fashions, complete with tie-dyed jeans. A small group of Buddhist monks were also present, their shaved heads and saffron robes attracting curious stares on the streets of Baghdad. After 12 years of sanctions and embargoes, Iraqis were not used to seeing such strangers in their midst, and the motley collection of human shields created a small spectacle wherever they went.

Observing the press conference in his hotel's lobby, manager Haider Hindi expressed mixed emotions. "When I look at these people, I'm curious to know why it is that [Western] governments would think twice about bombing them?" Haider asked. "There are already 23 million Iraqis here, including my wife and three daughters. Shouldn't *we* be enough reason not to bomb?"

Also in Baghdad trying to prevent a war were a number of religious groups, including the Christian Peacemaker Team (CPT). Among their numbers were two dairy farmers from southern Ontario. Both Allan Slater and Stewart Viresinga were quick to point out they were not human shields. "We're made of flesh and blood; we're not here to shield anything," said Viresinga. "It is our objective to try to stop a potential humanitarian crisis through raising awareness. And if that fails, then we shall bear witness to the tragedy."

At 67, the father of four and grandfather to seven explained his motivation for making the trip to Iraq. "It has always been the case that old men start wars and young men go off to fight them," said Slater. "I felt it was time to change that. Old men should know better and we must do all we can to prevent war."

Although Slater planned to return to Canada by mid-February, Viresinga intended to stay in Baghdad "for the duration of whatever transpires."

Another Canadian expected to remain in Iraq in the event of a war was Kassandra Vartell, the Protection Co-ordinator for the Baghdad office of the International Committee of the Red Cross (ICRC). Deemed to be part of the organization's essential staff, Vartell would be one of only a dozen international employees to remain at the Red Cross offices should war begin.

Originally from Calgary, Vartell had spent the past 12 years working in global hot spots, including the Balkans, Chechnya and South Sudan. Although she was not too concerned about the possible danger, she conceded that "no two situations are ever the same."

Inside the iron gates of the ICRC's compound, preparations for war were already well underway. To help withstand possible bomb-blast damage, a six-foot high wall of sandbags surrounded the entire ground floor of the building, and tape had been adhered to all the windows to limit the destructiveness of flying glass shards. In addition to preparing themselves, the ICRC has also been feverishly working over the past few months to help hospitals in Iraq brace for war.

The ICRC had managed to stockpile nearly one million one-litre bags of potable water at hospitals throughout Iraq. As for medicines and other emergency supplies, the Red Cross was able to distribute only a limited supply. "We estimate that there is sufficient stock to handle up to 7000 casualties, both civilian and military," said Roland Huguenin, a spokesman for the ICRC. "Even in the best-case scenario, we have to hope that a war will be over in a few days. We simply can't cope with a protracted conflict."

The only topic of discussion these days in Baghdad related to when the war would start. "Every shop owner and waiter that knows me asks for advice as to when to leave Baghdad or how to prepare themselves," said Vartell. "They think that we [the ICRC] have some inside information, but we are guessing just like everyone else."

Most people were watching the actions of Baghdad-based UN staff – and in particular the weapons inspectors – for clues about a start date. "As soon as I hear that the UN staff have left, I will take my family to our relatives' home in the north," said hotel manager Haider Hindi.

The Iraqi Ministry of Information was once again tightening control of the foreign media. Even those who had obtained prior official permission to travel were now restricted to the Baghdad area. In addition, Iraq began to cut down on the number of visas issued, and were cracking down on those whose visas had expired. The increased media security had intensified speculation among journalists that a war was only days away. Many reporters who had been in Baghdad reporting on the crisis since last October feared they would be asked to leave before hostilities erupted.

"It would be a shame to spend so much time here, only to miss out on the big show," said one Australian journalist, adding with a wink, "Not that we want a war."

With everyone discussing possible scenarios of how a war would develop, the most common belief, based on Pentagon statements, was that the initial airstrikes were going to be very intense. After the initial bombardment, the question remained of how much of a fight the Iraqi army could muster.

Although the Ministry of Information continued to proclaim defiance, few Iraqis shared this enthusiasm.

"The army consists of conscripts, not volunteers," explained Anmar. "They will return to their houses at the first opportunity," he continued. "It is not that we are afraid to fight the Americans; it is just that we want to protect our families from being violated."

Official stories had been circulating about how U.S. soldiers would ravage the local populace if they succeeded in their invasion. The propaganda was effective. "We have been told how Americans raped young girls in Korea and Kosovo – everywhere that their soldiers are stationed," said Anmar. "I will not sacrifice myself senselessly for Saddam, but I will kill every American who approaches my family."

To defend his wife and young son, Anmar stockpiled a small arsenal in his family home. "My brother is an expert hunter, so we have many shotguns, rifles and three Kalashnikovs," he said. "But we do not have nearly as many weapons as our neighbours."

Average citizens were not the only ones preparing to defend their homes. Outside Saddam's many palaces, the number of guards increased during the day, while at night they completely sealed off all entrances. Spiked metal barricades were placed along the roadways and grim-looking soldiers manned watchtowers along the perimeter walls. It was estimated that Saddam had 17 presidential residences throughout Baghdad and his exact whereabouts remained a closely guarded secret.

At the main palatial compound located on the banks of the Tigris, it appeared as though the presidential bodyguard was preparing for a last stand. Numerous bunkers had been constructed around the palace and along the riverbank. And in recent days, the number of troops evident inside this compound had increased dramatically. The Iraqi air force had also flown in three Russian-built Mi-8 combat helicopters, which were based out of an airstrip on the palace grounds.

"These Mi-8s are not capable of stopping the Americans. They are not so sophisticated and modern," explained Anmar, who, as a commando, had served as a member of the elite presidential bodyguard. "But they will be a deadly deterrent to any Iraqis who try to storm the palace to attempt a coup."

Despite widespread fears, life on the streets of Baghdad continued with an almost surreal sense of normalcy. Iraq hosted an international trade furniture exhibition that was attended by many senior government and military officials. And the televised images of good-news stories on the nightly newscast airing immediately after coverage of events taking place at the UN Security Council seemed almost ludicrous.

On the weekend of March 8 and 9, there was almost non-stop coverage in Iraq of the feverish American and British attempts to win over a majority of the 15-member Security Council. Although everyone was closely following the critical debate surrounding the United States' second resolution sanctioning a war against Iraq, the end result was no longer in doubt.

"I think the only thing that we will discover is whether the UN will be destroyed along with Iraq, and how many days are left before the U.S. starts bombing," said Dr. Amal Slash, a director with the Baytol Hikma Institute.

Despite the clampdown on foreign media, I had taken a walk along the Tigris to visit my old acquaintances at the Institute. Normally, the heavyset Dr. Slash was a diehard optimist buoyed by Baath party propaganda. Today was different and her nerves seemed to be getting the better of her. "If the UN issues a second resolution, then Iraq will have at least until the 17th of March to pray for a miracle. If the motion is vetoed, I'm afraid that Bush will launch his attack within hours."

The Baytol Hikma Institute was located right beside the Defence department's headquarters. This military facility had been completely destroyed by attacks in the 1991 Gulf War and again during the 1998 allied airstrikes. It had been rebuilt, but there was no doubt that it would again be targeted in the event of war. Despite the danger, Dr. Slash and her staff had no intention of relocating their offices. For the first time since I had met her in May 2001, Dr. Slash dared to speak about defeat. "We are still actively planning for an international conference in mid-April and we hope you will attend again," she said. "However, it seems no one can commit themselves in these circumstances... War will come and Iraq cannot defeat the Americans – no one can," she trailed off.

The official Iraqi position remained one of belligerent defiance. Following chief UN weapons inspector Hans Blix's March 7 report, and as the U.S. and Britain demanded approval for war, Iraq demanded an end to the inspections and a complete lifting of all economic sanctions. The president also issued a formal statement decrying the "crazy" U.S. policy

"If the U.S. commits aggression, it will in fact perpetrate a lunacy," Saddam said. "Besides, we will fight them like in 1991, whether they come alone or with international cover."

Walking back past the Defence department complex, I noticed there was little evidence of such bravado. Many of the offices had been evacuated and the remaining staff were frantically moving the last of their equipment to safer premises. As a result, equipment began to accumulate on the street in front of the building; traffic slowed and then clogged on the narrow street adjacent to the headquarters. With dozens of cars jammed into a gridlock, tempers flared and a full-scale fistfight broke out between a group of departing soldiers and local drivers.

A similar exodus occurred at the landmark Al-Rasheed, the hotel that had become home to the majority of the foreign press corps and to the numerous dignitaries who had come to Baghdad. When Mohammed Al-Sahaf announced on March 8 that the Al-Rasheed was on the U.S. target list, everyone hurriedly checked out and sought safer accommodations. Most headed across the Tigris and set up new residences at either the Palestine or the adjacent Sheraton.

Freelancers (and journalists without hefty expense accounts, like me) who were on the lower end of the press-corps ladder were the ones who typically stayed in this part of Baghdad. In better days, the Sheraton and the Palestine had been magnificent hotels, but years of sanctions had taken their toll. Although fairly close to the central core of Baghdad, this hotel district was isolated enough that the Iraqi authorities had used it to house the steady stream of Shiites – about 3,000 a day – who came to Baghdad. Although the Iranian Shiites were permitted access to their holy pilgrimage sites during the day, at night their whereabouts were strictly controlled and they were barred from leaving the hotel grounds.

During most of my visits, the Mukhabarat had booked me in advance into the Sheraton. Mohammad, in particular, seemed to take great delight in having me housed among hundreds of filthy pilgrims. Often, the only other Westerner staying in the hotel was the coach of the Iraqi soccer team, a German national.

With the pilgrimages halted by the threat of war, the empty rooms were now filled by those who had abandoned the Al-Rasheed. For security reasons, the Sheraton did not have an outgoing international phone or fax service, so I was in the habit of filing my stories from the Al-Rasheed's business centre. It was strange to see the normally bustling lobby now virtually deserted.

Rahim, the 27-year-old concierge, told me he would continue to come to work, even during the airstrikes. "I don't know why Bush would want to target us? We even have a picture of his father on our floor," joked Rahim.

In 1991, following the Gulf War, the Al-Rasheed had a marble mosaic portrait of George Bush Senior installed on the floor so that all guests would walk over his likeness upon entering the hotel's front doors. However, in recent months and as the crisis intensified, the Al-Rasheed's staff had covered the tile portrait with a red carpet. When numerous journalists insisted on lifting the rug to film the landmark mosaic, the hotel management prudently glued the covering in place.

Now that airstrikes seemed imminent, many of the human shields had had second thoughts and had begun leaving Iraq. As for Ken O'Keefe, the 33-year-old ex-Marine organizer of the human-shield initiative, he had been asked by Dr. Al-Hashimi to leave Baghdad in mid-March. O'Keefe and several of his followers had fallen victim to political infighting. In an effort to appease the majority of the shields remaining, it was decided that O'Keefe should leave the country. When O'Keefe refused to co-operate with the deportation order, he was arrested and escorted to the border.

Al-Hashimi, who had been responsible for bringing the human shields to Iraq, insisted on the deportation despite the consequences O'Keefe might face as a result. "It will prove difficult for him to get back into America, I think," said Al-Hashimi. "He burned his passport when he entered Iraq from Syria. Now I think he may regret having been so extreme."

Each morning, outside many of central Baghdad's hotels, similar scenes of foreigners packing their belongings into orange and white Suburbans to make the long trek across the desert to the Jordanian border were taking place. With only four flights a week, reservations for Amman were fetching a hefty bribe. With only a tiny number of journalists, dignitaries, and human shields still entering the country, the majority of the human tide was fleeing Iraq to safety.

Although I had fully intended to stay in Iraq for the duration of any hostilities, I would soon find myself part of the exodus.

~ ~ ~ ~ ~ ~ ~ ~ ~ ~

I had sensed that something was amiss on my second morning back in Baghdad. Haider Hindi, the desk manager at my hotel, was not his usual jovial self. When he gave me back my passport, he whispered dramatically, "Be careful, Mister Scott. Big eyes are watching you."

As the Mukhabarat were always watching me, I was perplexed and somewhat alarmed. When I pressed for an explanation, all he would say was, "I've said too much already." Later that day, when I visited the Al-Rasheed Hotel, the staff were similarly standoffish. After an absence of two or three weeks, these people had normally greeted me like a long-lost cousin. But this time I was shunned.

The following day, a note had been left for me at the hotel. It read: "I will see you tomorrow at 9 a.m. Wait for me," and was signed "Sami."

The fact that Sami had stopped by my hotel on the holiday of the Islamic New Year was surprising, but even more startling was that he and Mohammad were actually at my hotel room five minutes before nine the next morning. Anyone who has worked in Iraq knows punctuality is not a local custom. And with the Iraqi secret service, you could normally expect to wait for hours – if they decided to show up at all.

This time, there was no cordiality or smiles, and they did not waste any time on pleasantries.

"How did you obtain your visa?" Sami demanded.

Admittedly, this time the visa process had been difficult. With the crisis intensifying, I had assumed the Iraqi bureaucracy was simply unable to cope with the overwhelming number of visa demands from foreign journalists. Since the process appeared to be stalled, and because I had already made an airline reservation in anticipation of a routine acceptance, I had called my old friend Al-Hashimi in the hope that he could accelerate the issuing process. He, in turn, had called the Iraqi embassy in Ottawa and had issued a formal invitation for me to visit Baghdad, thus clearing the way for my visa.

When I explained all of this to Sami and Mohammad, they checked the visa notation in my passport. "We were the ones denying your visa," said Sami. "You were not to return to Iraq."

Incredulous, I asked why. The agents exchanged glances. There was a pause, then Sami said, "Because you are an agent for Mossad. If you were not an invited guest, you would be in jail."

"Or worse," added Mohammad, drawing a finger across his throat. He had never liked me very much, but today he looked especially sinister, deigning to once again address me in English.

At any other time, it would be one hell of a damning allegation for anyone to be accused of working for the Israeli intelligence agency inside Iraq. But at this particular pre-war moment of panic and paranoia, it could have been a potential death sentence. As the gravity of the accusation sank in, I realized that, this time, Sami and Mohammad were not playing games. In the past few months, I had tested their patience by disappearing into the north of Iraq, and there had been the Basra referendum episode, which had led to my first formal expulsion. However, this time I knew it was different. I could sense the tension.

"You are to pack up your things and leave as quickly and quietly as possible," Sami told me. "Until you depart, we will watch your every move and listen to all of your calls. Consider yourself lucky."

The only information the Iraqi agents would give me on the source of the

Mossad allegations was that it had been forwarded to them "by another journalist." Although I know that, in the media game, there's a perception that "all is fair," I couldn't believe a colleague would recklessly endanger someone's life – my life – in this fashion.

Because my intention had been to remain in Iraq for the duration of whatever might transpire, I was in no rush to leave Baghdad at this critical time. So I decided to take a rather liberal interpretation of Sami's directive, and put the emphasis on the "quiet" rather than the "quickly" part of his demand and book myself on a flight out five days later.

I knew it was risky to push the Mukhabarat in this way, but I wanted to experience as much as I could and gather as much information as possible. One other reason I wanted to stay in Baghdad as long as possible was that, prior to leaving Ottawa, I had made arrangements to assist Sacha Trudeau upon his arrival in Iraq. The 28-year-old documentary filmmaker had done a brief stint in the Canadian Forces and had travelled to a number of global hotspots – including Yugoslavia where we first met – but he had never been to Iraq. When he contacted me, I offered to help with his visa and get him settled in.

Since I would probably not be meeting up with Sacha at the airport – I was scheduled to depart on the return portion of his flight – I arranged to pass on this responsibility to Anmar and Mitch Potter, a reporter for the *Toronto Star*. I had met Potter on several occasions in Baghdad and I felt he was one of the few reporters I could trust with the news of my expulsion and the arrival of Sacha, who did not want a lot of publicity about his presence in Iraq. He told me he wanted to make it clear that he was "not a human shield" and that he was definitely "not making a political statement, just bearing witness to a potential tragedy."

~ ~ ~ ~ ~ ~ ~ ~ ~ ~

Diyarbakir, March 12-14, 2003   Upon landing in Amman, Jordan, I began making arrangements to fly to Turkey in the hopes of getting into northern Iraq. Officially the border had been closed, but some of my Turkish colleagues suggested this might not be the case for long. When I arrived at the Anatolian city of Diyarbakir, located just 150 kilometres from the Iraqi border, the pre-war build-up was in full gear, and the region had been transformed into an armed camp. Busloads of Turkish soldiers were pouring in to this army staging area, while police and paramilitary *jendarma* units patrolled the streets in armoured personnel carriers.

The Diyarbakir airport was now home to several squadrons of F-16 fighter jets, and the sound of combat aircraft flying overhead was almost continuous. Twin Huey helicopters, ferrying troops in and out of military casernes, were also a regular sight in the airspace above this ancient walled city.

At the airport, two batteries of Patriot missile defence systems were manned by Dutch soldiers, there as part of NATO's contribution to the defence of Turkey in the event of a war with Iraq. Although the locals welcomed the foreign currency that the Dutch soldiers were spending at hotels and restaurants, no one really viewed them as protectors.

"We do not need to be protected from Iraq," said Salen Ostunc, a 24-year-old hostess at an upscale café in central Diyarbakir. "The Turkish army could capture Baghdad and defeat Saddam Hussein by itself," she said. "The only thing we are afraid of is a resurgence of the Kurdish nationalist movement here should the war destabilize the entire region."

In the early 1990s, Kurdish separatists waged a long and bloody struggle in this remote corner of Turkey. Following a series of military reversals at the hands of Turkish security forces and a number of political reforms, the Kurdish uprising was eventually all but quelled. The hard-line guerrilla group known as the PKK (the Kurdish acronym for the "Kurdistan Workers' Party," which has been linked to terrorist activities), were forced into northern Iraq, while the moderates continued to seek additional reforms through the diplomatic process.

With the Turkish army poised to enter northern Iraq in support of a U.S. intervention – but against the wishes of the Iraqi Kurdish leaders – tensions between the Kurds and Turks had increased dramatically in the past few weeks.

Massoud Barzani, leader of the Iraqi Kurdistan Democratic Party (KDP), had moved a number of his peshmerga militias to the border to block a possible Turkish military incursion. Although his lightly armed peshmergas could offer little more than token resistance against the heavily armed Turks, the rebel leaders of the PKK have also threatened a renewed terror campaign in eastern Turkey should the Turkish army attempt to occupy northern Iraq.

The constant threat of civil disobedience and protests against the war were also present. Over 90 per cent of the Turkish population was opposed to a U.S.-led war in Iraq, and in early March thousands of citizens took to the streets to rejoice when their parliament rejected a bill that would have permitted American forces to deploy into Turkey.

However, I soon learned that, despite a public proclamation that denied the U.S. military access to Turkey, American forces were in fact disembarking at the Mediterranean port of Iskenderun. When the locals discovered this duplicity, there were protests at the Turkish port's facilities. One such protest had become violent, and several shots were fired by security forces to disperse the crowd.

On my drive to the border town of Silopi, I witnessed one such violent confrontation. Assembled in the parking lot of a roadside truck stop, the protest had begun peacefully. In total, about 1000 demonstrators, mostly young Turkish-Kurd males, chanted anti-U.S. slogans and denounced a possible war with Iraq.

Several meters away, about 200 local Turkish military police – clad in complete riot gear and backed up by two armoured personnel carriers – had turned out in force to observe the proceedings. When word spread that a U.S. military convoy was en route and fast approaching, the protesters attempted to move onto the highway to block its passage.

Without hesitation, the jendarma assembled their ranks into a 'V' formation and advanced on the crowd. Wielding their truncheons furiously, the riot police quickly dispersed the crowd and arrested several of the bloodied participants.

A small convoy of U.S. military vehicles rolled past only minutes later, presumably without being aware that a protest had even been staged at this intersection. There was no other media present at this particular demonstration, and it was only by chance that Erdinc, my driver, and I had stopped there for lunch.

Following our meal, and as we were attempting to leave the now virtually empty parking lot, one policeman shouted out an inquiry as to my identity. Erdinc explained to the young jendarma lieutenant that I was a tourist, and not a journalist, because the Turkish government was desperately trying to keep the media from reporting on the U.S. military buildup which was proceeding covertly, despite Turkey's parliamentary proclamation on March 2 which denied America access.

After scanning my passport – which is full of entry visas for Iraq and numerous Balkan countries – the lieutenant proclaimed, "I don't believe you are a tourist, but today I will take you at your word. However, I caution you not to take away the wrong impression of what you witnessed here today."

The lieutenant went on to say that he and his men were serving out their mandatory conscription service. "Beneath these uniforms we are still Turks. And like our countrymen, we too are opposed to this U.S. war with Iraq," he said. "How do you think we feel, having to do America's dirty work here in our own country?"

Despite attempts to suppress the coverage, video images of U.S. convoys rolling through southeastern Turkey were still aired on every newscast.

"The government tries to explain that these troop movements are part of a routine base expansion program that was approved last September," said Tashkin Tivelek, a 37-year-old correspondent for *Sabah*, Turkey's largest national newspaper. "Except no one can explain why there is no construction equipment."

While most of the convoys filmed have been of Hummers, Jeeps, personnel carriers and communication vehicles being carried aboard flatbed trucks, one column contained about a dozen armoured ambulances.

"I can't believe that the Americans really expect to encounter so many casualties on a construction site," joked Tivelek.

Already present at hotels in Diyarbakir were dozens of U.S. personnel. Wearing civilian clothes but unmistakable with their crewcuts and Harvard sweatshirts, the American GIs were paving the way for thousands of their countrymen who were expected to arrive in the next few days.

As there was only one American fast-food restaurant in Diyarbakir, I had only to set up shop in the Burger King and wait for the U.S. troops to appear.

Doug, a burly Special Forces sergeant, explained to me that his unit had been reassigned to Turkey from Camp Bondsteel in Kosovo.

"We only just received word that we'd be coming here about 48 hours before we left Kosovo," explained Doug in his mid-western American accent.

"I had just shaved my head and then they tell us to go to Turkey and try to 'blend in with the locals' until we get the deployment officially approved. I stand out like a sore thumb," he said.

A female corporal with the U.S. advance team looked equally out of place in this corner of the Muslim world, where burqhas are not uncommon and headscarves for women are the norm. Her tight blue jeans and *Victoria's Secret* baseball cap were somewhat conspicuous, to say the least.

When asked how he and his comrades felt about deploying into Turkey under such duplicitous circumstances – that is, without official approval and against the wishes of the local population – Doug replied, "Like our dollar bill says, 'In God We Trust.' All the rest we have to second guess. As soldiers in the American army, we don't worry about public opinion, and we don't care what they say about us on CNN," he said.

Taking off his sunglasses for dramatic effect, Doug looked me in the eyes and said, "When George Bush, our Commander in Chief, tells us to start the music, we are going to rock and roll."

OPPOSITE PAGE, TOP LEFT: *Peshmerga fighters of Massoud Barzani's Kurdish Democratic Party rejoice at the news of Saddam's toppling. Although independent of the Baath party regime, the KDP was also in conflict with Jalal Talabani's rival Patriotic Union of Kurdistan.* (AP) / **TOP RIGHT:** *Although UN chief weapons inspector Hans Blix requested more time to complete his work, he did not use the opportunity to attack the U.S. propaganda machine. In the end, Blix reported that Iraq was not fully co-operating.* (UN PHOTO BY ESKINDER DEBEBE) / **BOTTOM:** *When he presented his January 20, 2003 State of the Union address, George Bush left no doubt as to his intentions: The countdown to war had begun.* (AP)

Zwei britische Soldaten vor einem Schützengraben im Südirak, in dem zwei irakische Soldaten trotz weißer Flagge den Tod fanden

ABOVE: *This photo, published in the early days of fighting, served to fuel the anti-war cause. It is obvious that the Iraqis were killed while attempting to surrender.* (AKRAM SALEH/ REUTERS)

OPPOSITE PAGE: *Intended to rattle the Iraqi regime, the U.S. launched its "shock and awe" bombing campaign in the first days of war. The attacks primarily targeted government complexes, which had been abandoned weeks before in anticipation of war.* (RAMZI HAIDER)

CHAPTER EIGHT:
War Reports

When the U.S. Commander of Chief gave the final order launching the long-planned invasion of Iraq on March 20, 2003, I had just left Turkey to go on a promotional book tour in Europe that had been arranged months earlier. I was dining with Laci Zoldi and his wife in Budapest when we learned that the bombing of Iraq had started. Our supper was cut short as Laci had to return to his office at the *Magyar Nemzet* (*Hungarian Nation*) to rewrite the next day's headlines. Already the wires were alive with rumours, the most bizarre being that Saddam had surrendered himself to Kurdish warlord Massoud Barzani in Erbil. While the initial coverage was often contradictory, there was no doubt the war had begun.

As American and British armoured columns poured into southern Iraq, easily overcoming Iraqi defences, anti-war movements all around the globe intensified their efforts. Peace protesters soon flooded European streets in the tens of thousands.

On March 21, at a major rally in Yemen, police had opened fire on peace protestors, killing three and wounding scores of others; Egyptians burned U.S. flags in Cairo; over 25,000 Aussies took to the streets of Melbourne; while Indonesian protestors set effigies of President George Bush ablaze.

In the European press, the anti-war backlash was receiving almost as much play as coverage of the developing war in Iraq. This was in stark contrast to the coverage on CNN and BBC, which focused on up-to-the-minute reports of allied troop deployments, and made only rare mention of the large-scale protests taking place world-wide.

While it was apparent the U.S. military was attempting to win the war as quickly as possible, its initial rapid success seriously undermined George Bush's premise that Saddam Hussein posed a "clear and present danger" to global security. Televised images of dazed-looking Iraqi soldiers surrendering en masse with even senior officers wearing rag-tag uniforms and sneakers, hardly supported the notion of Iraq as a dangerous, heavily armed enemy.

As one commentator quipped, "It looks like the world's mightiest superpower has gone to war against the Flintstones."

Senior U.S. officials repeatedly stated that the target was Saddam Hussein's regime not the Iraqi people. The initial missile strikes into Baghdad, which were aimed at "decapitating the Iraqi leadership," certainly supported this claim. However, once the U.S. began the "shock and awe" phase of its war plan – an overwhelming bombardment of government facilities throughout Iraq – one had to question the American judgement.

Everyone in Baghdad knew months beforehand which buildings would be likely targets. Most of the key installations had, therefore, long since been relocated to residential areas or commercial districts.

U.S. Secretary of Defense Donald Rumsfeld stated that the destruction of those government buildings would be viewed by the Iraqi people as a "symbol of Saddam's regime crumbling." However, the massive explosions and rolling thunder barrages aimed at what everyone knew to be empty real estate, did little to reassure the average Iraqi that George Bush was coming to "liberate" them.

Although the U.S. was using precision-guided munitions against selected targets, when launching so much explosive ordnance into a city populated by 8 million people, inevitably, innocent lives would be lost. The human collateral damage created through the elimination of 'symbols' could not, therefore, be justified as either a strategic or tactical necessity.

Over the previous three years Baghdad had become something of a second home for me. I had made many friends, most of whom had little love for Saddam. However, when I watched the television newscasts showing attacks against familiar landmarks, it left me with a sick, empty feeling. I could only guess at how the Iraqis felt.

One hint of their continued defiance came in an e-mail sent to my office from the Baytol Hikma Institute. As a result of the Mossad allegation, my invitation to the April 2003 conference was being rescinded. I marvelled that, in the middle of

Rumsfeld's "shock and awe" bombing the Iraqis still had time for such pettiness.

Just four days into the war, a photo was published by the international media which I felt could prove to be one of the defining images of the coalition of the willing's foray into Iraq. Looking dumbfounded, two heavily armed British soldiers were shown peering down into an Iraqi slit trench. In the bottom of the shallow bunker lay the crumpled corpses of two pathetic-looking Iraqi conscripts. What I found so disturbing about the photo was the clearly evident white flag of surrender.

Many of the European newspapers displayed the image on their front pages, while the Turkish editions made a point of enlarging a portion of the photo to clearly illustrate the dirty white rag tied to a stick. While there could be no telling exactly what had happened, the image would, I was certain, further fuel anti-war protestors.

While it was possible that the two Iraqi soldiers had been gunned down by their own comrades, who might have viewed their surrender attempt as disloyal, the impression one was left with is that the British soldiers refused to take these men prisoner.

When I flew back into Turkey on March 23, I learned the photo had sparked the already incensed Turks into further violent anti-American and anti-British demonstrations. Few Europeans actually bought into the U.S. State Department's claim that this military intervention was to "liberate Iraq," and the image had further strengthened the anti-war groups.

For the beleaguered Iraqi president, however, the photo must have seemed like a Godsend. Although the white flag of surrender belied the official line that 8 million Iraqi soldiers would be prepared to fight to the death, Saddam used this image to illustrate how the allied coalition was not taking prisoners. If young Iraqi soldiers truly believed they would be killed regardless, then they might instead choose to fight with suicidal ferocity.

The ability of photographers to capture such a sight, just moments after actual event, was facilitated by the new U.S. and British policies of embedding journalists within front-line units. Unlike Gulf War One, where media access was strictly controlled, this time around the allies actually encouraged journalists to record events as they unfolded – although the information disseminated to the public would still be strictly controlled by the military.

Obviously, the decision to embed journalists stemmed, in part, from the fact U.S. planners really did not expect much of a fight from the Iraqi forces. If soldiers were entering into heavy combat, the last thing they would want would be some idiot with a video camera getting in the way. So far, the planners' assessment had proven correct. With few exceptions, the Iraqi army had put up little resistance. Already, thousands of Iraqi soldiers had surrendered and hundreds more were being killed in a very one-sided combat. Nevertheless, it now appears that one controversial photo may have done more to damage to the U.S.-led war effort in those first few days than the entire Iraqi army.

On the fourth day of fighting, the U.S. acknowledged that only a dozen of their personnel had been killed as a direct result of enemy action. (Another twelve allied soldiers were killed when their helicopter crashed, but the Pentagon maintains this was the result of an accident, and not hostile fire.)

The news on the morning of March 23 was a startling shock and presented a severe setback for the allied forces. A support company was ambushed near Nasiriya. It was estimated that 11 U.S. soldiers had been killed, 50 wounded and 7 others – including Private Jessica Lynch – had been captured.

When I heard the news, I recalled a January breakfast discussion at the Al-Rasheed, where a number of journalists had been discussing the possible start date of a U.S. intervention in Iraq. The words of one American reporter now seemed, in hindsight, to have been prophetic.

"Whatever they do, the last thing the Iraqis want to achieve is any initial success against the U.S. forces," he said. "Because the only thing more dangerous than the U.S. military is the U.S. military when it's scared."

To illustrate his point, the American journalist had cited the example of the loss of American helicopters in Somalia, immortalised by the 2002 Hollywood blockbuster *Black Hawk Down*.

"Although everyone focused on the American losses (18 killed and dozens more badly wounded), what is overlooked is that the U.S. shot the hell out of the Somalis in the battle," explained the journalist. "Only when the final credits [of the movie] roll past do they note that some 500 Somalis were killed and 1,000 more were injured in that firefight."

With Iraqi resistance stiffening and U.S. forces suffering an increase in fatalities, it seemed as though the frontline forces were no longer so confident that this operation would be a cakewalk. Compounding the situation was the old axiom that ignorance breeds fear. And from initial media reports, it was evident that both the allied soldiers and the embedded journalists who accompanied them had virtually no understanding of the circumstances they now found themselves in.

Following the March 23 setback in Nasiriya –dubbed "Ambush Alley" by the U.S. forces – the Marines had become understandably jumpy. Judging by published quotes, however, it would appear U.S. personnel had never been properly briefed about Iraq. On Monday, a number of Iraqi men, dressed in civilian clothes, were detained by a U.S. Marine security detail in Nasiriya after a search revealed they were carrying a large amount of Iraqi dinar notes. Lieutenant Matt Neely, the U.S. Marine officer responsible for overseeing security in this city, was quoted as saying, "These individuals were suspicious because who carries a wad of cash in their pocket but has no shoes on?"

Obviously, this must have been Neely's first contact with the local population as he clearly had no idea about the Iraqi economy. With the Iraqi dinar devalued by some 7000% since 1990, everyone in Iraq carried "a wad of cash." (For example, $20 Canadian would amount to a stack of dinars about 10 centimetres thick.) As for the lack of footwear, shoes were in such short supply and relatively expensive that even Iraqi soldiers often went without boots. Yet anyone who had done a modicum of research would have known this since many journalists commented upon this to exemplify the sorry state of Saddam's forces.

A Kuwait City-based reporter for the BBC showed an equal lack of understanding. He repeated a Pentagon statement that the U.S. Third Division had captured what it believed to be a site containing weapons of mass destruction. While the news anchor noted that no proof had been offered as yet, the field reporter added his own speculation.

"What made this site particularly suspicious is that it was hidden behind a sand berm – or wall of sand – so as to make it invisible from the air," he had said.

If the presence of a sand berm was grounds for suspicion, then all of Iraq was littered with potential sites of weapons of mass destruction. Anyone who has driven outside of Baghdad, regardless of the direction taken, would recognise the ignorance of this BBC correspondent's statement. The Iraqi military – and even most civilian firms – used sand berms to surround all of its facilities. While offering only the most primitive protection from munitions, sand berms do provide protection from the wind and are simply an inexpensive means of marking out territory.

Likewise, the allied forces' discovery that Iraqi soldiers had been issued with gas masks was also misreported. Many reporters speculated that the equipping of Iraqi soldiers with such protective measures could only mean that Saddam Hussein intended to use his chemical arsenal. "After all," they concluded, "the Iraqis know that the U.S. and British troops would *never* use such illegal weapons."

The fact is, the Iraqi army, like virtually every other military in the world, had always issued gas masks to its soldiers. In fact, many Iraqi civilians had stocked up on military surplus gas masks as well. This was not to protect their families from Saddam's chemical weapons, but because they were under the mistaken belief that the gas masks would offer them a measure of protection against radioactive fallout in the event of a U.S. nuclear strike.

Fear mongering continued to be incited at the highest levels. When images of U.S. prisoners from Nasiriya were first broadcast on Iraqi television, U.S. President George Bush and British Prime Minister Tony Blair immediately denounced the spectacle as a "war crime, contravening the Geneva convention." While the fact that U.S. personnel had been captured was certainly embarrassing to the allies, it was a hell of a stretch to call it a war crime. (After all, weren't Western media outlets televising images of captured Iraqis?)

George Bush's warning to Iraqi officials "not to harm" the prisoners seemed unnecessary given the footage that was broadcast. The U.S. service members appeared to be unharmed by their captors as they sat sipping water in front of the cameras. What was disturbing was that they all looked terrified, and that wasn't a good omen.

In addition to the mounting casualties, Bush briefed Congress on March 24 on the estimated costs ($75-$90 billion U.S.) of the war against Iraq. The same day Bush tabled his estimates, Iraqi television proudly displayed the shattered wreckage of a U.S. Apache attack helicopter.

During the heavy combat around the city of Nasiriya, an Iraqi farmer, using only his personal Kalashnikov assault rifle, had supposedly brought down this high-tech aircraft. According to the Iraqi media, the farmer fired his entire 30-round magazine at the Apache, and the bullets had done enough damage to the rotor tips to force a crash landing.

At $22 million U.S. apiece, the sophisticated armoured Apache helicopters are the most expensive combat aircraft in the world. Given the street value of Kalashnikov bullets in Iraq (about 10 cents each), it cost the farmer just three dollars to topple the high-priced attack helicopter.

Similarly, if one did the math on the war's opening salvo – the allied coalition's attempt to "decapitate the Iraqi leadership" – there was very little bang for their tremendous bucks. The firing of an estimated 39 precision-guided Tomahawk cruise missiles – with a unit price tag in the vicinity of $3 million U.S. each – means the Pentagon budgeted close to $100 million on its assassination attempt.

Spokespersons immediately claimed the target choice had been based on "solid intelligence" and the chance to remove Saddam Hussein "was too good an opportunity to pass up." In the days following this strike, however, the International Committee of the Red Cross (ICRC) confirmed only one Iraqi had been killed as a result of this massive air strike.

Despite rumours to the contrary, Saddam Hussein, his two sons and all of Iraq's top ministers were still very much alive. While the question remained as to just who the U.S. had killed in their attack, you can bet that whoever the dead man was, he never thought he would be worth $100 million to the Pentagon.

The enormous amount of money President Bush had initially earmarked for the war was predicated on a number of variables which seemed to be eroding daily. The premise that this would be a quick war, with U.S. troops welcomed as liberators by the Iraqi people had been disproved almost from the beginning.

Similarly, the notion that post-Saddam Iraq would be quickly restored to normalcy, thereby enabling the U.S. to withdraw its troops inside of six months, was a pipe dream. Before the fighting had even ceased, squabbling factions of the so-called Iraqi opposition were battling for post-war supremacy. Added to this was the potential for the U.S.-Iraq conflict to blow up into a much wider regional conflict, particularly if Turkey pursued its aim of occupying the Kurd-controlled territory of northern Iraq.

Other 'hidden' costs not tabled by Bush included expenses incurred by the rest of the world as a result of this widely unpopular war. International markets plummeted with news of each allied setback; major industries such as airlines suffered tremendous losses; and increased security measures were costing all counties – not just the coalition of the willing – a small fortune.

While Bush's announced U.S. war budget allowed for $4 billion in additional funds for homeland security, most other countries had to absorb their own sizeable costs. Not only was there an increased threat of global terrorism, but there was also the problem of dealing with large-scale and often violent civil disobedience aimed at protesting the war.

In Berlin, the German police had to convert the British, American and Israeli embassies into virtual fortresses in the face of violent antiwar protests. Sandbags, barbed wire and squads of riot police had to put in place to hold back the crowds, which regularly numbered in the tens of thousands.

~ ~ ~ ~ ~ ~ ~ ~ ~ ~

SILOPI, MARCH 24-31, 2003   The Turkish Army had completely sealed off the border with Kurd-controlled northern Iraq and journalists were not permitted within six kilometres of the frontier.

With the U.S. Army's airborne forces being parachuted into the Kurdish region and the peshmerga militia of the Patriotic Union of Kurdistan (PUK) pushing forward toward the Kirkuk oilfields, tensions along the border had increased dramatically. One of the key conditions for Turkey's remaining outside of northern Iraq was the U.S. promise that the Kurds would not take possession of Iraq's strategic oilfields.

In an unexpected development on March 27, Saddam's troops in the north withdrew from their forward positions back to the outskirts of Kirkuk. Realizing the Iraqis had abandoned their posts, PUK leader Jalal Talabani ordered his troops forward. Without firing a shot, his peshmerga militiamen occupied the town of Chemchemal and moved 20 kilometres closer to the oil-rich regional prize of Baba Gurgur. If either Talabani's PUK or rival Kurdish warlord Massoud Barzani's Kurdistan Democratic Party seize this valuable resource, the Turks fear that an independent Kurdistan could become a post-war reality.

To prevent this from occurring and thereby inciting the separatist movement among Turkey's large Kurdish minority, the Ankara administration maintained that it would resort to military force. The U.S. administration repeatedly warned Turkey against any "unilateral entry" into northern Iraq. In fact, Turkish authorities view the hasty deployment of the American 173rd Airborne Brigade into this region to be as much a deterrent to Ankara as it is a threat to Saddam Hussein's northern front.

Officially, the Turkish government downplayed these developments in the local media. The advance of Talabani's peshmerga was officially reported as "insignificant," but on condition of anonymity a federal spokesperson confirmed the PUK's capture of Chemchemal as "serious" and "potentially destabilizing to the entire frontier."

The media also made only casual mention of the fact that four U.S. cruise missiles had gone astray and landed on Turkish soil in the vicinity of Sanli Urfa. This southeastern city, also known in Turkey as the City of Prophets, is on the flight path of Baghdad-headed Tomahawk cruise missiles.

"So far there have been no casualties, thank God," said Heksul, a Turkish television correspondent based in Sanli Urfa. "But I'm afraid that if there is a tragedy, the Pentagon will simply say that they are not to blame because they are 'not targeting Turkey' – the same way they dismiss errant missiles which kill Iraqis."

Ironically, NATO had pre-deployed a large number of military resources into eastern Turkey to protect the local civilians from attacks by Iraqi missiles. Several fire units (batteries) of Dutch Patriot anti-missile systems were positioned around the regional capital of Diyarbakir. In addition to this air defence, the Norwegian government had also supplied a large number of gas masks and chemical suits along with several teams of military instructors. Registered foreign journalists were taken by bus to observe the Norwegians providing local Kurdish and Turkish citizens with a crash course in nuclear, biological and chemical warfare.

"We know that there is absolutely no direct threat to this vicinity," admitted Lieutenant Colonel Hans Breeman, the NATO spokesperson based in Diyarbakir. "That is why it is not very serious that we do not have nearly enough protective gear to outfit even a small fraction of the population."

Given that Diyarbakir was outside of the maximum range of any missiles held by Saddam Hussein – and that there is no direct threat of chemical attack – Breeman tried to justify NATO's efforts. "You have to remember that this is a media war, and we are just one part of a much bigger show," he said.

~ ~ ~ ~ ~ ~ ~ ~ ~ ~

Although we had already tried to take the main road to the Iraqi border and been turned back by the Turkish military police, we decided to see if a less-travelled side road might still be accessible.

My old friend Sasha Uzunov, an Australian soldier-turned-photojournalist, had left Macedonia and linked up with me in Silopi. We decided to rent a couple of bicycles from a local Kurdish teenager and see if we could cross into Iraq. Without any camera gear or any distinguishing 'journo-jackets,' the roving Turkish jendarma paid us no heed. Even at the final checkpoint before the border, the Turkish conscript merely waved and returned our greeting of "Salam-ali."

We rode a further eight kilometres to the junction of the Syrian-Turkish border and then headed northwards toward the mountain ridge that marks the Iraqi boundary. Daylight had begun to fade and we were now covering muddy, ploughed fields on foot, carrying our bicycles on our backs. We eventually reached the fence that marked the border, but with complete darkness now almost upon us, the sight of the red triangular signs marking a minefield were enough of a deterrent to send us heading back towards Silopi.

We retraced our steps, but when we passed the final border checkpoint, the one where we had at first been waved through, we were "apprehended" by a jendarma's challenge. As we tried to continue pedalling past the guardhouse, whistles were blown and searchlights were switched on. Exhausted after nearly five hours of constant exertion, we were more relieved at being halted than anxious. After being escorted to the commander's quarters and offered tea, the young Turkish officer, who could not speak English, conducted a translated interrogation with us by telephoning his girlfriend in Silopi.

We told him that we had rented bicycles to go sightseeing, but when one of the bikes broke down (which was true), we were stranded in the dark. Seeing two exhausted, muddy and sweat-soaked characters in front of him, he obviously didn't believe our story.

He was very concerned by the fact that we had been allowed such easy access to the forbidden area. To stress his point, the Turkish officer drew a small map and indicated the area beyond his checkpoint with a skull and crossbones. He was obviously worried that his detachment would be in serious trouble if his superiors learned that journalists had got past his outpost. As such, it was agreed by all that Sasha and I had never ridden beyond the checkpoint, and that no formal report would be filed.

During the previous weeks, numerous news outlets reported that the Turkish military was massing hundreds of armoured vehicles in this "forbidden zone" in anticipation of them pushing into Kurdish-controlled northern Iraq.

However, after covering most of this off-limits territory on foot or bicycle, Sasha and I had found no evidence of any Turkish armoured forces having been in this area. Only the regular border guards and jendarma checkpoints were seen, plus the heavily rutted farmers' fields that *could* have been churned up by wheeled – or tracked – armoured personnel carriers.

If there had been Turkish forces here, they were now gone – either into northern Iraq or simply back to their casernes. As for other reports that a large number of Turkish troops had advanced into the Kurdish region of Iraq from a northern mountain pass, one Turkish reporter recently embedded with the unit in question said that such a large-scale penetration had not yet occurred.

"There are thousands of soldiers marshalled around Hakkari waiting to enter Iraq, but there are at least two meters of snow in the area," said Selver, a television reporter with the federal Turkish broadcaster TRT. "Some Special Forces troops have been able to cross, but not the main units," he reported.

Given the political sensitivity of this issue – Kurdish forces had threatened to engage the Turks and the U.S. administration repeatedly warned Turkey against any unilateral entry into Iraq – it was proving extremely difficult to ascertain exactly what was transpiring along this front. This despite the fact I was actually there.

Likewise, even with all the media's preparation of 'war teams' – including the new technology of videophones and the inclusion of embedded journalists within front-line units – the coverage of Gulf War II remained largely an exercise in bluff and deception. Confirmed information was in scarce supply, and eyewitness accounts often differed greatly from official Pentagon and Iraqi statements.

While no news agency can possibly have enough correspondents to cover all of the potential and actual flash points, each wants to give their viewers/readers the impression that they were presenting them with first-hand accounts of the war. To pull this off successfully, networks were relying heavily on the general public's relative ignorance of this region and its geography, and the basic premises of newsgathering and dissemination.

For instance, a journalistic low point occurred during one of Fox Television's weekend reports about the allied military buildup just south of Baghdad. To provide analysis of this subject, the anchor went live to his correspondent in Amman to ask, "Just how capable are the Iraqi Republican Guard units after the allied softening-up bombardments?"

Without a pause, the young woman in Jordan went on at great length describing the troop strength and possible morale of Saddam's Medina division of the elite Republican Guard. Most viewers would simply accept this report at face value, without questioning how an American reporter based 1,200 kilometres from the fighting – and with no access to Iraqi military officials – could possibly know anything more than what had been included in the Pentagon's assessments. However, by tagging the information with a Middle Eastern dateline, mere speculation suddenly appeared to be credible reporting.

Another media shortcoming was the almost complete absence of critical assessment after the actual fighting began. We were repeatedly told by the Bush administration that this was going to be a war of "liberation" for the "long-repressed" and "brutalized" people of Iraq. The U.S. operation was dubbed *Iraqi Freedom* and, after the initial successes in the first hours of the campaign, everyone predicted a short, virtually bloodless war.

However, once things took a turn for the worse – Iraqi defences stiffened and the number of allied casualties began to mount – it became apparent that the U.S. and British troops were not welcome after all. Although they were unprepared for a protracted campaign, U.S. military planners repeated at every opportunity that things were unfolding exactly as planned.

When that was not enough, public relation officers began taking license with the facts – such as the media sideshow that became known as "Saving Private Lynch."

The whole affair had started with the U.S. military debacle on March 23. Up until then, coalition forces had suffered only a handful of casualties while achieving major successes over the first three days of the war. Iraqi resistance had stiffened suddenly around the city of Nasiriya and the fast-advancing U.S. Marine column had come to a halt.

Just south of Nasiriya, the commander of the 507th Maintenance Company made a wrong turn and drove his lightly armed column straight into an Iraqi ambush. In the confusion, a bloodbath ensued. Ten Americans were reported killed,

50 wounded and 12 had surrendered to Iraqi Fedayeen fighters. The 507th had been shattered, and the supporting Marine units had arrived too late to prevent the capture of the U.S. personnel.

While official U.S. Army spokesman Brigadier General Vince Brooks continued to report those soldiers as missing, the Iraqi media had already broadcast images of the terrified American captives.

To salvage some martial pride, unnamed Pentagon press officers began calling up reporters to plant tales of heroism. Before long, Private Jessica Lynch, an attractive 19-year-old, had become larger than life.

On April 3, the *Washington Post* ran the front-page story headline, "She was fighting to the death." Like some sort of GI Jane, Jessica was said to have fought back against overwhelming odds, even though she was wounded. She had killed several Iraqis, it was said, and surrendered only after firing her last bullet. Heady stuff, but highly improbable, given the circumstances. At that point, the only possible witnesses to Lynch's alleged heroics were either dead, retreating to safety, or in captivity with her.

From published reports, it seems safe to say that most members of the 507th Maintenance Company never considered themselves Rambo-like warriors. Specialist Shoshanna Johnson, who was also captured in Nasiriya, told her family that she had "joined the Army to learn cooking skills in a support unit." She had "never expected to see combat and violence in a real war."

Meanwhile, the myth continued to grow.

Following Lynch's dramatic April 1 rescue, Brooks told reporters that the evacuation team had "gone in under fire" to rescue one of their own. Night-vision video footage was released at the press conference showing Private Lynch being put aboard a helicopter by heavily armed U.S. Special Forces operatives.

When asked whether Private Lynch had been violated during her captivity, Brooks looked sternly at the reporter and said that he could not discuss that "in the interest of her privacy." Of course, this careful use of words is rarely used except when a sexual assault is involved. While the thought of a wounded young American girl being raped by vicious Iraqis would certainly help to demonize the enemy in a time of war, the fact is that it never happened.

When the Lynch family publicly denied that their daughter had been raped, the U.S. Army claimed Private Lynch suffered from amnesia (i.e., she was raped but she was traumatised into forgetting about the incident). When the Lynches disputed their daughter's mental state (i.e., she was not suffering any amnesia), the Pentagon put a gag order on them.

British reporters, anxious to follow up on the whole story, had made some startling discoveries when they visited the hospital where Lynch had been held. Apparently, the Fedayeen fighters had pulled out on March 30, two days before her rescue. Despite some sporadic fighting on the outskirts of the city, medical orderlies who had treated Jessica decided to take her by ambulance towards the advancing Marines. Still jumpy and taking no chances, the U.S. soldiers opened fire and the ambulance was forced to return to the hospital.

Iraqi lawyer Mohammed Odeh Al-Rehaief had then made separate contact with the U.S. military to alert them to Lynch's whereabouts and condition. (Al-Rehaief would later be granted asylum in the U.S. for his actions.) Although the military knew the hospital was deserted, the U.S. Special Forces arrived on the scene with guns blazing. However, the spent shell casings that were found at the hospital by the British reporters were from blank munitions.

When the details about this staged rescue were made public, the Pentagon would backtrack only slightly. Apparently, when Brooks had claimed that the rescue team went in "under fire," what he had really meant to say was that the soldiers had witnessed tracer fire as they flew into Nasiriya, and not at the hospital itself.

No U.S. official could explain why soldiers on a real mission would be carrying and firing such a large quantity of blanks. As for the combat wounds Private Lynch had sustained in the attack, the Iraqi doctor who treated her stated she had suffered a broken foot when her vehicle crashed and that she had no gunshot injuries of any kind.

~ ~ ~ ~ ~ ~ ~ ~ ~ ~

As frustrating as it was being unable to cross into Iraq, it had been interesting to watch the war coverage on television, particularly the British Broadcasting Corp.'s world report segments. Whenever the local anchor – whether in London or with the U.S. command centre in Doha, Qatar – introduced their Baghdad-based correspondent, they would always include a cautionary phrase: "Viewers, please keep in mind that the following commentary is being closely monitored and controlled by the Iraqi authorities."

While this was undoubtedly true, such an introduction only served to cast doubt on everything the reporter said. Unfortunately, the BBC did not issue similar warnings about the information that was passed along by all their other journalists who were either embedded with allied units or attending official press conferences. The truth was that almost *all* of the media's reporting on this conflict was being closely monitored and controlled by whichever faction or organisation they were in contact with.

One need only look at the case of Peter Arnett, who was fired by NBC for having stated during an interview with Iraqi television that the initial U.S. attack had "failed to meet its objectives." While there can be no denying that this was a private opinion (and a very valid one at that), the executives at NBC quickly realised the impact Arnett's opinions had had and just how sensitive the Bush administration was to any kind of negative commentary on the war.

Despite Arnett's vast knowledge of Iraq and his depth of wartime experience, the network summarily fired him, thereby sending a very clear message to all its correspondents that negativity (even when supported by fact) will not be tolerated in this war. Journalists who were lucky enough to be embedded with front-line units knew there was a tremendously long waiting list of eager, young reporters who were anxious to take their place. Obviously, any commentary that would be embarrassing to either the detachment or to the commander involved would result in a one-way ticket home. The military mindset has never been known for its tolerance of criticism.

Likewise, those few journalists who were able to enter northern Iraq and report on the activities of the Kurdish peshmerga were equally reluctant to offend their 'hosts.' Almost unheard of in the media reports from inside Iraq was the Turkmen. This large minority group, estimated to number 2 million in Iraq, had little official representation within either of the two Kurdish factions ruling the north or within Saddam's Baghdad-based regime. Despite the important role the Turkmen stood to play in a post-Saddam Iraqi federation, the ruling Kurdish parties – Massoud Barzani's KDP and Jalal Talabani's PUK – were dissuading the foreign media from presenting the Turkmen platform.

Along with Sasha Uzunov and I, about 750 journalists were stuck inside Turkey, all trying to find some way to get across the closed border into Iraq. Tales were shared about the few daring reporters who actually managed this difficult feat. One Spanish reporter apparently paid $2,500 U.S. to be smuggled across the border in the fake bottom of a truck's cab, while another of his countrymen bribed an aid worker to trade places with him as the driver of a humanitarian delivery vehicle. Meanwhile, a television crew managed to race through a remote crossing point, but only after the Turkish border patrol riddled their car with bullets.

Most of the remaining reporters hoped that either the border would be opened shortly or that Turkish authorities would grant them some sort of special access. With this in mind, very few reports were published that could be construed as critical of either the Turkish military or of the government's duplicity in officially denying the U.S. access while covertly permitting the military buildup to continue unabated.

Also for fear of losing their media credentials, our media colleagues only complained privately about the fact they were being monitored and controlled by the Turkish intelligence service. Located above the Silopi press centre, squads of operatives made little attempt to conceal their activities from the media. The recording of all Internet message traffic, viewing of all web sites visited, and analysing of all published media clips were routinely performed. In addition, foreign journalists were required to register their lodgings with the local police, and middle-of-the-night bed checks by the jendarma were not uncommon.

Keeping this in mind, the general public must be made to realise that when they were viewing any coverage of the war, what they were getting may have been the 'truth,' but it certainly wasn't the 'whole truth.'

~ ~ ~ ~ ~ ~ ~ ~ ~ ~

One of the first images shown after U.S. and British troops entered Iraqi cities were of them shooting holes in portraits of Saddam Hussein and toppling over statues of the Iraqi president. Such scenes would be repeated in every town and village the coalition troops captured over the next three weeks.

On April 7, the U.S. Third Division brought a detachment of combat engineers with them into Baghdad to blow up a monument of Saddam on horseback. Their goal: To send a clear message to the Iraqi people that regime change was inevitable.

However, never was the media 'truth' more manipulated than during the staged statue toppling scene on April 9 that was meant to symbolise the end of Saddam's regime. Watching CNN's senior correspondent, Christiane Amanpour, give a live report on the supposedly spontaneous incident, I suspected this would be one of the United States' largest staged news events. What a coincidence for Amanpour and her crew to be on hand in Firdos Square to capture on video a mob of Iraqis as they tried to bring down a large statue of Saddam. Unable to achieve this feat alone, a detachment of U.S. Marines just happened to be in the area to lend a hand.

I listened incredulously as Amanpour told CNN's viewers that this was Baghdad's central square and that this particular statue was "deeply symbolic" to the Iraqi people. As Firdos Square sits between the Sheraton and the Palestine hotels, I was very familiar with it. Contrary to her claims, Firdos Square certainly was not "the centre of Baghdad." The real city centre – Revolution Square – was some two kilometres away and was still very much under the control of Saddam loyalists. Furthermore, this particular statue was cast from a standard mould and identical copies could be found all over Iraq. In fact, up until the previous October when the statue had been erected, Firdos Square had been nothing more than an empty traffic circle.

When other media outlets housed in the Palestine Hotel began broadcasting images of the statue's toppling, they actually provided a different perspective. By pulling back from the action, it became obvious that the Iraqi mob was in fact just a tiny crowd. American tanks completely surrounded the square, so the Iraqis were operating inside a protected perimeter. One Iraqi who camped it up for the cameras by banging his shoe on the toppled Saddam was later recognised to be one of Ahmed Chalabi's INC bodyguards. Two days earlier this individual – wearing the same shirt – had appeared beside the Iraqi National Congress president when he returned to the town of Nasiriya.

By comparison, in October 1989, when the people of East Germany had risen up as one to overthrow the Communist regime, thousands of long-oppressed citizens attacked the Berlin Wall with hammers and picks to bring it down. After suffering four and a half decades of Soviet occupation, the East Germans openly vented their suppressed hatred against the concrete barrier that symbolised their suffering.

Likewise, in December of that same year, when the Romanians overthrew Communist dictator Nicolae Ceausescu, thousands of people took to the streets to celebrate in a violent fashion. Senior officials and police were targeted for public reprisals, and statues representing the Communist regime under which the Romanians had suffered were toppled to the cheers of onlookers.

In October 2000, nearly one million Serbs took to the streets of Belgrade to demand the removal of Yugoslav President Slobodan Milosevic. When the police turned and joined ranks with the protestors, the parliament buildings were stormed and occupied by the dissidents. Joyful Serbs burned files and furniture, then marched on the state television building to wreak further destruction. Radio Television Serbia (RTS) broadcasts had long been considered as nothing more than Milosevic's propaganda machine, and the vandalising of these premises was symbolic of a nation's pent up hatred for Slobo's socialist regime.

While there can be no denying that a large percentage of Iraqi citizens were happy to see Saddam's rule brought to an end, it must have seemed odd for those who had endured so much suffering for so many years to see foreign soldiers exhibiting such aggression and hatred towards a man whose torment they had never experienced.

The media reports of U.S. soldiers sitting in one of Saddam's palaces, smoking, looting ashtrays, and using the presidential toilet were undoubtedly morale boosters aimed at the coalition forces. In contrast, for the average Iraqi, those images created the perception that the allies were arrogant conquerors, not liberators.

As became clearly evident, the incident at Firdos Square had been orchestrated by the U.S. military in conjunction with CNN. While it would certainly not fool Iraq's citizens, it effectively convinced North American audiences that the war was over.

During that evening's newscast, Global Television anchor Kevin Newman interviewed correspondent Patrick Graham, one of the few Canadian reporters who had stuck it out in Baghdad. From the Palestine Hotel's rooftop, Graham explained how this particular incident had involved "only a handful" of Iraqis. He went on to say that, in reality, the Fedayeen fighters still controlled most of Baghdad.

Nevertheless, the following morning virtually every North American headline read "Saddam Toppled" and CNN had switched its "War in Iraq" logo to a new "Iraq Rebuilds."

Instead of waiting for the Iraqis to rise up en masse to celebrate their "liberation," the Bush administration had decided the time was right to start celebrating for them.

ABOVE: *The April 9, 2003 toppling of Saddam's statue in Firdos Square was a carefully stage-managed event – symbolizing the end of Iraq's organized resistance* (JEROME DELAY/AP)

ABOVE: *It was several weeks after the collapse of Saddam's regime before the U.S. military began making a serious effort to stop the looting. In the initial occupation phase, the American mandate was limited to self-protection – the Iraqi citizenry was left to fend for itself against the thieves. (BENJAIMIN LOWY/ CORBIS FOR TIME MAGAZINE)*

OPPOSITE PAGE: *Destroyed Iraqi armoured vehicles in Baghdad's northern suburbs. Even though many of these vehicles were abandoned (without putting up a fight), the advancing Americans had taken no chances and destroyed them anyway. (S. TAYLOR)*

CHAPTER NINE

Back to Iraq

Although the Pentagon, the State Department and the American news chains proclaimed "victory" over Saddam Hussein on April 9, 2003, in reality the war in Iraq would create international reverberations for months to come.

On the ground, coalition forces had shattered most of Saddam's security forces, but a number of "regime loyalists" would continue to offer sporadic resistance. The decision by U.S. Secretary of Defense Donald Rumsfeld to initiate the intervention in Iraq with a relatively small number of combat troops in theatre meant the coalition was unable to create a secure environment in large urban centres.

The minute the Iraqi authority was officially dissolved, chaos ensued. As many Western journalists in Baghdad had repeatedly predicted, the nearly three million impoverished Shiite residents of the capital's Saddam City ghetto wasted little time in looting upper-middle-class suburbs. Without the manpower to protect all of Baghdad's key installations, the U.S. military had been selective when choosing sites to secure. Topping their list were the Iraqi Ministry of Oil complex, oil pipelines, petroleum refineries, and the Al-Rasheed Hotel. One of the few unscathed buildings in central Baghdad, this luxurious hotel was quickly seized by U.S. Marines before looters could do any serious damage and became the U.S. military's command centre in Iraq. But first some renovations were required. Immediately following the first patrol's entry into the Al-Rasheed's lobby was a combat engineer detachment armed with a jackhammer. As the fighting and looting continued on the streets outside, the soldiers set to work chiselling out the infamous "Bush is Criminal" mosaic that had graced the hotel's floor since 1991.

American officers confirmed to *Toronto Star* reporter Mitch Potter that the instructions to remove the mosaic had come "from the top." In all the madness, it's difficult to imagine that either the Bush administration or senior Pentagon planners would have had time for such pettiness. As the Marine detachment smashed up the portrait of George Bush Senior, outside the Al-Rasheed relatively small groups of Iraqis engaged in the desecration of portraits and statues of Saddam. However, most of the mobs were busy vandalising and looting what was left of the buildings occupied by the former Iraqi government. What seemed to be an incredible stroke of luck for allied propaganda occurred in the first few days of scavenging through the burnt debris and scattered wreckage of the heavily bombed building that served as headquarters for the Mukhabarat. It was here that journalists from the *London Daily Telegraph* and U.S.-based *Christian Science Monitor* found a number of damaging documents linking George Galloway to Saddam's regime.

One of the loudest voices objecting to a military campaign prior to the U.S.-led intervention in Iraq was George Galloway, Britain's maverick Labour Party MP. During the pre-war months of sabre rattling between the Bush administration and the Iraqi regime, Galloway had made a number of trips to Baghdad, often as the head of high-profile peace delegations. Undoubtedly, the efforts of such individuals as Galloway and the well-organized peace activists in Britain helped to undermine Prime Minister Tony Blair's efforts to sell the war to his constituents.

As testimony to the confidence placed in his abilities by the Iraqi authorities, Galloway was even granted a rare private interview with the reclusive Saddam Hussein. With no other international journalist being granted such access (the interview pre-dated *60 Minutes'* Dan Rather's), Galloway's relayed message from Saddam had received huge play in British papers and around the world.

According to the documents found at the Mukhabarat headquarters, the British MP had been siphoning millions of dollars from the UN-administered oil-for-food program. Large payments were allegedly made as a commission or lifting fee and had been reportedly authorized in recognition of Galloway's public relations work on behalf of Iraq.

Naturally, the British papers had a field day with this revelation of despicable treachery, and several of Galloway's colleagues began demanding that charges of treason be levelled against him. The fact that Galloway himself denied the accusations and protested desperately that the documents were forgeries made the beleaguered MP seem all the more pitiable.

Although one of their most damaging critics had now been silenced, the British (and the U.S.) still faced a daunting task on the international front. Anti-war sentiment throughout the world was supposed to be quieted by the unearthing of proof that Saddam possessed weapons of mass destruction (WMD). Even after hostilities had started, Donald Rumsfeld had remained adamant that Saddam's illegal arsenal would be uncovered. "We know where they are," he told reporters on March 23, 2003.

Several months later, with the coalition forces having completely overrun Iraq, they had yet to come up with a wet peashooter let alone a "smoking gun" to justify their claim that this intervention was about the "self-defence" of America. Other than a few captured gas masks and several drums of pesticide, no doomsday weapons had yet been located, and certainly none that had been used by the "Butcher of Baghdad," even as the coalition forces smashed their way into his country.

Incredibly, the repeated media coverage of "false alarms" of suspected Iraqi weapons sites – video footage of U.S. inspectors in chemical suits testing artillery shells and suspicious trucks – had convinced a majority of Americans that WMD actually had been found. While the remainder of the American public was diverted into believing that President Bush had brought freedom and liberty to Iraq, the rest of the world was still waiting to see the evidence that would justify the unilateral and unsanctioned military intervention into Iraq.

For anyone who closely followed official U.S. statements, it would not come as a shock to learn that allied intelligence reports had been anything but solid. When U.S. Secretary of State Colin Powell made his final presentation to the UN Security Council on February 5, 2003, he claimed that Iraq had attempted to purchase uranium from Niger as part of an illicit attempt to create a nuclear bomb. However, after close examination of the documents, Mohamed El Baradei, Director General of the International Atomic Energy Agency (IAEA), declared that Powell's proof was nothing more than a "clumsy forgery."

Both the U.S. and British intelligence agencies had apparently been aware of this fact since as early as January 2001 – when it was pointed out that the signature on the document was from a minister long since removed from his post. Nevertheless, the same "yellow cake" claim would be repeated by President Bush in his January 2003 State of the Union address. And again by Powell at the UN a month later.

Similarly, Powell's shocking revelation that Iraq possessed two secret "unmanned aircraft capable of dispensing chemical weapons" quickly became a farce when the Iraqis allowed Western journalists to inspect these so-called WMD.

The deadly drones were in fact nothing more than primitive, oversized model aircraft capable of flying a mere 150 kilometres – providing it was unarmed and had no warhead.

On April 7, nearly three weeks into the campaign and with U.S. troops on the outskirts of Baghdad, the Pentagon once again relied upon solid intelligence reports to launch yet another attempt on Saddam's life. Although a barrage of cruise missiles and bunker-busting bombs turned an upscale restaurant into a 40-foot crater, Saddam was still believed to be alive and well. (Tragically, 16 bodies were recovered from the rubble, most of them women and children.) The restaurant targeted was actually a frequent haunt of Western reporters as it was the only American-style fast food restaurant in Baghdad. I found it difficult to believe that at the height of a war, with the enemy at his gates, the reclusive Saddam would take himself out to a burger joint that served Kentucky Fried Chicken on a plastic tray.

It was also "solid" American intelligence that predicted allied troops would be welcomed by the oppressed Iraqis as liberators. When the expected jubilation failed to materialise, and Iraqi cities instead erupted into an orgy of violent looting, the U.S. administration did its best to put a positive spin on things. The looters were simply "getting a taste of freedom," explained U.S. Secretary of Defense Donald Rumsfeld. Of course, that did not explain why U.S. soldiers and journalists had also jubilantly joined in the looting.

However, it was also evident from the immediate increase in Shiite fundamentalism in the south and the outbreak of interfactional violence in the north, that "solid" U.S. intelligence had failed to properly assess the post-Saddam chaos that would occur throughout Iraq.

On April 10, a U.S.-supported Shiite cleric, Abdul Majid al-Khoei, and his Baghdad-based, Saddam-loyalist counterpart, Haider al-Kadar, were hacked to death by an angry mob at what was supposed to be a reconciliation meeting at Imam Ali, one of Shiite Islam's holiest shrines. After killing the two clerics, the furious crowd then dumped the bodies on the road in front of the mosque.

While U.S. post-war religious preparations were in trouble, things on the political front were even worse. Ahmed Chalabi, president of the Iraqi National Congress opposition party and a possible successor to Saddam, has been met with open hostility. Viewed as an American stooge by most Iraqis, Chalabi, who had lived primarily in the U.S. and London since leaving Iraq in 1956, has already survived one attempt on his life. After a number of his Taszar-trained Iraqi bodyguards were killed in the attack, Chalabi had to rely on U.S. military personnel for around-the-clock protection.

As for the CIA-funded training camp in Taszar, Hungary, the entire Iraqi liberation army experiment had proven to be a colossal waste of resources and time. The first two planned drafts, each intended to produce 1500 American-trained Iraqi soldiers, had graduated a mere 80 qualified candidates. Many Iraqis simply disappeared after pocketing their $3,000 signing bonus. Of those who did go to Taszar, the majority left without completing the program.

The fact that the Iraqi training base in Taszar was quietly shut down due to lack of interest should have set off alarm bells for the Bush administration. The U.S. candidate earmarked to rule Iraq couldn't even buy himself an army.

~ ~ ~ ~ ~ ~ ~ ~ ~ ~

As a result of the press corps' collective ignorance or wilful blindness, the U.S. was able to stage a "liberation parade" in the northern town of Sulaimaniyah on April 22. Jay Garner, a former general who had been appointed by the U.S. State Department as Iraqi interim military governor, was welcomed by crowds of cheering Kurds as he casually walked down the main street. While no doubt this image was reassuring to the American public, anxious to see their soldiers greeted as liberators, not one reporter pointed out that this region had first been "liberated" by a Kurdish warlord in 1991. Since the post-Gulf war uprising, Jalal Talabani had ruled this province as his own personal fiefdom, completely free of Saddam Hussein's authority.

In his post-9/11 address to the nation, George Bush had made it clear that America's foreign policy would follow a black-and-white guideline of "you're either with us or against us," defiantly proclaiming, "You're on the side of good… or evil."

The problem with such simplistic declarations is that the world's complexities cannot clearly be divided into these two categories. Nevertheless, the American media (and, to a lesser extent, their pro-U.S. Canadian counterparts) had patriotically tried to mould their coverage of international events within Bush's good guy/bad guy framework.

And as long as Saddam Hussein controlled Iraq, the war had been relatively simple to catalogue in this manner. Everything pertaining to Saddam's regime was "evil" and anyone opposed to his rule was automatically considered a supporter of America. One problem with the old any-enemy-of-my-enemy-is-my-friend school of thought is that, in this case, not all parties shared the same post-Saddam goal for Iraq.

The Bush administration was now faced with the conundrum of trying to

militarily impose a Western-style democracy on an occupied country. Unfortunately, the majority of Iraqis are Shiite Muslims whose desire is to establish a fundamentalist state. Of course, America did not stage a military intervention in Iraq
in order to facilitate a Taliban-style religious regime that would undermine
Saddam's secular reforms and abolish minority rights and freedoms.

Western reporters, most of them in Iraq for the first time, tried to put a positive
spin on the post-Saddam surge of Shiite fundamentalism. Almost every one of
them erroneously reported that, under American liberation, the Shiites were once
again free to stage pilgrimages to Iraqi holy sites.

However, while Saddam had certainly limited the number of participants, foreign Shiite pilgrims had been a major source of income for Iraq. An estimated
3000 visitors had entered Iraq every day prior to the war and the standard pack-
age tour cost $800 U.S. Ironically, it was only the threat of U.S. military action that
halted the flow of worshippers.

Another oft-reported misrepresentation of new-found freedom was that the
Iraqis were now free to sell and consume alcohol. Of course, anyone who had
visited Iraq prior to the war knew that Iraqis had always had access to booze. The
only stipulation was that it could not be consumed in a public place such as a bar
or restaurant. Of course this law was only loosely enforced and it never took long
for intrepid journalists to track down the Baghdad speakeasies.

One Canadian journalist actually reported that cigarettes had been banned
under Saddam's oppression, and that liberation now meant that Iraqis were once
again free to smoke openly. If only this were true, my lungs would not be full of
the second-hand smoke that has always been utterly unavoidable in Iraq. Another
inexperienced reporter claimed that the post-Saddam looting was so pervasive
that even "the toilets had been taken, leaving just a hole in the floor" – apparently
unaware that in this region of the world this sort of plumbing is the norm.

Admittedly, it is sometimes difficult for journalists unfamiliar with a particular region to sort out fact from fiction, particularly when so many "sources" are
anxious to say anything to make their case. However, I am still amazed at how
some journalists can put a positive, pro-American spin on cases of tragic suffering. One classic example was when a Baghdad resident told an American television crew that, despite the fact he had lost all 12 members of his family to a U.S.
missile, he was thankful to America for having removed Saddam from power.
Another was the story of the little girl who suffered burns to a large part of her
body and was brought to the U.S. for hospitalization. Although her burns were
the result of a U.S. bomb, her family was grateful for the medical care their daughter was now receiving thanks to the Americans.

It seemed as though common sense was rarely applied by either the interim U.S. authorities or the media reporting on developments. For instance, when U.S. troops pushed into Iraq and captured the country's penitentiaries, the first thing the soldiers did was release all of the prisoners. When interviewed by embedded journalists, the newly freed Iraqi prisoners singularly professed to being political prisoners, jailed because they had opposed Saddam. And their tales of torture and brutality committed by Saddam's police helped reinforce the justification for the facilitation of a regime change by the U.S.

While there is no doubt that Saddam's intelligence service had a zero-tolerance policy for political dissent, it was ludicrous to simply empty the prisons. Equally ignorant is the fact that no one in the media questioned how Iraq, with a population of 23 million, could have been bereft of any actual criminals – the murderers, rapists, thieves, paedophiles, etc., that exist in every society. Yet nobody seems to see a connection between their liberation and the violent anarchy and widespread looting that has since resulted. In retrospect it seems probable that at least some of those jailed actually deserved to be kept separate from civil society.

As part of the pre-war propaganda, U.S. analysts and Iraq's opposition exiles claimed that among his many crimes Saddam had jailed children as young as five years old if they showed signs of political dissent. Now anyone with a young child – and a modicum of intelligence – would have recognised that at this young age such an assessment would be impossible. Nevertheless, U.S. troops advancing into Baghdad obviously believed this nonsense. As such they claimed to have liberated a number of suspected "youth jails" that were, in fact, orphanages.

"They saw children wearing uniforms and presumed they were prisoners," said Julia Guest, a British reporter with a wealth of experience in Iraq. "Once these children were set free, they had nowhere to go and no one to look after them." Aged between 5 and 12 years, these Iraqi children had turned to begging food in their streets and sniffing glue. "They are dying," said Guest.

Another issue which the media had repeatedly failed to put into context was the ongoing discovery of mass graves. To follow just the headlines and photos, one could be forgiven for believing that George W. Bush intervened in Iraq to halt an ongoing genocide. The first revelation of an alleged slaughter came during the first week of fighting. In a warehouse outside of Basra, U.S. troops found the remains of 400 corpses. America's military spokesman in Qatar, Brigadier General Vince Brooks, told reporters that there was evidence "that many of the dead had been … executed" and that the case was being handled as a "possible war crime."

It mattered not that these decomposing bodies were the remains of Iraqi soldiers that had been killed nearly two decades earlier by the Iranians during the Iran-Iraq War. Furthermore, the International Committee of the Red Cross had been in the process of repatriating the soldiers' remains when the war started. Since the collapse of Saddam's regime, a number of other mass graves have been discovered, with the majority of them containing the bodies of Shiite rebels killed during their failed uprising in 1991.

While these burial pits provided stark evidence that Saddam's security forces were capable of extreme brutality, very few reports in the Western media bothered to put this rebellion into context. Immediately following Gulf War One, the U.S.-led coalition had over 500,000 troops poised along the Kuwait-Iraq border. The allied air forces had just destroyed the bulk of Saddam's heavy weaponry and the Iraqi president was hard-pressed to retain control over his people. In fact, by the summer of 1991, Saddam's loyalists had lost all but 3 of Iraq's 18 provinces to rebel forces — Kurds in the north and Shiites in the south — before the Iraqi president was eventually able to regain control of 12 of them.

Following *Operation Desert Storm*, George Bush Senior obviously considered Saddam Hussein as less of a regional threat than did his son. At the time, the U.S. did not want an Iranian-sponsored Shiite fundamentalist regime to seize power in oil-rich Iraq. Consequently, the U.S. turned a deaf ear to the rebels' pleas for assistance. (In fact, the U.S. actually helped to facilitate Saddam's rearming by allowing his troops to recover their abandoned weaponry from Kuwaiti territory.)

Of course, for journalists to provide all the background on the United States' complicity in these old gravesites would be to think outside of Bush's black-and-white template. In reviewing the Iraqi people's suffering over the past two decades, no one could argue that Saddam was not evil. However, it is wrong to believe he held the monopoly on it.

~ ~ ~ ~ ~ ~ ~ ~ ~ ~

On May 1, CNN began broadcasting almost continual updates on President Bush's planned flight out to the homeward-bound USS *Abraham Lincoln*. All day long, North American television viewers were informed of how the Commander in Chief was a former Air National Guard pilot, and that he would likely take the controls of the S-3B Viking during the aircraft's brief flight to the carrier. Everything from what clothing the President would wear down to speculation of his possible airsickness was discussed by the news anchors. Everyone knew that Bush was going to use this opportunity to proclaim a victory. And when he finally announced an "end to all major combat operations in Iraq," the whole thing seemed contrived and anti-climactic.

However, by giving so much coverage to the President's flight, the U.S. media neglected to report on the massive May Day parades that were taking place in Europe. Millions of people had turned out on the streets to mark this annual event, but this year the assembled masses carried a singularly anti-U.S. message. Inflamed over the war, many of the marches turned into violent protests. (In Berlin, over 7,000 police had been deployed to control the crowds.)

Although the killing continued unabated in Iraq and global anti-U.S. sentiment was at its zenith, Bush's proclamation of victory was the signal for major media outlets to redirect their priorities. The war was now a civil reconstruction project, and most of the foreign correspondents and embedded journalists began heading home.

Wanting to see the aftermath for myself, I headed back to Iraq.

~ ~ ~ ~ ~ ~ ~ ~ ~ ~

NORTHERN IRAQ, MAY 14-20, 2003   It was almost surreal travelling back through southeastern Turkey, which, little more than a month earlier, had been abuzz with wartime activity. If I had not seen it for myself, I would never have believed that this area had been the site of both a U.S. and a Turkish military buildup along the Iraq-Kurdistan border.

All the American transport aircraft and freight containers, never officially authorised to be there in the first place, had left the Diyarbakir airport. Also gone were the batteries of Dutch Patriot missile batteries that had constituted NATO's wartime commitment to the defence of Turkey. Ironically, many of the Turkish troops that had massed along the border to facilitate a possible pre-emptive offensive intervention into Iraq had not yet fully returned to their casernes.

Officially the border between Turkey and Kurdish-controlled Iraq remained closed. Until January of this year, this crossing point had been a major oil tanker route dubbed Turkey's "rolling pipeline." Closed as a result of pre-war U.S. diplomatic pressure, there was still a massive parking lot of idle oil tankers that stretched back nearly 30 kilometres inside the Turkish side of the border.

Unofficially, a small amount of daily traffic had increased somewhat now that the war in Iraq had been declared over by President Bush. Although there were only a handful of foreign journalists being processed, it took nearly three hours to walk through and receive approval from the various authorities on both sides of the border.

It had been over a month since Saddam Hussein's regime collapsed, but without a new central government in Baghdad the Kurdish side of the border remained under the control of Massoud Barzani's KDP. No U.S. soldiers were in evidence at the border, but it was interesting to note that Barzani's peshmergas had recently been issued with American-style camouflage uniforms and were no longer wearing their traditional cloth caps and baggy trousers.

Although not a formally recognised authority, the KDP was issuing visitors a $50 U.S. visa fee as well as levy entry taxes, seemingly based on the entrant's ability to afford the price. "Welcome to the new liberated Iraq," said Hosad Ahmet, a 24-year-old Iraqi Turkmen who lived in the border town of Zakho. "We are now free to charge and be charged just about anything."

As a volunteer with the Iraqi Turkmen Front, Ahmet was helping to facilitate the re-entry of several of his countrymen. One if those hardest hit by the Kurdish taxes was Zygon Chechen, a 53-year-old Iraqi Turkmen who emigrated to Toronto in 1991. After buying a used car in Germany for about $3000 U.S., Chechen was obliged to pay the Kurds a $1600 U.S. entry tax.

"Not exactly a grateful welcome home for an old soldier," complained Chechen.

During the post-Gulf War uprising in 1991, Chechen and some of his Turkmen compatriots had taken up arms against Saddam Hussein. Although they were briefly able to gain control of the area around the oil-rich city of Kirkuk, Saddam's forces were able to regroup and quickly smash the revolt. During the grim fighting and their bloody retreat through the northern Kurdish provinces, Chechen lost part of his left foot to an armour-piercing shell and his fourteen-year-old son to a deadly fusillade from an Iraqi helicopter gunship.

After a twelve-year absence from his homeland, Chechen returned to search out the fate of his family members and to assist the Turkmen in attaining fair representation in a post-Saddam Iraq.

"Everyone thinks there are only Kurds and Arabs living in Iraq," said Chechen. "That is because the Turkmen live as an oppressed minority, without rights under Saddam's regime and in the northern provinces controlled by the two Kurdish militias."

With a deep-seated historical enmity between the Turkmen and the Kurds, the resentment that greeted Chechen's return was not surprising. Many international analysts believe the Kurds were anxious to lay singular claim to the oil resources of Kirkuk, which would then allow them economic security to declare an independent Kurdish state.

"The Americans have taken the cake away from Saddam and now all the factions are demanding their slice," said Hidayet Eris, a spokesman for Turkey's Foreign Ministry.

With its large ethnic Kurdish population, Turkey still feared that an independent Kurdistan would re-ignite the separatist movement in its eastern provinces. For this reason, along with cultural, linguistic and historical ties, Turkey had been openly supporting the Iraqi Turkmen Front (ITF). Nevertheless, with no existing military forces and being unwilling to fight for Saddam, the Turkmen were unable to counter the advances made by Kurdish peshmergas during the U.S.-led offensive from the north.

"On April 8 Saddam's army just ran away and the Kurdish troops entered Kirkuk without any real fighting," explained Mustafa Kemal, leader of the ITF in Kirkuk. "Immediately, the Kurds began to loot Turkmen homes, and ten of our volunteer fighters were killed trying to fight them off."

With the arrival of American troops in Kirkuk, the violence and looting had abated somewhat. However, despite working towards achieving equitable representation in a new Iraqi government through peaceful means, the ITF continue to organise themselves for future self defence.

"We must protect ourselves," explained Kemal, who admitted that his uniformed ITF guards were only "about 200 volunteers," adding that "all Turkmen have had military training and will be prepared to fight."

It did not take long for the American soldiers patrolling the streets of Kirkuk to realize that cultural complexities and bitter hatreds exist in northern Iraq. "There is no doubt in my mind that these buggers will go after each other like fighting dogs the minute the U.S. pulls out of here," said U.S. Special Forces Staff Sergeant Al Tifton. "But that's not our problem. All that matters right now is that Kirkuk is the safest town in Iraq." And with gunfire, looting and killing every night, that wasn't saying much.

My hotel room was a filthy pit – stains on the rug, fleas on the sheets, and a four-inch cockroach in the shower stall. The air conditioner was broken and the heat was stifling. Outside, I could see the glow of burning buildings and hear the shouts of looters. However, as I watched that night's BBC news on a tiny black and white television, I realized that my circumstances could have been worse. It was reported that on May 6, 2003, Sierra Leone rebel leader Sam Bockarie had been gunned down in his home in Monrovia. According to reports, the news of his death had been delayed by over a week because positive identification of the corpse had been difficult. I was glad I had not followed up on the war criminal's invitation to attend one of his hunting parties.

~ ~ ~ ~ ~ ~ ~ ~ ~ ~

The Kirkuk gas pumps opened at 7:00 a.m. and the altercation began almost immediately. Shouts and punches were exchanged between the attendants and a disturbed customer. A mob of angry Iraqi men soon joined in to haul away the perpetrator so that service could resume.

Almost hysterical over his expulsion from the queue, Sezqin Mirkhan pleaded his case with the U.S. security detail stationed at the gas pumps. "I have been waiting in line here for four days and now they won't serve me because they say I'm a Kurdish *shroog*, a thief," said Mirkhan through an interpreter. "Please do something to help me."

Corporal Amy Johnson, the young U.S. soldier Mirkhan had asked to intervene, looked exasperated and a bit frightened. "We can't help you. This is an internal problem," Johnson said. "We are only here to provide security and we don't have enough people to get involved in these affairs."

The potential for violence in Iraq is a constant threat. Along the nearly six-kilometre line-up of cars waiting for gas, tension often mounted between frustrated patrons and would-be queue jumpers and at times erupted into clashes. Believing me to be an American, I endured a barrage of anti-U.S. insults as I walked the length of the line-up. Stopping me on the sidewalk, one rather large man began shouting in English, "Where the fuck is our gas? What have you Americans done with all of Iraq's oil?"

It did not take long for a crowd to gather round, all of them yelling similar accusations in Arabic. Seeing my plight, a pair of the U.S. Special Forces personnel I had met the previous day stopped and ordered the mob to disperse at gunpoint. As we departed the scene, Staff Sergeant Al Tifton began laughing and said, "We've got plenty of gas up at the (U.S.) airbase. Hell, we'll probably have to start drinking the stuff now that we've run out of places to put it."

During Saddam Hussein's rule, the Iraqi government heavily subsidised domestic gasoline and there were never any shortages. "This is an entirely new experience for Iraqis to be concerned about petrol," said Aydin Aslin, an Iraqi Turkmen who is the chief oil advisor at the Kirkuk-based North Oil Company. "The price has quadrupled in a month (up from 6 cents to 24 cents a litre) and black market gas has become an overnight industry."

Former government workers and soldiers, now unemployed and working on the black market to support their families, would wait in line for up to four days. Once they received their allotment of gas, they immediately siphoned their tanks dry before getting back in line. The fuel was then sold at a one hundred per cent mark-up to taxi and bus drivers who cannot afford to wait in line.

"It's not much of a job, but without any infrastructure in Iraq the only alternative employment is looting," explained Aslin.

As a top oil executive, however, Aslin only missed two days of work because of the war. When the Americans arrived, they quickly put him back to work. "It was their top priority to get Kirkuk's oil wells pumping and the three refineries back in operation. And so far we've made good progress," he said.

Having been a Baath party member of Saddam's regime – at 6 foot 5 inches the big Turkmen joked that he played for their basketball team – was not a deterrent to the Americans' rehiring him immediately. "I'm an engineer, not a politician," Aslin explained.

In revisiting Kirkuk for the first time since Saddam's ouster, it was interesting to see how quickly the former president's presence had been eradicated, with the more obvious signs, of course, being the toppled statues and defaced portraits. In the power vacuum that still existed, symbols of the old regime had also changed ownership. For instance the once dreaded Mukhabarat building was now, ironically, the headquarters for the Communist Party of Kurdistan.

In the pre-war days there was only one hotel in Kirkuk – the Palace – that had been open to foreigners. To show his gratitude for being favoured with such a lucrative monopoly, the proprietor, Mohammad, had turned his lobby into a shrine dedicated to Saddam Hussein. However, when I stopped by the Palace on this return visit, Mohammad nervously pretended not to recognise me. And when I asked about the contents of his now-empty glass shelves, he excused himself to attend to other duties elsewhere.

It is with good reason that Mohammad did not want his past devotion to Saddam revealed: The Palace was now rented out entirely to U.S. Special Forces personnel stationed in Kirkuk.

~ ~ ~ ~ ~ ~ ~ ~ ~ ~

Many Iraqis living in the north had dubbed the recent conflict "the war that wasn't." With Turkey's refusal to allow U.S. forces a staging area and with most of the early fighting taking place in the south, the campaign in the north had been a virtually unopposed occupation.

From the Kurdish-controlled provinces in the north down to the northern outskirts of Baghdad, very little evidence of any combat was visible, despite the fact that extensive defensive positions had been constructed. The earthwork bunkers lining the main highway were all virtually intact, and the artillery and tanks that had once occupied them had been removed.

"Our biggest mystery is wondering where all the Iraqi equipment disappeared to," said Sergeant Fred Walker, one of the U.S. Special Forces personnel that had been assigned to assist the Kurdish peshmerga. "Our guys knocked out 12 Iraqi tanks with hand-held missiles, but we sure as hell didn't kill them all. Hell, they had an entire armoured division here that's just up and gone."

On the drive south, a large number of Iraqi army vehicle carcasses lined the shoulders of the highway. My driver, Droued, said these trucks had not been hit by coalition forces, but had been abandoned and then looted, right down to the chassis, after the war.

It was on the approach to Baghdad that I first saw signs of the massive destruction caused by the allied forces and of the ongoing anarchy that had seized the capital. Dozens of T-72 tanks – the most modern heavy weapon in Saddam's arsenal – lined the highway, their blackened hulks twisted and many with the turrets blown completely off. The Americans had slowly started to clear away some of these shattered vehicles, but, given the scale of the task, it would take months to completely clear away the battle debris.

Right into the central core of Baghdad, wherever the Iraqis had established defensive positions, shattered artillery pieces and destroyed armoured vehicles remained. Although there were two days of combat in Baghdad, after the April 9 collapse most of the Iraqi equipment was abandoned. The advancing Americans, however, had taken no chances and had shot up everything in sight. Although the U.S. military had a tremendous number of soldiers stationed in Baghdad, their presence remained limited to vehicle patrols and checkpoints. With no Iraqi police visible on the streets, looting and arson continued unabated five weeks after Saddam's regime had been toppled. Fires were being set daily throughout Baghdad, with many of them being deliberately started even in buildings that had already been torched.

During the day, *shroogs* openly plundered what was left in unattended government buildings, carting away even the bricks. At night, with the power still out in most districts, armed looters roamed in gangs, looking to seize cars and 'liberate' homes. In most suburban neighbourhoods, citizens formed their own civil defence forces, patrolling nightly to protect their homes, with bloody clashes often erupting between the *shroogs* and homeowners.

When I returned to Baghdad, my first objective was to locate Anmar. I had heard from Sacha Trudeau that, when he had left Iraq two weeks earlier, the Saadi family was alive and safe. With the phone systems partially destroyed, phone calls could be made only within local exchanges. So my plan of contacting Anmar was not an easy one. However, after a circuitous trek through Baghdad's dangerous streets, I finally arrived outside his small bungalow just before dusk. "Where have you been?" asked Anmar. "You missed all the fun!"

As it would soon be dark, Anmar and I set out right away to pick up the necessary food and drinks to celebrate our reunion. Pointing to a shattered bus just a few hundred metres from his home, Anmar proudly said, "That is where we ambushed the thieves. They were coming to rob this district and everyone just opened fire on them. We killed many, and so far they have not returned."

That night, with loaded Kalashnikovs stacked behind the door, we ate, drank and discussed our adventures while gunfire sounded in nearby neighbourhoods.

American troops were becoming more responsive to the violence, sending armoured patrols to the locations where the sound of gunfire was particularly heavy. Their mandate, however, remained primarily that of self-protection. Given that Iraqi hostility towards the continued U.S. presence remained high, the U.S. soldiers' limited directive was understandable.

"We are suffering at least a casualty a day in Baghdad, and we've had two killed last week in separate sniper incidents," said Corporal Dave Jackson, a U.S. military policeman. It was not exactly a one-sided affair. Through Anmar I had learned that my old friend Wahib Hindi had lost two brothers at a U.S. checkpoint. When an Iraqi vehicle failed to slow down, the Americans began shooting and the two brothers had been caught in the deadly crossfire. The U.S. forces' wanton use of deadly force coupled with their singular failure to restore law and order in this war-torn country have only further angered the Iraqi people.

In one incident Anmar and I witnessed, a carload of shroogs drove past us on the highway. They soon began firing their Kalashnikovs at the tires of a new truck that was ahead of us. Riddled with bullets, the truck rolled to a halt. The driver got out quickly and ran away. The thieves then jumped out of their car and began stripping the truck for parts.

This whole scene played out in broad daylight with a clearly visible American patrol of three armoured Hummers no more than 200 metres behind. Although witnesses to the incident, the American soldiers simply rolled past. Anmar was choked with emotion.

"Why the fuck are they even here in Iraq?" he asked angrily. "Would they simply drive by and let people be robbed like this in America?"

Despite his outrage, Anmar admitted he had taken part in the initial looting. "The Kurds had entered Baghdad from the north and immediately begun stealing any automobile with a blue (government) license plate," he explained. "Sometimes these vehicles were previously abandoned, or the Kurds killed the occupant." Once enough cars were collected to form a convoy, the Kurds hired drivers to take the stolen vehicles north. "Most of these vehicles were the new four-wheel drive Toyotas or Nissan Pathfinders," said Anmar

"We were paid $200 to drive them to the Iranian border and the Kurds had arranged for buses to bring us back."

It has been estimated that nearly 30,000 government vehicles were stolen in the first month following Saddam's collapse. It would have taken only a couple of U.S. tanks and a dozen soldiers to block this massive theft as there is only one highway between Baghdad and Sulaimaniyah. As denoted by their government plates, these vehicles belonged to the people of Iraq, and would certainly have been a valuable asset in the rebuilding phase of the country. But since Saddam had previously implemented an embargo on U.S. products, all government vehicles were Japanese models. Under the new U.S. administration, that policy would soon change.

~ ~ ~ ~ ~ ~ ~ ~ ~ ~

"The current situation in Iraq is as close as you can possibly get to total anarchy," said Osman Paksut, the recently returned Turkish ambassador in Baghdad. Paksut is one of about 20 foreign diplomats that had returned to the Iraqi capital, only to find himself operating in a virtual power vacuum. "There is literally no one in control for us to establish diplomatic relations with," he explained.

I had met Osman at a diplomatic function in Ankara several weeks earlier. At that point the war was still raging and he had been temporarily recalled from Baghdad for safety reasons. His wife had optimistically invited me to dine with them, when and if we ever returned to Iraq. Not really expecting a meal, Anmar and I had driven to the Turkish compound for a visit.

The countries that had reopened their embassies had done so against the express wishes of the U.S. State Department, claiming their troops had not yet established a secure environment. That assessment was not without merit. When we arrived at the desk, we heard the sound of gunfire. We were told that, for the first three nights, the Turkish diplomats and their Palestinian security guards had exchanged gunfire with gangs of armed looters on several occasions. In preparation for nightfall, the guards were test-firing their weapons.

"As the only residence with a generator in this neighbourhood, when our lights went on again it was like sending out a beacon to the thieves," said Paksut. "The Americans send tanks to protect us whenever they hear the gunfire, but the U.S. does not yet have enough troops to be everywhere there is trouble in Baghdad."

As for re-establishing some form of federal administration, the U.S. announced earlier in May that Iraq's first interim government would soon be in place. This appointed committee, composed of representatives from a variety of former Iraqi opposition organisations, would hopefully start rebuilding Iraq's shattered bureaucracy and begin preparations to hold a general election sometime in the near future.

However, even the interim U.S. authority had been unable to show any cohesive progress. After only a few months, Director of Reconstruction and Humanitarian Assistance Jay Garner was replaced on May 11 by former diplomat Paul Bremer. The sudden shuffle had a whiff of desperation to it. Although the State Department tried to put a positive spin on it, there was little doubt that Garner had been overwhelmed. With his predecessor unable to restore either law and order or basic utilities, Bremmer was now expected to rush Iraq into a democracy.

In the wake of Saddam's Baath party regime, over 60 political parties had been established and registered in Iraq. With names like the Kurdistan Communist Party, the Islamic Turkmen Front and the Army Officers' Party, it was apparent that the fractured political scene had not broken down along the already complex religious, ethnic and linguistic divisions that exist in Iraq.

There was even a political party to represent the interests of the expatriate Iranian Mujahadeen Khalq. Numbering nearly 60,000 men, women and children, this group resided on three special reservations in Iraq, provided as a token of Saddam's gratitude for their service against Ayatollah Khomeini during the Iran-Iraq War. In driving down from Kirkuk to Baghdad, my Turkmen driver, Droued, had casually pointed out a Mujahadeen Khalq encampment. At the gates were a pair of U.S. military Abrahams tanks and a sentry hut at which several Mujahadeen stood. Further down the road sat an entire U.S. armoured brigade, obviously intent on keeping a close watch on this rogue Iranian military force. Although the Khalqs had proven loyal to Saddam in suppressing the Kurdish and Shiite uprising of 1991, this time they had signed a separate non-aggression pact with the Americans. Nevertheless, a final decision on the future of the Mujahadeen Khalqs had yet to be determined.

Despite the rush of delegations to enrol in this new democratic process, many Iraqis feared this political restructuring was doomed to fail. After tracking down Sami Shallal at his home to bring him mail from his brother Najeeb, he called Jabar Abu Marwan for me. The Mukhabarat agent had survived the war and was anxious to see me again. "The Iraqi people are too splintered and have no experience with Western-style democracy," said Jabar.

As for his wartime experience, Jabar explained that by the time the U.S. bombed the Mukhabarat headquarters everyone had already gone. Only an estimated "2 to 3 per cent" of the intelligence operators had been killed. Apparently my old friends Sami and Mohammad were also alive and well and in hiding, although Salin Said Khalaf al-Jumayli, the former head of the Mukhabarat's North American operations, had been arrested on April 23.

"When Saddam's regime collapsed on April 8, Iraqi intelligence officers simply melted away like ice cream in the hot sun. But we remain in contact and continue to monitor all developments," said Jabar. He gloomily predicted that "the most likely scenario would be that Iraq would divide into two halves, which would then erupt into two separate civil wars. In the south, fundamentalist Shiites will fight each other for control, while in the north it will be a three-way battle between the Kurds, Turkmen and Arabs."

Several recent events would appear to support Jabar's theories. When long-exiled cleric Mohammed Al-Hakim had returned to Iraq after 23 years, nearly six million Iraqi Shiites lined the roads to welcome him. Al-Hakim had repeatedly stated that his intention was to establish an Islamic fundamentalist state in Iraq. If his group gains control, they would certainly repeal the secular reforms made by Saddam's Baath regime. Although he himself was a Shiite, the hard-drinking Jabar vowed to fight any increase in fundamentalism.

Before leaving Iraq, I returned to the Baghdad offices of the International Committee of the Red Cross, hoping to catch up with Kassandra Vartell and find out how she had fared during the war. While she had stuck things out as planned, I was told that she had left Iraq for some long-overdue R & R. For the six ICRC members that had stayed behind, the conflict had taken its toll. Canadian Red Cross worker Vatche Arslanian, 48, was killed on April 8 when he and two other ICRC staff (who managed to escape) were caught in the crossfire between U.S. and Iraqi forces.

In the chaotic aftermath of the war, the danger and stress continued. One of the ICRC's primary concerns was unexploded munitions. In an attempt to alert civilians to the many hazards they posed, the ICRC set up a large-scale awareness campaign.

"Our analysts have reported that the scale of this current situation in Iraq is without parallel," said Nada Doumani, the Baghdad-based ICRC media officer. "It wasn't just that a lot of the combat took place in or near urban centres, but in the aftermath we have to also deal with the wholesale abandonment of weaponry by the Iraqi army."

When I asked whether or not the ICRC would be providing any information to Iraqis to protect themselves from possible exposure to depleted uranium, Doumani had shook her head. "It's not that we are not aware of the potential risks, it's just that there is a lot of political pressure for us to avoid causing any unnecessary

ABOVE: *Anmar Saadi (also inset) inspects a disabled Luna missile at an abandoned Iraqi artillery position. The missile base had been hit by cluster bombs and those defenders not killed had deserted their post. (S. TAYLOR)* ***LEFT:*** *Even six weeks after the Americans occupied Iraq, the shroogs were still openly looting in Baghdad. (ALEXANDRE ZEMLIANICHENKO/AP)*

panic."

When I had entered Kuwait following the first Gulf War, no one had any idea about the potential hazards caused by DU rounds. As such, Allied troops had immediately climbed all over destroyed Iraqi armoured vehicles, with many of them painting graffiti on the hulks and posing for troop photos. By contrast, I noticed that not a single one of the hundreds of abandoned Iraqi vehicles in Baghdad had been defaced. Whether this was due to the American soldiers' heightened awareness of DU residue or the result of an official directive to give such sites a wide berth I couldn't confirm. However, it was disturbing to see that Iraqi children had no such fears and I often saw them playing on the shattered tanks as though they were play structures.

"The long-term health concerns are very disturbing," said Doumani. "But right now we must concentrate our efforts on the immediate situation."

First and foremost, the Red Cross wanted the U.S. coalition forces to establish an interim authority that could restore law and order. "It sounds rather strange that a humanitarian organisation would be calling for additional security measures," said Doumani. "But it can't be a priority to worry about unexploded shells as long as people are still shooting."

One of the last stops I made in Baghdad was to visit the staff at the Sheraton Hotel. It was a tremendous lift to see so many familiar faces, who welcomed me as an old friend. On the day that I last left Iraq, the local papers had run a front-page story about my being a Mossad spy. "Our Mukhabarat have scored a victory over the Zionists by thwarting their espionage," or some such nonsense had been the press line. Haider Hindi, the hotel's manager, had kept a copy of the article for me. "You are famous Mr. Scot," he said.

On a more serious note, Haider wanted to know what legal recourse the Sheraton had to recover money from foreigners. Apparently, a large number of the American journalists who had entered Baghdad after the collapse had run up extensive bills and then left the country without paying. Most had snuck out of the premises, but one individual had been incensed that he was expected to pay for his room. Crumpling his invoice into a ball, the reporter had thrown it at Haider and said, "Consider that the price of your freedom."

~ ~ ~ ~ ~ ~ ~ ~ ~ ~

Heading north to Mosul, it didn't take long to comprehend the scale of the war's deadly legacy. Anmar and I had barely exited the Baghdad suburbs when we came upon the scene of what must have been a ferocious battle on the road to Tikrit.

From the position and disbursement of the shattered Iraqi tanks, it appeared as though the column had been caught by surprise as it tried to reinforce Baghdad in the final days of the fighting.

Pulling off the road to take some photographs, I thought I would get behind the debris and use a northward-bound U.S. truck convoy as a dramatic backdrop. Just over a slight rise, I could see a blackened, twisted armoured personnel carrier, several discarded helmets and about 50 unexploded anti-tank rockets.

These projectiles were fully assembled, primed for firing and left lying in the blistering sun. Realising the danger posed by this abandoned ammo (particularly given its proximity to a major highway), Anmar and I raced after the tail end of the American convoy.

Once parallel to the last armoured Hummer, I yelled through the window to the sergeant and asked him to whom we should report our discovery. He replied, much to the amusement of his three comrades, "Tell someone who gives a shit." The Hummer had a Confederate flag fluttering from the radio antenna, and the four white crew members looked to be the epitome of the "Good ol' Boys" slogan that was painted of the driver's door.

We decided to try our luck with the next vehicle in line. When we overtook the aptly named Hummer "The Boom Box," there was no point in us even trying to communicate with the four African-American soldiers over the gangsta rap music blaring from a stereo. We gave up and continued on our way.

Later that day, about 40 kilometres north of Tikrit and near the village of Makbul, we pulled over to refuel Anmar's old Volkswagen Passat. Taking advantage of the break to make a "nature call," I headed well off the roadway in search of some suitable cover.

What I discovered instead was a six-foot-deep trench that stretched about half a kilometre and contained ten white cylinders. These metal tanks – each about three metres long and a metre and a half in diameter – were adorned with both Arabic script and a metal identification plaque written in the Russian Cyrillic alphabet. The Arab text, a combination of letters and numbers, meant nothing to Anmar, but in bringing the car around to join me, he stumbled upon another find.

In the field next to the cylinders was a number of earthwork bunkers along with what I presumed to be abandoned pipes. Being a former soldier in the Iraqi army, Anmar recognised these tubes as the containers for Luna missiles, a tactical guided weapon with a range of 65 kilometres. In these three bunkers and on the open ground in between them, we counted as many as 24 of these missiles. Although the majority were disabled, at least four were intact, complete with warheads.

As we looked around, a curious young goatherd approached us and eagerly explained that this Luna battery had been heavily hit by U.S. aircraft during the first days of the war. He explained that the white containers were rocket fuel for the missiles. After the air strike, the surviving Iraqis had fled, and no one had visited this site except for a few looters. But after opening one and discovering that this fuel did not work in cars, the looters left empty-handed.

Realizing that some short-range missiles, even complete with fuel, did not constitute one of the elusive "smoking gun" weapons of mass destruction, and despite the lackadaisical reaction we received only hours before, we still wanted to pass along the location of the Luna site to the next Americans we found. Although taking a Pepsi break at a roadside restaurant, the handful of officers from the 101st Airborne Division were much more receptive to this information than the comical sergeant I had talked to earlier.

"We have been receiving a lot of Iraqi civilian casualties in our sector as a result of this sort of unexploded ordnance going off," said Lieutenant Clayton Curtis. "With thousands of potential sites for us to search and secure, we are beginning to appreciate why the UN inspectors needed so much time."

To facilitate my exit back through Turkey, Anmar drove me north all the way to the border town of Zakho. We had been careful to stockpile enough gasoline for his return trip prior to leaving Baghdad, however, with black market fuel, the quality was usually questionable. A mixture of bad gas and searing daytime temperatures had played havoc on the old Volkswagen Passat. A ham-fisted mechanic out of necessity, Anmar had been challenged to keep his car running. Over the final 40-kilometre stretch we averaged just 10 kilometres per hour. In Zakho, a delegation of Turkmen was waiting to escort me through the border. With luck I could still catch my flight from Diyarbakir that afternoon. Although it wasn't much, I gave Anmar what remained of my cash and wished him well.

He would have to drive nearly 700 kilometres, along extremely dangerous roads, in his seized-up car to return to his home in the chaotic hell of Baghdad. When I asked if he'd be okay, he gave me a reassuring smile. "Believe me, I'll be fine. I have my faith in Allah and, just to be sure, I've got a litre of arak in my back seat."

After what we'd been through together, I believed him.

TOP: *A cache of abandoned Iraqi anti-tank weapons lies only metres from the main Baghdad-Mosul highway. (S.TAYLOR)*

ABOVE: *It did not take long for the Iraqi people to express their anger at the American occupation, and protests outside the U.S. compound became commonplace. (AP)*

ABOVE: *Attacks against U.S. personnel have intensified since George Bush pronounced major combat operations ceased on May 1, 2003. On August 28, 2003, more American soldiers had been killed after the war ended than during actual combat. (JOE RAEDLE/GETTY IMAGES)*

OPPOSITE PAGE: *Often not included in the media tally of casualties is the staggering total of nearly 4,000 wounded allied personnel (as of 1 September 2003). (BRITISH DEPARTMENT OF DEFENCE)*

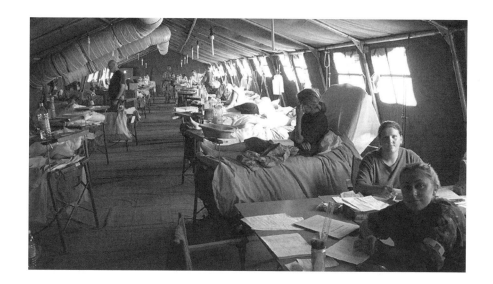

CHAPTER TEN:
Bring 'Em On

On July 1, 2003, over 25 separate attacks were mounted in a 24-hour period against U.S. personnel in Iraq, and accounted for 14 casualties. Many of the attacks followed a similar pattern: Iraqi resistance fighters target a small, three-vehicle U.S. army patrol and fire a rocket-propelled grenade (RPG) at the lead vehicle as it turns the corner at an intersection. The next two vehicles are forced to stop, and are unable to either see or engage the ambushers.

One journalist had witnessed one of these attacks and reported that three U.S. soldiers fled from their Hummer, their clothing ablaze from the ignited fuel. As their comrades tried to douse the flames and provide emergency medical attention, the American reporter was aghast as he watched a crowd of bystanders cheer and dance in celebration. He was unable to comprehend the Iraqis' jubilation over the attack nor their ungratefulness for having been liberated.

The U.S. State Department and Pentagon steadfastly denied that the escalating guerrilla attacks were gaining in popular support, maintaining the ambushes were the handiwork of Saddam's former Mukhabarat agents and a number of foreign Mujahadeen fanatics. Early speculation was that the ambushes were even being organized by Saddam or his two sons, Uday and Qusay, who had yet to be apprehended.

On July 2, as he strolled across the White House lawn like a Texan gunslinger,

George Bush told reporters, "There are some (Iraqis) who feel like conditions are such that they can attack us there... My answer is, bring 'em on. We have the force necessary to deal with the situation."

Much to the resentment of the 150,000 coalition troops stationed in Iraq, the resistance movement did indeed 'bring it on.' In addition to the relentless attacks on U.S. patrols, the Iraqis began to mount larger terror attacks aimed at key targets and the vital infrastructure. A suicide bomber attacked the Jordanian embassy on August 7, killing 17. The message was clear: any Arab country perceived as a U.S. ally would also be punished. On August 19, another suicide bomber detonated a massive truck bomb outside the UN headquarters in Baghdad. Injuring 100 and killing 22 people, including Sergio Vieira de Mello, the head of the mission, the incident rocked the coalition. In its wake, the UN openly criticized the U.S. for failing to protect its personnel and the International Committee of the Red Cross announced days later that it would withdraw the majority of its personnel from Iraq, fearing it might be a target for terrorists. Although several key employees of the ICRC had remained throughout the "Shock and Awe" bombing campaign, spokesperson Nada Doumani said, "We are concerned about the security of the staff working with us and the people who come to visit us."

In addition to terrorizing international aid agencies into leaving the country, the guerrillas also attacked vital oil pipelines. Since the collapse of Saddam's regime, the U.S. interim administration was anxious to restart the export of Iraq's oil in order to help offset the massive reconstruction costs. On August 18, just two days after the reopening of the Kirkuk-Turkey pipeline, Iraqi revolutionaries detonated a bomb and brought all pumping to a halt. An exasperated Paul Bremer, the U.S. civil administrator in Iraq, admitted that the interruption of oil shipments was "costing the Iraqi people over $7 million a day."

While this lost revenue is significant, it's a drop in the bucket when compared to the fact that the occupation of Iraq is costing the U.S. about $1 billion a week. The pre-war export totals of Iraqi oil were approximately $20 billion annually. The United States' original budget for the war – based on a smooth liberation and the establishment of a transitional government within six months – was estimated at $75-90 billion.

While U.S. costs continue to climb, the first post-war survey of Iraq's oil fields contained some sobering news for the Bush administration. Without access to replacement parts or new machinery during 12 years of sanctions, the Iraqis were driven to desperate measures in an attempt to keep up production.

Although Iraq Program Director Benon Sevan's August 2000 report to the UN clearly stated that if the sanctions against Iraq were not eased so as to permit the necessary upgrades and repairs to the oil extracting equipment, long-term irreparable damage would be done to Iraq's oilfields, U.S. engineers were apparently shocked at the condition of the machinery. Furthermore, the Iraqis had been forced to pump a large amount of water into the oil fields to make up for the loss of pumping capacity. As a stopgap measure, this permitted the oil company to maintain production quotas; in the long term, however, serious harm was done to untapped deposits. The U.S. engineering assessment concluded that several billion dollars would be required to refurbish Iraq's entire oil infrastructure and, even then, the fields would not yield anywhere near previous expectations of output.

With the coalition force unable to provide a secure environment and with operational costs continuing to mount in the face of questionable oil returns, U.S. Secretary of State Colin Powell sought additional international commitment for the rebuilding of Iraq. At the end of August 2003, Powell was reportedly 'working the phones' trying to convince other nations to provide security forces and donate additional relief funds.

Although the United States' coalition of the willing was comprised of some 40 countries, for the majority of the participants this meant little more than allowing the U.S.-British forces to use their military bases and/or access to airspace. Although everyone realized the U.S.-led war would be a short, swift, one-sided campaign, few countries were willing to commit combat troops. Now that the situation in Iraq has degenerated into anarchy and violence, it will be extremely difficult for Powell to find any country willing to put its soldiers' lives on the line.

As the weeks turn into months, it is becoming clear that the U.S. did not have a clear exit strategy from the Iraqi quagmire, nor did it even have a firm handle on the scale and scope of the threat and complexities facing the new administration. American military intelligence was proving to be an oxymoron and Pentagon statements were so contradictory they would be laughable under different circumstances.

On April 7, the U.S. military claimed General Ali Hassan al-Majid (a.k.a. Chemical Ali) had been killed in an airstrike on his home. Two days later this claim was 'confirmed' by British troops who 'positively identified' the body. When the coalition updated its deck of the 55 most-wanted Iraqis, Chemical Ali was crossed off and listed as killed. On August 21, the Pentagon was pleased to announce they had successfully captured this very same individual, without ever having corrected the earlier statement or even suggesting there could have been doubt on the body's identification. Similarly, on April 24 the U.S. proudly boasted that soldiers had General Zuhayr al-Naqib, Iraq's intelligence chief, in custody. Al-Naqib was reportedly picked up in the same sweep that had captured my old Mukhabarat contact Salim Said Kalaf al-Jumayli. Much to everyone's embarrassment, the real al-Naqib willingly turned himself in to the U.S. in late August – again, no explanation was given nor was a name provided for the person apprehended in error.

After cornering Saddam's fugitive sons at a house in Mosul, U.S. forces killed Uday and Qusay in a vicious six-hour firefight on July 22. Pronounced by the Pentagon as a major setback to the Saddam loyalists it claimed were conducting the attacks against allied troops, the guerrilla war, nevertheless, steadily escalated after their deaths.

By the end of August, the U.S. military admitted it was recruiting former Mukhabarat agents to assist in counterinsurgency operations when, only weeks earlier, these same individuals were being blamed for the coordination of the guerrilla attacks. Following the new alliance, the U.S. began attributing the attacks to al-Qaeda terrorists cells. There can be no question, however, that the Mukhabarat agents had a better understanding of Iraq than the U.S. authorities.

The August 29 suicide bombing that claimed the life of popular cleric Ayatollah Muhammad Baqir al-Hakim is an example of the widening rifts occurring between Shiite factions in the south, while, in the north, clashes between Turkmen militia and Kurdish peshmerga escalated around Kirkuk – this territorial division into two separate civil wars was the exact scenario Jabar Abu Marwan, my guide and a former Mukhabarat agent, had forecasted for a post-Saddam Iraq.

Colin Powell's postwar attempts to lure additional international support, however, have been hampered by the ongoing instability in Iraq while, prior to the war, the U.S. could not convince either the UN or NATO on the necessity for invading Iraq. Although the military's failure to find Saddam's alleged weapons of mass destruction has not come as a shock, it has served to undermine whatever credibility the Bush administration once had.

To further cloud the issue, U.S. officials have begun distancing themselves from the charge of WMD possession. Spokespersons have instead begun spinning the invasion of Iraq as a humanitarian mission aimed at alleviating the Iraqi people's suffering. Before he was replaced as interim governor in May 2003 after just five months as U.S. civil administrator in charge of reconstruction and humanitarian aid in post-Saddam Iraq, Jay Garner told the media that "up to one million bodies" could be found buried in Saddam's mass graves. On August 27, Vice President Dick Cheney deflected the issue of WMDs by claiming that if the U.S. had not intervened in Iraq, "the torture chambers would still be operating" and Saddam would be on target to kill his annual "10,000" civilians.

Unfortunately, as the U.S. military continues to average one soldier killed every day in Iraq, the American public is no longer so easily diverted. In polls taken in mid-August 2003, President George Bush's approval rating had fallen to 44 per cent from a post-September 11, 2001 high of 96 per cent.

A HIGHER PRICE WAS PAID politically by Bush's staunchest ally, British Prime Minister Tony Blair. First was a minor scandal, when scientists proved that damaging documents discovered in post-Saddam Baghdad concerning George Galloway's alleged bribes were forgeries. The maverick Labour Party MP had been publicly smeared in April when several letters were found by reporters following the looting of the Iraqi Foreign Ministry office. The paperwork appeared to be a series of communiqués outlining millions of dollars in payment which had been made to Galloway by Iraqi authorities in the mid-1990s. Paper and ink tests, however, proved that the documents were fabricated in 2003. Galloway had always professed his innocence.

Following his vindication, he insisted on a full investigation into the forging of the dossier, demanding to know who was responsible for both creating and then planting it in order to discredit him. While Blair was able to hold off Galloway's demands and limit the reverberations of this whole affair, he was unable to prevent a bigger scandal from erupting.

Under the condition of anonymity, British Ministry of Defence (MOD) scientist David Kelly had told BBC Radio that it was Alistair Campbell, Tony Blair's own press secretary, that had "sexed up" the Iraqi weapons dossier. Of particular note in the document was the allegation that Iraq had been "within 45 minutes" of deploying weapons of mass destruction. In an effort to discredit Kelly, the MOD revealed his identity to the media at large. The following day, the distraught whistleblower had taken his own life. In the subsequent parliamentary hearings surrounding Kelly's suicide, all of Blair's top officials denied having either "sexed up" the dodgy dossier or pressured British intelligence officials to do so.

What quickly became lost in all the finger-pointing surrounding David Kelly's death, however, was the fact that the intelligence file *was* wrong. Saddam had not possessed nuclear arms nor did he employ chemical or biological weapons – even when his country was completely overrun by coalition forces.

Following his historical July 18, 2003, address to the U.S. Congress, Tony Blair was awarded the Congressional Gold Medal in recognition of his staunch support of Bush's war. The event was planned months in advance and was to have been the culminating celebration of a victory in Iraq. However, with Blair under tremendous political pressure in Britain and American casualties still mounting, the taste of victory had somewhat soured. Having all but admitted that he no longer expected to find WMDs in Iraq, Blair suggested he felt confident that "history will forgive" the allied intervention.

And, as it is usually the victors who write popular history, there is little doubt Blair's statement will ultimately prove prophetic. Regrettably, without admitting mistakes lessons remain unlearned, ensuring that tragedies such as this violent chapter in Iraq's history are destined to be repeated.

~ ~ ~ ~ ~ ~ ~ ~ ~ ~

POSTSCRIPT

SAMARA, IRAQ, SEPTEMBER *14, 2003*   A little Iraqi girl, no more than eight years old – squatted beside the road with tears of humiliation streaming down her cheeks. Twenty feet away, three American soldiers had their rifles aimed at her as she was forced to relieve herself in full view of a long line of parked cars. From inside their vehicles, the Iraqi onlookers screamed with rage at the U.S. troops. Whenever one the Iraqis ventured to get out of his vehicle, an American officer would yell, "Get back in the car, asshole!" and the .50 calibre machine gun mounted on the U.S. Hummer would swing menacingly towards the protester. The terrified little girl was weeping uncontrollably by the time she dropped her skirt and ran back to her mother. Her enraged father began working his horn, and other Iraqi drivers quickly took up the protest by doing the same. The Americans laughed as they drove off, their weapons still trained on the Iraqi vehicles.

This incident took place after a detachment of the U.S. 101st Airborne Division set up a roadblock on the Samara-Kirkuk highway. In order to conduct a thorough weapons search of all traffic along this route. However, without enough person- nel to man the roadblock, cars and trucks had backed up for at least two kilome- tres in each direction. The afternoon temperatures had reached over 40° Celsius and there was not a bit of shade on that desert stretch of highway. As part of their operational doctrine, the Americans would not allow anyone to step out of their vehicles until they had been searched, despite the fact that the waiting time at the roadblock was upwards of four hours. To ensure that no Iraqi ventured onto the roadway, First Lieutenant Fisher and his detachment raced up and down the queue in their armoured Hummer, pointing their weapons and hurling verbal abuse at any violator.

The little girl had been sitting in a small Mazda with six other family members for over three hours before she left the car. Her older brother, who was about 10, had bravely taken her by the hand and attempted to reach a small depression in the sand which might have offered her a modicum of privacy. Lieutenant Fisher's Hummer had roared down the unpaved shoulder and braked to a halt in a cloud of dust. With guns fixed, the young boy abandoned his sister, who had no choice but to squat where she was.

While Fisher and his men may have carried out their orders efficiently, their aggressive behaviour and lack of empathy had done little to win over the hearts and minds of the Iraqi people who witnessed this overwhelming show of force.

Admittedly, there was good reason for the U.S. occupation troops to be jumpy since, over the past few months the number of ambushes mounted by Saddam loyalists against coalition forces have increased dramatically. On average, allied troops are coming under attack a dozen times a day, and the casualty list for *Operation Iraqi Freedom* continues to increase at a rate of about 10 killed and 60 wounded per week.

"If you do the math, with 150,000 U.S. personnel each serving at least a 12-month tour of duty in Iraq, the chance for one of us being killed or wounded is a one in 50 possibility," said Sergeant Chris Jones, a tank commander with the U.S. First Armored (Old Ironsides) Division in Baghdad. "Those are not exactly comforting odds, and its something which most soldiers think about every day."

The constant stress and demanding workload have taken a tremendous toll on both the U.S. forces' individual psyches and their collective morale. Units such as the 173rd Airborne Brigade, which was stationed in northern Iraq, have spent over seven months in-theatre, without any of these soldiers being able to enjoy so much as a weekend off for R & R. "We've been living on hard rations, working 24 [hours a day], 7 [days a week] not knowing when the next incident might occur," said Staff-Sergeant Spry, a 17-year veteran with the 173rd. "How long can they expect our guys to go without sex and alcohol?"

More than the physical hardship, the lack of American progress in restoring stability to Iraq has seriously undermined the resolve of the coalition troops. "Our guys are disillusioned," said Corporal Miller, one of the U.S. soldiers stationed in central Baghdad. "First they told us that we would be welcomed as liberators. And Bush promised us that we would not have to stay in Iraq; but 'stabilization' is just another word for 'occupation,' no matter what Bush tells America."

Since the U.S. President declared an end to major combat operations on May 1, the American forces in Iraq have developed a bunker mentality. While armoured patrols are mounted and weapons searches are conducted on Iraqi streets, for the most part U.S. troops remain completely isolated from the general population. Their barracks and camps are ringed by barbed-wire fences and cement bastions complete with watchtowers and floodlights. "I've not been outside the camp wall since we moved into this bivouac on April 20," said Corporal David Slaughter, a 22-year-old West Virginian serving with the 4th Infantry Division in the central Iraq town of Taji. When asked whether he would like the opportunity to venture into town to meet with the locals during his tour, Slaughter replied, "Are you out of your mind? I can't stand these Iraqis." When pressed as to how many Iraqis he had actually met, Slaughter confessed that he had never so much as spoken to one of the local civilians. "But I know that I wouldn't like them. All they do is sit around in cafés on little stools drinking tea. That's just stupid."

For most of the young American troops, Iraq is a living hell that they can't wait to leave. "The women [serving in Iraq] know that getting knocked up is a one-way ticket out of this shit-hole," said Corporal Slaughter. Four of the 10 females assigned to the U.S. compound in Taji had already been shipped home as a result of pregnancy. "For the guys, it's not so easy. The only way to get out of Iraq early is either in a body bag or on a stretcher."

While senior members of the U.S. administration continue to deny that Iraq is fast becoming another Vietnam, the troops on the ground have no problem making such an analogy. "My only mission here is to survive my tour," said Sergeant Chris Jones. "If I get home alive, I plan to get out of the army and forget forever that there is a place on earth called Iraq."

ABOVE: *Whatever develops from America's long-term exit strategy from Iraq, in the short haul the troops on the ground must first establish a secure environment.* (TIM SLOAN/AFP)

SADDAM HUSSEIN
President of Iraq. He was a key figure in the CIA-sponsored Baath party coup in 1963 that toppled President Kassem. As a deputy to President Ahmed Hasa Al-Bakr, Saddam initiated the pan-Arab movement, culminating with the nationalization of Iraq's oil (1972) and the creation of OPEC (1973). When he came to power in 1979, the U.S. 'encouraged' Saddam to attack the Ayatollah Khomeni's new Shiite fundamentalist regime in Iran then, in 1990, led him to believe that Iraq would not suffer from sanctions for invading Kuwait. Following the devastating Gulf War, President Bush Senior found it preferable to keep a 'weakened Saddam' as leader of Iraq. The U.S. position changed on September 11, 2001.

TARIQ AZIZ
Deputy Prime Minister of Iraq. A longtime survivor on the Middle East diplomatic scene, Aziz received international acclaim during the first Gulf War. In spite of the Western media's demonization of Saddam and his regime, the charismatic Aziz had always been recognized as a statesman. In September 2002, Aziz met with UN Secretary General Koffi Annan in Johannesburg to present a list of Iraqi demands. At that time, Iraq still believed the U.S. would not resort to force if weapons inspectors were refused entry into Iraq and that the UN would withstand pressure from the Bush administration and support Iraq's cause. Aziz was captured by U.S. troops on April 25, 2003, near his hometown of Mosul.

TAHA YASSIN RAMADAN
Vice President, Iraqi Revolutionary Council. A close confidante of Saddam Hussein, Ramadan was a longtime member of Iraq's inner circle. His unquestioned authority became readily apparent in 1996, when he ordered the execution of dozens of senior Iraqi army officers; the generals were foiled in their attempt to overthrow Saddam Hussein as part of a CIA-sponsored coup. Following the April 8, 2003, collapse of Saddam's regime, Ramadan remained on the run until he was arrested on August 19, 2003. U.S. press officers dubbed him "Saddam's Knuckles" at the time of his capture, although no Iraqi had ever heard Ramadan addressed by such a Hollywood-style moniker.

ALL ABOUT OIL: A BRIEF HISTORY OF IRAQ

1914 – In order to protect its oil interests in neighbouring Iran, the British launch an offensive into Mesopotamia against the Ottoman Turks.

1915 – After some initial success against the Turks around Basra, the British expeditionary forces push north where they suffer a devastating defeat at the city of Kut.

1917 – With additional reinforce-ments and the assistance of Arab allies, the Turks are pushed out of Mesopotamia and the British occupy the provinces of Basra,

Baghdad and Mosul.

1918 – Although it was not previously known that the Turk-occupied Mesopotamian provinces possessed oil resources, by the end of World War I British naval engineers had forecasted that this region contained "the worlds largest deposits."

1919 – With proven oil reserves located in Basra, the British hesitate on turning this region over to the Arabs as they had previously promised.

1920 – After being snubbed by

both Britain and France, Faisal declares himself the King of Syria and his brother Abdullah is named the king of Mesopotamia. The French and British suppress Faisal and ignore Abdullah, setting in motion a regional wave of violence and anarchy.

1921 – Unable to suppress the revolt in Mesopotamia, the exiled King Faisal I is recalled from Lebanon and proclaimed 'king' of the newly created State of Iraq.

1927 – The natural gas fires of Baba Gurgur are finally explored and the oil deposits of northern

MOHAMMED AL-SAHAF
*Iraqi Minister of Information.
Probably the most infamous Iraqi
politician of the U.S. intervention.
As the official spokesperson, al-
Sahaf spouted the Baath party line
right to the bitter end. Even as CNN
showed American tanks approaching the center of Baghdad, al-Sahaf
continued to deny the crumbling of
the regime to the Iraqi people. "The
U.S. will never capture Baghdad"
was one of his final comments –
before casting off his own uniform
and going into hiding. Al-Sahaf
antics, however, caused little worry
for the Bush administration. When
he tried to surrender to U.S. troops,
they turned him away. Al-Sahaf is
now a commentator for the Al-
Jazeera news network.*

UDAY HUSSEIN
*Saddam's oldest son. Although he
fancied himself a playboy, most
Iraqis considered him a violent
pervert. Although a failed
assassination attempt had left him
confined to a wheelchair, Uday
maintained a Baghdad harem of
prostitutes. Embarrassed by his
eldest son's numerous scandals
and reported tales of debauchery,
Saddam considered the younger,
more ambitious Uday his heir
apparent. The animosity between
these two brothers was well known.
When U.S. forces stormed a Mosul
residence and reportedly killed both
of Saddam's sons on July 22, 2003,
many Iraqis were suspicious of the
circumstances that would have
brought the two brothers-in-hiding
together.*

AHMED CHALABI
*President of the Iraqi National
Congress. The exiled opposition
leader was believed to be the U.S.'s
prime candidate as a successful
replacement to Saddam Hussein.
Unfortunately, the CIA-sponsored,
long-exiled Chalabi had never
suffered under the Baath regime
and was viewed as a complete
outsider. His résumé also contained
a few blemishes – a fraud
conviction in Jordan and the
embarrassing embezzlement of INC
funds. One of the first clues of
Chalabi's inability to gather the
requisite support for Iraq's post-war
presidency should have been his
abject failure to attract exiles into
the U.S.-funded Iraqi liberation
army.*

Iraq are proven to be among the
world's richest.

1932 – King Faisal I attains Iraq's
independence from Britain. Iraq is
admitted into the League of
Nations, but British troops and
aircraft remain in the country which
has now been declared a
protectorate.

1938 – Oil is discovered in the
sheikdom of Kuwait and Faisal's
son, King Ghazi, lays claim to this
territory as Iraq's 19th province.
With both Kuwait and Iraq being
under British protection, the issue
of Kuwait's appropriation is soon
dropped.

1939 – King Ghazi is killed in a
suspicious automobile accident.
His three-year-old son, Faisal II,
assumes the throne with his uncle,
Abdul Illah, serving as regent.

1941 – At the height of World War
II, with British troops stretched thin
around the globe, Iraqi military
officers stage a rebellion. The
British rush reinforcements from
India and Palestine to restore
Faisal II's monarchy and secure
British oil investments.

1958 – General Abdul Karim
Kassem stages a military coup.
King Faisal II is killed and the last
of the British troops are withdrawn

from Iraq.

1963 – With the backing of the
CIA, the Baath party seize power
briefly. In the wake of the coup,
President Kassem and thousands
of his followers are slaughtered.

1968 – Although they had in turn
been ousted from power by a
military junta, the Baathists regain
control of Iraq. As deputy to
President Ahmed Hasa Al-Bakr,
young Saddam Hussein was seen
as the controlling force in Iraq.

1972 – Iraq nationalizes its oil
resources and calls on other Arab
nations to do the same.

(PUK)

MASSOUD BARZANI

Leader of the Kurdistan Democratic Party (KDP). Although technically an elected official within northern Iraq's autonomous Kurdistan parliament, in reality, Barzani is more akin to a tribal warlord. Since the 1991 Gulf War, the KDP's peshmerga fighters controlled the two provinces of Dohuk and Erbil. In 1996, when the U.S. supported his rival, Jalal Talabani, Barzani cut a separate deal with Saddam. Iraqi tanks assisted Barzani's troops in pushing into Talabani's area of operation and, in the process, Saddam's operatives were able to successfully dismantle the extensive CIA operation that had been established in northern Iraq.

JALAL TALABANI

President of the Patriotic Union of Kurdistan (PUK). Considered to be more a hardline nationalist than rival Barzani, the PUK leader made a number of strange alliances over the past decades. Alternately supported by Iran and the CIA, Talabani retained close contacts with the al-Qaeda movement. In order to increase his prominence in the post-war Iraq administration, Talabani had his people stage elaborate 'liberation parades' for the benefit of the Western media and interim U.S. military governor Jay Garner, however, most neglected to mention that the Kurds had liberated themselves in a 1991 revolt.

SANAN AHMET AGA

Former leader of the Iraqi Turkmen Front (ITF). Although the ITF established its own headquarters in the Kurdish-controlled city of Erbil following the 1991 uprising, Aga's organization was not in good standing with Barzani's ruling KDP. Historically based around the oil-rich city of Kirkuk, the Iraqi Turkmen have been openly supported by the Turkish government. The Turkmen's claim to Iraq's oil resources is considered an important obstacle to the possible postwar creation of an independent Kurdistan. The Turkmen hope to raise their profile and autonomy within a restructured post-war Iraqi federation.

1973 – The creation of the Organization of Petroleum Exporting Countries (OPEC) sets the U.S. economy into turmoil, as oil prices skyrocket.

1975 – After the CIA and the Shah of Iran had successfully supported a Kurdish rebellion in Iraq, Saddam signed a treaty in Algeria: In exchange for Iran's use of the Shatt-al-Arab waterway, Iraq's military was allowed a free hand to crush the Kurds.

1979 – Saddam Hussein becomes President of Iraq at the same time the Shah of Iran is toppled. With Shiite fundamentalists in control of

Iran, Saddam is encouraged by the U.S. State Department to declare war against the Ayatollah Khomeini.

1980 – Saddam believes his forces can easily defeat the Iranian army since it had been recently purged of its officers corps. However, after only limited initial gains, the Iraqi offensive bogs down into a war of attrition.

1984 – With his forces pushed back against the Shatt-al-Arab, Saddam indicates he will end the war. President Ronald Reagan's special envoy, Donald Rumsfeld, flies to Baghdad. Saddam is

promised full U.S. support – including chemical weaponry.

1988 – Iran and Iraq sign a peace agreement; the Pentagon begins conducting war games based on the scenario that Iraq is attacking Kuwait.

1990 – Forced to repay Kuwait a $30 billion loan yet unable to increase oil prices, Iraq issues an ultimatum to Kuwait to cease their overproduction of oil. The U.S. advises Saddam that it has no position on Arab-Arab affairs. On August 2, Iraq invades Kuwait. Four days later the UN Security Council imposes sanctions against

(U.S. DOD)

GEORGE W. BUSH
President of the United States of America. Since becoming president in 2001, Bush has never wavered from his stated desire of removing Saddam Hussein from power. The events of September 11, 2001 provided the Bush administration with the impetus to include Iraq on its "axis of evil" hit list. From that point forward war was inevitable. Winning the peace has proven far more difficult however, as the U.S. intelligence services seemed to completely misunderstand the complex social structure of Iraq. With casualties mounting steadily in the post-war chaos, Bush overflew Iraq at 34,000 feet and urged Iraqi resistance fighters to "bring it on."

DONALD RUMSFELD
United States Secretary of Defense. "Rummy's" first experience in Iraq was in the mid-80s when he was Ronald Reagan's special envoy to Iraq, which, at that time, was a useful ally in undermining the Iranian fundamentalist movement. When Saddam wanted to pull out of the Iran-Iraq War due to escalating casualties, Rumsfeld had promised to deliver to Iraq whatever support was necessary to continue fighting – including the sale of chemical weapons. In the run up to the 2003 intervention in Iraq, Rumsfeld demonized Saddam as "evil" for having used chemical weapons to quell the Kurd uprising while neglecting to mention the U.S. had sold them to Iraq in the late 1980s.

PAUL WOLFOWITZ
United States Deputy Secretary of Defense. Undeniably the leading 'hawk' on Bush's war team, Wolfowitz had first advocated Saddam's removal during the 1991 Gulf War. A protégé of then-CIA Director George Bush Sr., Wolfowitz accelerated his career by heading up Special Project B. This team revised intelligence data (in the final days of the Cold War), portraying the Soviet Union as far more of a military threat than it actually was. President Reagan used the revised document to justify increased defence spending until the USSR collapsed. Later reports revealed that Wolfowitz's dossier had been "sexed up" in a fashion similar to the 2003 reports used to justify the attack on Iraq.

Iraq. On August 7, George Bush Senior launches *Operation Desert Shield.*

1991 – On January 17, the U.S.-led coalition initiates 48 days of airstrikes against Iraq and occupied Kuwait. On February 24, the ground assault goes in and Saddam's forces are routed. Four days later, Iraq signs a cease-fire agreement with the coalition forces. With the collapse of his army, Saddam faces rebellion within Iraq. After months of heavy fighting, Saddam regains 15 of his 18 provinces; the three northern provinces remain under the control

of Kurdish rebels.

1996 – Saddam assists Kurdish warlord Massoud Barzani in an incursion into the territory controlled by rival Kurd, Jalal Talabani. In the process, Saddam destroys a CIA operation in northern Iraq. After 6 years of sanctions, the Iraqi people have suffered nearly 1.5 million deaths. As a result of this carnage, the United Nations eases the embargo and initiates the oil-for-food program. Saddam's exports are completely controlled by the UN, which allows him to buy only food and medicine.

1998 – The U.S. passes the Iraq Liberation Act in October. In December, the UN weapons inspectors are withdrawn from Baghdad. This act precipitates a massive assassination attempt against Saddam in the form of "leadership target" airstrikes.

2000 – Saddam meets with Venezuelan President Hugo Chavez to discuss the strategy of trading their oil exports in the new Euro currency rather than the U.S. dollar.

2001 – On February 17, newly elected President George Bush

(GETTY IMAGES)

DICK CHENEY

Vice President of the United States. Like Rumsfeld and Wolfowitz, Cheney had a long history in dealing with Saddam Hussein since, during the first Gulf War, he was Secretary of Defense. While the Republicans were out of power during the Clinton era, Cheney solidified his extensive corporate contracts within the U.S. military industrial complex. Even before the first bomb fell on Iraq on March 20, 2003, Cheney's former employer, Kellog, Brown and Root, had been issued substantial contracts to support the U.S. forces deployed to the Persian Gulf and in the reconstruction of Iraq. One of Kellog, Brown and Root's major accounts was the Iraqi exile training facility in Taszar, Hungary.

COLIN POWELL

U.S. Secretary of State. Of all the members of Bush's inner circle, Powell appeared to be the strongest opponent of a military intervention in Iraq. The former Vietnam veteran had risen through the ranks to become the Joint Chief of Staff at the time of the first Gulf War. Despite Powell's reluctance, Bush continued to push the 'moderate' Secretary of State as his point man for war. Powell's suspect final presentation at the UN Security Council failed to win unanimous international consent, but it was enough to convince the American public of the necessity for war. One of Powell's strongest arguments at the UN – that Iraq had purchased uranium from Niger – was based on documents known by the U.S. to be forgeries.

VINCENT BROOKS

Brigadier General, U.S. Army Spokesman. In the media's coverage of the war, Brooks has been one of the United States' most visible spokespersons and has successfully disseminated coalition disinformation and deflected negative reports. When U.S. Special Forces troops staged the elaborate rescue of Private Jessica Lynch, Brooks refused to comment on whether or not Lynch had been raped, "for privacy reasons." Brooks' implication of rape helped to demonize the Iraqis in America's eyes. After her recovery, Lynch denied the allegations of rape until the Pentagon imposed a gag order on her. Brooks repeatedly denounced reports of errant U.S. missile strikes and civilian casualties as Iraqi propaganda.

sends a message to Saddam in the form of airstrikes. The world condemns the U.S. aggression. On September 11, the U.S. suffers a devastating terror attack. Saddam issues a statement proclaiming that America has "reaped what it has sown." Although Osama bin Laden is the primary suspect, Bush warns Saddam to "watch his step."

2002 – On August 15, the U.S. Joint Chiefs of Staff approve a strategic plan to invade Iraq. On October 15, Saddam stages a presidential referendum and wins a 100 per cent majority. On November 20, Iraq agrees to

readmit weapons inspectors and turns over its weapons dossier to the UN on December 6. UN chief weapons inspector Hans Blix labels the dossier "incomplete."

2003 – On January 27, Hans Blix tables his final report. The following day George Bush denounces Iraq's "lack of cooperation" in his State of the Union address. After they fail to win consensus among the UN Security Council members, the U.S., Britain and Spain announce on March 10 that they will proceed against Iraq without a second UN resolution. On March 18, President Bush delivers an ultimatum to

Saddam: Leave Iraq within 48 hours or face the consequences.

THE WAR IN IRAQ

MARCH 20, 2003 – Baghdad is blasted by a massive aerial bombardment described by the Pentagon as a "leadership strike."

MARCH 21 – A still alive but somewhat shaken Saddam Hussein goes on Iraqi television to announce his continued defiance.

MARCH 23 – Coalition forces meet little initial resistance, but Iraqi defenses tighten around the city of Nasiriya. The 507th Maintenance

(PETER MARSHALL)

(GETTY IMAGES)

TONY BLAIR

British Prime Minister. Heralded as a staunch ally and supporter of President Bush, Blair faced intense opposition to the Iraq war. With his own Labour Party divided over the issue, Blair relied upon the support of the opposition Conservatives to ensure parliamentary approval. When evidence of Iraq's WMDs failed to materialize, Blair faced increased criticism when reports indicated that his officials had deliberately "sexed up" the Iraqi weapons dossier to justify the war. Blair's situation worsened when David Kelly, a Defence Department scientist who had released evidence of altered documents, committed suicide. Kelly's name had been leaked to the media, and he was then labelled a traitor.

GEORGE GALLOWAY

British Member of Parliament. Considered to be something of a maverick, he had long been a vocal opponent of the sanctions imposed against Iraq. The British MP had made numerous trips to Iraq to publicize the effects of the crippling embargo. As a result of Galloway's influence in Baghdad, Saddam Hussein granted the politician a rare, personal interview. In the looting spree that followed the Baath regime's collapse, British journalists found documents detailing massive illicit payments allegedly paid to Galloway. Tests would later prove the planted documents were forgeries but, like the sexing up of the weapons dossier, no culprit has yet been identified.

DAVID KELLY

Scientist, British Ministry of Defence. A senior advisor on biological warfare for the UN, Kelly spent many months in Iraq prior to 1998 as a member of the inspection teams. In compiling the pre-war dossier on Iraq, British intelligence had used Kelly's input. Following the war, and on the condition of anonymity, Kelly approached BBC radio alleging that Blair's press secretary, Alastair Campbell, had "sexed up" the Iraqi weapons file to support the claim that "Saddam was 45 minutes away" from possessing a nuclear bomb. When defence officials revealed Kelly's identity to the media, the devastated scientist cut his wrists. His suicide sparked a national scandal and investigation.

Company is ambushed leaving 10 killed, 50 wounded and 12 taken prisoner.

APRIL 6 – U.S. forces seize Baghdad's Saddam International airport. On the northern front, the allied Kurdish militia launches an offensive towards Kirkuk. U.S. jets mistake the Kurdish advance for Iraqis and 18 Kurds are killed in a friendly fire incident.

APRIL 7 – The U.S. Third Division launches a surprise armoured thrust into the center of Baghdad. An estimated 3000 Iraqi soldiers and civilians are killed with little loss of American life. An airstrike

against a Baghdad restaurant was initially thought to have killed Saddam.

APRIL 8 – All Iraqi army resistance collapses unexpectedly. Kurdish troops enter Mosul and Kirkuk.

APRIL 9 – Although irregular Arab Fedayeen fighters retain control of most of Baghdad, the U.S. Marines assist a group of Iraqi exiles in pulling down a statue of Saddam in Firdos Square. CNN proclaims Saddam's regime "toppled."

APRIL 10 – In the absence of any law and order, widespread looting and arson erupts throughout Iraq.

While critics chastise the Americans forces for not quelling the riots, U.S. Secretary of Defense Donald Rumsfeld says that Iraqis are simply "enjoying their freedom."

APRIL 11 – What was supposed to be a U.S.-Iraq reconciliation event turns ugly when two Shiite clerics are stabbed to death outside a mosque by an angry mob.

MAY 1 – Aboard USS *Abraham Lincoln*, George Bush announces a victory in Iraq and that "all major combat operations" have ceased. Looting and sporadic resistance continue unabated. U.S.

(BOISE STATE UNIVERSITY)

(GETTY IMAGES)

HANS BLIX

Chief UN Weapons Inspector. While the Iraqis refused to grant his UN inspection teams entry, Blix was the champion of the U.S. propaganda machine. But, after Iraq capitulated and Blix's teams arrived in Baghdad, he became the target of ridicule from the U.S. State Department. When Blix asked for additional time due to the complexities involved, Bush impatiently rejected the inspector's request. Reporting to the UN on January 26, 2003, Blix had the opportunity to clear Iraq. Instead, his ambiguous statements allowed the U.S. to proceed with an attack on Iraq. In the war's aftermath, however, when the U.S. had not found evidence of WMDs, Bush asked his critics for "more time."

SCOTT RITTER

Former UN Weapons Inspector. This hard-nosed ex-Marine lieutenant colonel was the Baghdad regime's worst nemesis during the eight years he had led the weapon searches in Iraq. As the U.S. tried to drum up support for war however, Ritter attacked the Bush administration for being fearmongers. Speaking to Iraq's National Assembly, Ritter admitted that his inspectors had been used to spy for the U.S. and that the 1998 airstrikes were primarily an assassination attempt on Saddam Hussein. Following the U.S. attack, which had been a betrayal of the UN's trust, Ritter quit his post in protest and launched his own campaign to encourage the lifting of UN sanctions against Iraq.

MOHAMED ELBARADEI

Director General, International Atomic Energy Association (IAEA). Although the UN withdrew its weapons inspectors from Iraq in 1998, the IAEA had continued to monitor Baghdad's dormant nuclear program. The Tamuze nuclear reactor site, destroyed by Israeli jets in 1981, was routinely inspected. Contrary to coalition claims, ElBaradei had reported that Iraq had not reconstructed those facilities. Also denounced as "clumsy forgeries" by ElBaradei were the U.S. intelligence documents alleging that Saddam had tried to buy uranium from Niger. First exposed as fakes in 2001, Bush and Powell continued to use these known-to-be-forged documents as justification for war.

---

commanders say the rampant violence is *not* organized and *not* a guerrilla war.

MAY 26 – It is announced that interim U.S. military governor Jay Garner will be replaced by former diplomat Paul Bremer. Although the State Department denies Garner was fired, it is a sign that America's original postwar plan is rapidly falling apart.

JULY 2 – After Iraqis launch a series of deadly ambushes George Bush challenges the rebels to "bring it on." U.S. commanders now admit they are engaged in a guerilla war – but deny that Iraq is

a potential quagmire.

JULY 23 – With attacks against U.S. forces still escalating, the Americans succeed in killing Saddam's two sons – Uday and Qusay – after a shootout in Mosul. American commanders now use the word *quagmire* to define the worsening situation – but deny that Iraq will become another Vietnam.

AUGUST 19 – A massive car bomb explodes at the UN compound in Baghdad, killing 20 and injuring 40 aid workers. The U.S. captures Iraq's former vice-president, Taha Yassin Ramadan, but the attacks continue. The UN,

Red Cross and other aid agencies begin pulling their personnel out of an "unsafe" Iraq.

AUGUST 28 – The death of a U.S. soldier brings the postwar American death toll to 139 – one more than during actual combat operations. Not included in this total are non-U.S. coalition forces and American-funded Iraqi security guards who have also lost their lives in Iraq.

SEPTEMBER 14 – U.S. soldiers stationed in Iraq simply want to go home. "This is just like Vietnam – a war we cannot win," admits one sergeant.

INDEX

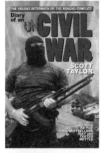